Soldiers in Peacemaking

Assistant Volume Editor: Lena Harding

New Approaches to International History

Series Editor: Thomas Zeiler, Professor of American Diplomatic History, University of Colorado Boulder, USA

New Approaches to International History covers international history during the modern period and across the globe. The series incorporates new developments in the field, such as the cultural turn and transnationalism, as well as the classical high politics of state-centric policymaking and diplomatic relations. Written with upper level undergraduate and postgraduate students in mind, texts in the series provide an accessible overview of international diplomatic and transnational issues, events and actors.

Published:

Decolonization and the Cold War, edited by Leslie James and Elisabeth Leake (2015)
Cold War Summits, Chris Tudda (2015)
The United Nations in International History, Amy Sayward (2017)
Latin American Nationalism, James F. Siekmeier (2017)
The History of United States Cultural Diplomacy, Michael L. Krenn (2017)
International Cooperation in the Early 20th Century, Daniel Gorman (2017)
Women and Gender in International History, Karen Garner (2018)
International Development, Corinna Unger (2018)
The Environment and International History, Scott Kaufman (2018)
Scandinavia and the Great Powers in the First World War, Michael Jonas (2019)
Canada and the World since 1867, Asa McKercher (2019)
The First Age of Industrial Globalization, Maartje Abbenhuis and Gordon Morrell (2019)

Europe's Cold War Relations, Federico Romero, Kiran Klaus Patel, Ulrich Krotz (2019)

United States Relations with China and Iran, Osamah F. Khalil (2019)

Public Opinion and Twentieth-Century Diplomacy, Daniel Hucker (2020)

Globalizing the US Presidency, Cyrus Schayegh (2020)

The International LGBT Rights Movement, Laura Belmonte (2021)

Global War, Global Catastrophe, Maartje Abbenhuis and Ismee Tames (2021)

America's Road to Empire: Foreign Policy from Independence to World War One, Piero Gleijeses (2021)

Militarization and the American Century, David Fitzgerald (2022)

American Sport in International History, Daniel M. DuBois (2023)

Rebuilding the Postwar Order, Francine McKenzie (2023)

Forthcoming:

China and the United States since 1949, Elizabeth Ingleson

Soldiers in Peacemaking

*The Role of the Military at the End of War,
1800-present*

Edited by
Beatrice de Graaf, Frédéric Dessberg, and
Thomas Vaisset

Assistant Volume Editor: Lena Harding

BLOOMSBURY ACADEMIC
LONDON • NEW YORK • OXFORD • NEW DELHI • SYDNEY

BLOOMSBURY ACADEMIC
Bloomsbury Publishing Plc
50 Bedford Square, London, WC1B 3DP, UK
1385 Broadway, New York, NY 10018, USA
29 Earlsfort Terrace, Dublin 2, Ireland

BLOOMSBURY, BLOOMSBURY ACADEMIC and the Diana logo
are trademarks of Bloomsbury Publishing Plc

First published in Great Britain 2023
This paperback edition published in 2025

A catalogue record for this book is available from the British Library.

A catalog record for this book is available from the Library of Congress.

Library of Congress Cataloging-in-Publication Data

Names: Graaf, Beatrice de, editor. | Dessberg, Frédéric, editor. |
Vaisset, Thomas, editor.
Title: Soldiers in peacemaking : the role of the military at the end of war, 1800-present /
edited by Beatrice de Graaf, Frédéric Dessberg, Thomas Vaisset.
Other titles: Role of the military at the end of war, 1800-present
Description: London ; New York, NY : Bloomsbury Academic, 2023. | Series: New
approaches to international history | Includes bibliographical references and index. |
Summary: "Exploring the role of the military at the end of war, this volume of case
studies investigates how soldiers have contributed to the transition to peace
throughout the 19th and 20th centuries"– Provided by publisher.
Identifiers: LCCN 2023019431 | ISBN 9781350345027 (hardback) |
ISBN 9781350345027 (ebook) | ISBN 9781350345034 (epub)
Subjects: LCSH: Peace-building–Case studies. | Civil-military
relations–Case studies. | Armed Forces–Civic action–Case studies. |
Peacekeeping forces–Case studies.
Classification: LCC UH720 .S645 2023 | DDC 322/.5–dc23/eng/20230425

LC record available at https://lccn.loc.gov/2023019431

ISBN: HB: 978-1-3503-4501-0
PB: 978-1-3503-4504-1
ePDF: 978-1-3503-4502-7
eBook: 978-1-3503-4503-4

Series: New Approaches to International History

Typeset by Deanta Global Publishing Services, Chennai, India

To find out more about our authors and books visit www.bloomsbury.com
and sign up for our newsletters.

Contents

Illustrations

Acknowledgments

This book is the result of a colloquium organized by the Service historique de la Défense, the Research Center of the Military Academy of Saint-Cyr Coëtquidan, the Security History Network/Department of History and Art History of Utrecht University, and the Mixed Research Unit Sirice (Sorbonne-Identités, relations internationales et civilisations de l'Europe), with the support of German Armed Forces Zentrum für Militärgeschichte und Sozialwissenschaften der Bundeswehr, the Netherlands Institute for Military History and of Labex EHNE (Écrire une histoire nouvelle de l'Europe).

The editors would like to thank the members of the scientific board: Julie d'Andurain (University of Lorraine), Walter Bruyère-Ostells (IEP of Aix-en-Provence), Isabelle Davion (Sorbonne-University), Michal Epkenhans (Universität Hamburg, ZMS-Bw), Olivier Forcade (Sorbonne-University), Robert Frank (Paris 1 Panthéon-Sorbonne), Jean-Michel Guieu (Paris 1 Panthéon-Sorbonne), Jan Hoffenaar (Universiteit Utrecht and The Netherlands Institute for Military History), Stanislas Jeannesson (University of Nantes), Jean-François Klein (University de Bretagne Sud), Samuel Kruizinga (University of Amsterdam), Matthijs Lok (University of Amsterdam), Virginie Martin (Paris 1 Panthéon-Sorbonne), William Mulligan (University College of Dublin), Ozan Ozavci (Utrecht University), Ben Schoenmaker (University of Leiden and The Netherlands Institute for Military History), Mariusz Wołos (Pedagogical University of Krakow), and Thomas W. Zeiler (University of Colorado Boulder).

The editors of this volume would like to express their gratitude to all contributors. They have given much of their time, from the scientific conference at the origin of our project up until the many revisions to their chapter. We also would like to thank our home institutions that facilitated and enabled our reflection on the military in peacemaking and supported this publication: the Service historique de la Défense (SHD), Utrecht University, and the Military Academy of Saint-Cyr.

We particularly would like to thank Lena Harding for her ever-so-wise advice and helpful interventions in the making of this volume.

ACADÉMIE MILITAIRE SAINT-CYR COËTQUIDAN

SHD Service historique de la Défense

Utrecht University

1

Introduction

Beatrice de Graaf, Frédéric Dessberg, and Thomas Vaisset

Understanding the Role of the Military during "sortie de guerre" from the Nineteenth Century until the Present

Sortie de guerre

It is common to state that when the guns fall silent, diplomats take over. Yet this cliché stands to be corrected. Seeing war as the profession of the military and negotiations as the task of the diplomat is an overly simplistic binary. Wars require not only fighting but also include periods of negotiation. Take for example protracted wars such as the Eighty Years War, the Thirty Years War, or the First World War on the Eastern Front. Or even the Second World War in France. If we look beyond such characteristic all-out wars, there are even more instances where times of war interfere and interlock with times of peacebuilding, preparing for an armistice, or organizing a (partial) demobilization. During such hybrid situations of waging-war-and-preparing-for-peace, the military, diplomats, and politicians play a complementary role, where instead of taking turns, they often work closely together. The soldier and the diplomat intervene as parallel or joint actors in international relations, even when negotiations do not begin until the war proper has ended (which is rarely the case).[1] At the same time, "peace" is not a monolithic state of nonwar, with no more use for the military. Once signed, capitulations or armistice treaties need to be enforced on the ground, a transition period with an occupation sets in or external parties intervene to settle the conflict formally. Such enforcement is hardly conceivable without the support of armed forces, as in 1815 and 1945 when occupying armies were deployed to enforce a transition or during the Yugoslav Wars when armed forces were called in to enforce a ceasefire.

It is this hybrid, complex, and multilayered situation—the "sortie de guerre"—that this volume sets out to investigate. Scholars have only relatively recently started to devote attention to this phenomenon, mostly in the wake of the flood of academic publications that erupted from the First World War centennial. Bruno Cabanes, for example, introduces the importance of analyzing the "immediate aftermath of a war" as a "transition from war to peace," an exit from war.[2] He and others argue that this period of transition is highly ambiguous, combining grief and disillusionment with elation and feelings of liberation. It is a moment of enormous demobilization efforts and of governments struggling to gain oversight and influence on what happens on the ground, and when soldiers, local commanders, diplomats, and others "on the spot"—be they mayors, resistance fighters, militia leaders, or self-proclaimed authorities in charge—vie for control and legitimacy.[3]

It is true that in modern times, since the end of the eighteenth century, the different pillars of the centralizing (nation) state have emerged as distinct categories of governance. The military came to be considered, at least in European societies, as a separate branch of government, distinct from the political leadership of the state. Bureaucratic professionalization also entailed increasing compartmentalization and professional differentiation. State bureaucracies and ministries were divided along different functional lines. Yet in the post-Westphalian European states system, generals were not completely excluded from executing tasks outside the theater of war. In issues of "international relations," they were not limited only to signing acts of surrender. Sometimes they were also mandated to sign peace treaties, carry out negotiations, or even facilitate the creation of new states, as with a number of French generals in the revolutionary period.[4] Moreover, military victors have always been there to enforce armistice agreements or to help facilitate compliance with territorial clauses of peace treaties through, for example, military occupations. At the various Peace Congresses in early modern history, they indeed had to heed the instructions of their sovereigns, ministers, or political leaders. But they frequently acted as experts themselves, negotiated peace treaties on their own accord, or shaped the aftermath of wars by designing and overseeing large-scale demobilization programs. Since the second half of the twentieth century, they have also increasingly been an institutionalized part of peacekeeping and peacemaking missions and have appropriated roles outside "their" nation-states as assigned to them by international organizations. In short, there is no "sortie de guerre" without the military playing an intense and protracted role.

Ambiguous Roles

Yet there is still abundant ambiguity on how to understand and define the exact role of the military in such post-conflict situations. This ambiguity is enshrined in the fact that the military does and can be asked to undertake so many different tasks and activities during the transition from war to peace. Its functions in peacekeeping are multiple and have become even more diversified over time. International affairs have been diversifying for more than two centuries, implying the mobilization of an increasing number of actors. Post-conflict situations moreover have taken place in a trans-imperial setting or, since the twentieth century, in a globalized context of international organizations and institutions, and thus touch upon a whole range of aspects: from managing flows of displaced persons and war refugees to demobilizing troops and organizing homecomings of armies and from welfare (administering help in situations of food shortages, as in the Netherlands in 1944/45) to organizing on-the-spot adjudication and tribunals (such as the war tribunals in Japan). The role of the military in peacekeeping and peacemaking, therefore, evolves according to the makeup of different conflicts, the nature of warfare, and changes in international relations and the international system. At the same time, there are of course patterns of continuity and specific military logic that can be observed in times of transition, with most armed forces being mobilized to consolidate the end of the war situation, to prevent conflicts from continuing, and to enforce a peace settlement.

What stands out is how the impact of the military in "sortie de guerre" has not been a linear process. It varies, depending on the political regime and the context of the war itself. Take the role of the military in Germany, for example, to which we have not devoted a special chapter in this book, since it was a relatively minor one throughout the various "sorties de guerre." In 1815, the general staff and the military, most notably the generals Gebhard von Blücher and August Neidhardt von Gneisenau, did try their hands in launching a campaign of plunder and requisitions, during the time of the invasion in France and the ensuing military occupation. Yet, they were soon enough made to follow the lead of international coalition leaders or even foreign generals, such as the Duke of Wellington and British foreign minister Lord Castlereagh. Within the context of the allied occupation of Germany, the German generals had to subject themselves to the judgment of the Allied Council regarding the post-conflict situation in France (and the capture of Napoleon!)—though not without some degree of rumination and protest.[5] In 1871, the role of the Prussian military was equally minor, albeit for different reasons and in different circumstances (this time, there was no international coalition).[6] Although the Prussian chief of staff Helmuth von Moltke did demand equal authority for himself, on a par with Chancellor Otto von Bismarck in times of war, Emperor Wilhelm I did not meet his request and left diplomacy solely in the hands of his chancellor who wanted peace as soon as possible and did not feel to give in to the desire of Moltke to occupy more parts of France for a longer period of time. The role of the Prussian military in the transition toward war, therefore, remained minor.[7] Then again, in 1918, the story is familiar enough: here, the military made sure to abandon all responsibilities for ending the war and manage the peace themselves and intentionally left everything in the hands of the new democratically elected cabinet.[8] And in 1945, without any form of sovereignty left, the role of German diplomats and the military in managing the transition toward peace was officially nonexistent—although there was still some room left at the local level or in the field of intelligence. More work could be done there,[9] but for this volume we felt that in order to highlight the role of the military in peacemaking, it would make more sense to focus on the military in its official capacity of peacemakers and diplomats.

The Role of the Soldier

That leads us to the role of the soldier, in particular, during these times of transition, which we—for the purpose of clarity—summarize as situations of "peacemaking." The events that mark out the chronology covered by this book range from the end of the Napoleonic Wars, via the resolution of the two world wars, to the end of the Cold War and up to the present day. This rich (and dark) sequence of war exits reminds us of the extent to which peacemaking itself was never clear-cut but always required stamina, delicacy in negotiation, and a long-term commitment to completing the process. It is, therefore, necessary to underline the heuristic value of the notion of "exit from war" ("sortie de guerre") to designate this long and nonlinear process of transitioning from war to peace. Recent historiography has specifically underlined the role of individual actors in making peace, with the caveat that any action by the military in the aftermath of a war must be considered within the wider framework of global, institutionalized peacebuilding policies that were adopted and practiced at the time. This research has already produced some fascinating insights into the context and role of the military in negotiating the peace treaties of 1919–20.[10] Older and more recent literature on the First World War has made it clear that there were abundant prominent generals and military men, at the Paris Conference itself, and on the ground, who were highly influential in negotiating the treaties and trying to manage the manifold peace operations that continued after the armistice was signed.[11] And Robert Gerwarth, with his bestselling work on *The Vanquished*, has signaled that the role of the military could be exactly opposed to peacemaking and contributed to the onslaught of civil wars and insurrections in Eastern Europe, the Balkan and South Europe, staged by regular and irregular troops in equal parts.[12]

Yet, the military did not embark on peacemaking for the first time in 1919. On the contrary, it already played a role in enforcing the territorial clauses of earlier peace treaties. For example, during the occupations of guarantee that were initiated at the end of the Napoleonic Wars, when the armies of the Sixth and Seventh Coalition, under the guidance of the Allied Council and with the Duke of Wellington as the supreme commander, occupied French territory between 1814 and 1818,[13] or again after France was defeated by Prussia in 1871. Fortunately, there is an academic tendency to make the military a subject of research not only as a combatant but also as an actor in post-conflict missions, particularly when it is assigned the task of implementing peace agreements on the ground.[14] This volume addresses three scenarios for future research, which need to be studied in more detail.

First of all, to what extent has the military proved capable of taking on its role, how it has defined itself in relation to its civil and political leaders (and their instructions), and how it has implemented these general instructions in hybrid and complex situations on the ground? The second dimension that requires academic attention is the concrete relationship between the military and civilian populations, for example, during occupations or demobilizations or in relation to border demarcation commissions. The aftermaths of the Napoleonic Wars, the Franco-Russian War, the Crimean War, and especially the protracted aftermath of the First World War in Central and Eastern Europe provide a wealth of examples in this regard.[15]

The third aspect that gives salience to the role of the military in "sortie de guerre" is its capacity and quality to act as an expert on the spot. In times of uncertainty, emerging from the "fog of war" but not yet knowing how the transition toward peace will play out, the soldier emerges as an expert at hand. This is a fairly recent insight, in need of further exploration. In the realm of the political and social sciences, the role of experts, of expertise, and of social learning capacities has been studied for several decades.[16] Yet, for the military, such studies have only just begun to make their mark. With the bicentenary of the Congress of Vienna in 1815 and the centenary of the 1919–29 treaties, the notion of epistemic communities of experts (economists, jurists, geographers. and, of course, military specialists) was launched to map the levels of influence they exerted in the field of peacemaking. The scope and logic of a corps of peacemakers, including diplomats, sovereigns, ministers, generals, engineers, cartographers, financiers, and bankers during the Congress of Vienna, was further augmented after the First World War with specialists in aviation, undersea cables, judicial questions (on prisoners of war), and economic and technological questions who—working in fifty-two commissions—helped to design the new international order after 1918.[17] In a similar vein to studies on the birth of expertise in the diplomatic field,[18] the way now seems open to launch more research into the role of the military and its expertise, which is still lacking in comparison with other actors involved in making peace.[19] By adopting this approach, we also follow in the footsteps of the seminal work done by Séverine Autesserre on *The Frontlines of Peace*, where she shows how studying peacemaking should not only address topdown and outside help, by peacekeepers sent by the United Nations or international nongovernmental organizations, but also concentrate on "insiders (people living in conflict zones)," who oftentimes know far better what it takes to build peace.[20]

This volume starts by pointing out that the military has a set of specific characteristics in relation to expertise where peacemaking is concerned, which revolve, in particular, around the fact that it is the only actor able to use force to enforce a policy decision or treaty clause, be it commissioned by a state, a coalition, or an international organization. It is, therefore, necessary to carefully analyze the military's "specialties" in the different stages of the peace process and, even more importantly, in relation to the question of the legitimacy of military (even kinetic) action in the eyes of civil leaders and populations. In this volume, we focus on the three dimensions of the military's role in peacemaking referred to above in the three scenarios for further research. The volume is structured around these three aspects—politico-military relationships, the relationship with the civil populations, and the military as a source of expertise—with the chapters embedded in these three pillars in a chronological fashion.

Outline of the Book

The *first part of this volume* thus deals with how the military's role is (self-) defined and shaped in relation to political or civil authorities. The end of a war marks the threshold for the reconfiguration of politico-military relations disrupted by wartime, particularly in the age of all-out war. Civil authorities and populations can perceive soldiers engaging in making peace as a priori contrary to their raison d'être. This may place a burden on their contribution to the exit from war. A key point in making this relationship between the military and their leaders work is coherence and agreement on the strategy to be deployed. Hew Strachan clearly brings home this argument in his chapter, in which he carefully describes and analyzes how civil-military relations broke down at the end of the First World War, whereas a similar breakdown was avoided in 1945 when politicians did recognize the "strategic wisdom" of the soldiers.

Another striking example highlighting the often fraught relationship between the military and their leaders during a "sortie de guerre" is provided by David Fitzgerald, who discusses how, in the aftermath of the Cold War, politicians and military leaders projected their anxieties about the future of the US Army and its soldiers onto peacekeeping missions. Their public fights exposed deep fissures within the army and between the army and the US government about what attributes its soldiers would need in the twenty-first century. In the third chapter in this part of the volume, Wietse Stam unpacks the way a UN peacekeeping operation functioned as a hybrid form of diplomatic and military activity. He investigates how the leading military officers in Cambodia perceived and defined their role as peacekeepers and how they determined the balance between the military and diplomatic aspects of their mission when the cooperation of one party, in particular, was eroding. What does it mean, if we describe peacekeepers as "soldiers of diplomacy" or as "*la diplomatie en kaki*"?[21] The paradoxical identity of the peacekeeper became especially salient in the way the views of two generals, a French and an Australian diverged (and clashed) in dealing with the Khmer Rouge in the early 1990s.

The concluding chapter of this part is written by Dion Landstra and Thomas Wijnaendts van Resandt and explores the difficulties regarding the mandates given to international peacekeeping missions in conflict situations that are rapidly changing. He explains how, during the Yugoslav Wars, a lack of political will within the international community seriously hampered the use of force on the ground. While UNMO and UNPROFOR needed their mandate to be expanded and diversified "on the run," they were forced to remain at a distance and helpless under persistent attacks.

The *second part of this volume* focuses on the embeddedness and legitimacy of armed forces within civil populations, in the context of peacemaking and "sortie de guerre." We already touched upon this in the first part, where a peacekeeping mission was discussed, modeled on the framework of the UN Emergency Force sent to Egypt in 1957 (which was in turn based on the interallied peacekeeping force in Upper Silesia in 1921). Peacekeeping aims to maintain a ceasefire between belligerents, which often places troops *and the communities they need to protect* in a dangerous situation, especially since they can only use their weapons in self-defense. Peace enforcement allows missioned forces to use their weapons to protect civilian populations against armed forces that do not respect a ceasefire. Yet peacebuilding involves more than (successful or botched) protection; it also entails the rebuilding of administrative and (semi-)governmental structures in order to allow a community to function again. Since the early nineteenth century, such situations have arisen in particular during times of military occupation. Christine Haynes shares her findings based on a study of the occupation of Northern and Eastern France by the coalition armies in the first years of the *Restauration*. She demonstrates the flexibility and modernity of such early peacekeeping missions, where foreign troops fraternized with local elites, thus contributing not only to processes of cultural exchange but also to the reestablishment of "harmony" between victors and defeated.

As stated earlier, the role of the military in making peace cannot be separated from the impact of war on combatants and civilian populations. But what happens when armies interact with societies that have suffered tremendously and are traumatized and fragile due to the ordeals of war? The role of veterans here is highly relevant. In interbellum France and Germany, for example, veterans carried a substantial amount of political weight—accelerating processes of radicalization and lowering the threshold of violence in society.[22] Alexandros Makris, however, describes the case of Greece after the Great War, where veterans had a far lesser-known impact on Greek society, contributing to the spread of pacifist ideals and attitudes. The last chapter in this second part of the volume deals with the impact of armed forces on territorial transformations, in borderland areas, where demarcation lines and new borders have had to be drawn and enforced. Here, the deployment of armed forces can often be linked to ulterior motives and nationalist objectives. Paul Lenormand shows how, in the years following the Second World War, Czech and Slovak soldiers were garrisoning the main "German" cities in the north and the west in order to "pacify" the country, suppress German nationalists, and try to "win over" the inhabitants of the borderlands in the heart of the former Sudetenland.

The *third and final part of this volume* highlights the special skills, knowledge, and expertise of soldiers in times of transition. The traditional role of the military in maintaining peace and, if possible, achieving an advantageous peace involves not only kinetic action and operational skills but also a variety of alternative skills and capacities. In fact, a soldier may often become an agent of influence with his interlocutors and civil/political leaders on the basis of his knowledge of the terrain and intelligence on his opponents.

In times when reconnaissance relied on infantry and written letters, military officers—with their knowledge and expertise in the field—held the key to policy decisions. Elena Linkova vividly describes how Russian General Orlov wielded his impressive military skills to gather knowledge on fortifications and armaments and combined this with diplomatic and language skills to negotiate treaties between Russia and the Ottoman Empire and with France; no one else was better equipped or in the know in these matters than Orlov. A similar monopoly on information helped French officer-diplomats on their missions in overseas areas to shape the situation according to their expertise and insights, as Hélène Vencent argues. Naval officers in far-flung territories, such as in the Caribbean or in the Indian and Pacific Oceans, schooled and trained at the Ecoles spéciales de Marine established by Napoleon in 1811, emerged as agents of empire in the 1820s and 1830s, enforcing peace and consolidating French imperial rule wherever they went—often working with missionaries, local leaders, or even representatives of rival powers.

Another type of expertise is highlighted by Evan Wilson, who presents the fascinating case of Britain exiting the war in 1815 and using soldiers to "make peace with its people." Wilson describes how, in times when riot police had not yet been invented, British ministers relied heavily on the armed forces in dealing with social unrest, deploying troops returning home from France to suppress the manifold riots that occurred in the immediate post-1815 period. At the same time, however, discharged soldiers were also equipped and trained to engage in riots themselves. Military experience and expertise was thus of dual use in 1815, with soldiers emerging as both perpetrators and suppressors of riots. The volume concludes with a chapter on the importance of previous colonial experience and expertise within the French army in rolling out new situations of occupation and peace enforcement elsewhere. Renaud Dorlhiac observes how French soldiers in Albania toward the end and during the aftermath of the First World War mobilized their skills and expertise to cement the border with Greece and train Albanian elites, all the while trying to turn the region into a modern and Francophone country. Officers even initiated archaeological excavations and did not always heed orders from Paris, giving preference to their own assessment and expertise.

In summary, the role of the military during "sortie de guerre" is multifaceted and often entails conflicting objectives and strategies. Much more can be said and should be subjected to further research: What do soldiers themselves consider as achievements, how do they define peace, and what is a "good peace" in the eyes of men whose vocation is to wage war? If anything, the three dimensions and aspects laid out in this volume demonstrate how much a "sortie de guerre" is conditioned by the performance of the soldiers themselves. Naturally, the character of war and the international environment set the conditions for how peace is concluded. Yet, within the remit of the historical and geographical context, local forces can exert substantial influence and soldiers do leave an indelible mark on the way "sortie de guerre" plays out. This volume underscores that insight and can be considered a further call to research.

Notes

1   Stanislas Jeannesson, "Les diplomates français et la paix au lendemain de la Grande Guerre," *Matériaux pour l'histoire de notre temps*, no. 4 (2012): 18–22.

2   Bruno Cabanes, "Aftermath, 1919," in *The Cambridge History of the First World War: Global War*, ed. Jay Winter, vol. 1 (Cambridge: Cambridge University Press, 2014), 172–90.

3   See also Cosima Flateau, "Les sorties de guerre. Une introduction," *Les Cahiers Sirice* 3, no. 17 (2016): 5–14.

4   The best known example is that of General Napoléon Bonaparte after the campaign of Italy. He negotiated the Leoben peace preliminaries with Austria, signed on April 18, 1797, and then signed the Campo-Formio peace treaty on October 18, 1797, at the same time as he created the Cisalpine Republic.

5   See Beatrice de Graaf, *Fighting Terror after Napoleon: How Europe Became Secure after 1815* (Cambridge: Cambridge University Press, 2020).

6   Marcus Jones, "Vae Victoribus: Bismarck's Quest for Peace in the Franco-Prussian War, 1870–1871," in *The Making of Peace: Rulers, States and the Aftermath of War*, ed. Williamson Murray and Jim Lacey (Cambridge: Cambridge University Press, 2009), 177–208.

7   Dennis E. Showalter, "Diplomacy and the Military in France and Prussia, 1870," *Central European History* 4, no. 4 (1971): 346–53.

8   See Eckart Conze, *Die große Illusion. Versailles 1919 und die Neuordnung der Welt* (Frankfurt am Main: Siedler, 2018).

9   See, for example, this excellent volume and the introduction on the multilayered and ambiguous situation in Germany after 1945: Camilo Erlichman and Christopher Knowles, "Introduction: Reframing Occupation as a System of Rule,"

in *Transforming Occupation in the Western Zones of Germany: Politics, Everyday Life and Social Interactions, 1945–55,* (London: Bloomsbury Academic, 2018).

10 Frédéric Dessberg, "The Versailles Peace Settlement and the Collective Security System," in *A Companion to World War II,* ed. Thomas W. Zeiler and Daniel M. DuBois, vol. 1 (Chichester: Wiley-Blackwell, 2013), 29–46.

11 See, for example, Jürgen Heideking, *Areopag der Diplomaten. Die Pariser Botschafterkonferenz der alliierten Hauptmächte und die Probleme der europäischen Politik 1920–1931,* Historische Studien (Husum: Verlag Matthiesen, 1979), 436.

12 Robert Gerwarth, *The Vanquished: Why the First World War Failed to End, 1917–1923* (London: Allen Lane, 2016).

13 See Beatrice de Graaf, "The Allied Machine: The Conference of Ministers in Paris and the Management of Security, 1815–1818," in *Securing Europe after Napoleon: 1815 and the New European Security Culture,* ed. Beatrice de Graaf, Ido de Haan, and Brian E. Vick (Cambridge: Cambridge University Press, 2019), 130–49.

14 See Christine Haynes, *Our Friends the Enemies: The Occupation of France after Napoleon* (Cambridge, MA: Harvard University Press, 2018); de Graaf, *Fighting Terror after Napoleon.*

15 Isabelle Davion, "Les sorties de guerre en Europe centre-orientale (1918–1921): comment les peuples ont eux aussi tracé les frontières," *Matériaux pour l'histoire de notre temps,* no. 3 (2018): 35–41.

16 See, for example, Chris Argyris and Donald A. Schön, *Organizational Learning: A Theory of Action Perspective* (Reading: Addison-Wesley, 1978); Peter A. Hall, "Policy Paradigms, Social Learning and the State: The Case of Economic Policy-Making in Britain," *Comparative Politics* 25, no. 3 (1993): 275–96.

17 See, for example, Beatrice de Graaf, Ido de Haan, and Brian E. Vick, "Vienna 1815: Introducing a European Security Culture," in *Securing Europe after Napoleon: 1815 and the New European Security Culture,* ed. Idem (Cambridge: Cambridge University Press, 2019), 1–18, here: 9; Alan Sharp, *Versailles 1919: A Centennial Perspective* (London: Haus, 2018).

18 For example, Stanislas Jeannesson, Fabrice Jesné, and Éric Schnakenbourg eds., *Experts et expertises en diplomatie. La mobilisation des compétences dans les relations internationales du congrès de Westphalie à la naissance de l'ONU* (Rennes: Presses universitaires de Rennes, 2018).

19 Jean de Préneuf, Thomas Vaisset, and Philippe Vial, "La Marine nationale et la Première Guerre mondiale: une histoire à redécouvrir," *Revue d'histoire maritime,* no. 20 (2014).

20 Séverine Autesserre, "Insiders and Outsiders." In *The Frontlines of Peace: An Insider's Guide to Changing the World* (Oxford: Oxford University Press, 2021), see especially Chapter 3.

21 Jocelyn Coulon, *Soldiers of Diplomacy: The United Nations, Peacekeeping, and the New World Order* (Toronto: University of Toronto Press, 1998); Marie-Claude Smouts (ed.), *L'ONU et la guerre: la diplomatie en kaki* (Brussels: Éditions Complexe, 1994).
22 Antoine Prost, *Les anciens combattants et la société française* (Paris: PFNSP, 1977).

Part I

Politico-Military Relationship

2

Peacemaking and Civil-Military Relations, 1918–23

Hew Strachan

Civil-military relations during the First World War are conventionally seen as a source of recurrent friction, of "frocks" (or civilians) battling with "brasshats" (or generals). The result is portrayed as domestic discord and wasted effort during the war and a bout of splenetic and self-serving memoirs after it. Two factors, in particular, contributed to these tensions.

The first was the establishment and growth of general staffs between 1870 and 1914. The creation of what in 1938 Dallas D. Irvine called "capital staffs" meant that developed states set up military planning bodies at the heart of government, which prepared for major war in peacetime.[1] Given the still comparatively underdeveloped state of central government, these were significant bureaucracies with considerable latent powers over the functioning of the state should war break out, and yet the mechanisms for their political control and direction were ill developed.[2] Where general staffs were positioned in the hierarchy and to whom they answered were questions that were only fully resolved after the war broke out in 1914. It was this event, the onset of what we might now call, and some did then, existential conflict, which generated the second problem.

The scale of the First World War ensured that its conduct became the principal function of the state and of the nation. Within weeks soldiers—Joffre and Gallieni in France and Hindenburg and Ludendorff in Germany—became national heroes. After the war, in 1922, the American political commentator, Walter Lippmann, edited and quoted the words of Captain Peter Wright, who had served as the Assistant Secretary of the Supreme War Council:

All chiefs everywhere are now kept, painted by the busy work of numberless publicists, so as to be mistaken for Napoleons—at a distance. . . . It becomes almost impossible to displace these Napoleons, whatever their incompetence, because of the enormous public support created by hiding or glossing failure, and exaggerating or inventing success. . . . But the most insidious and worst effect . . . is on the generals themselves. . . . They themselves are ultimately affected by these universal illusions. . . . These various conditions . . . at last emancipate all General Staffs from all control. They no longer live for the nation: the nation lives, or dies, for them.[3]

By 1917–18 the democratic states, preeminently Britain, France, and Italy, had brought these two pressures under control. Civilian supremacy was reasserted, but in such a way that the military's voice was heard, not silenced. The result was the institutionalization of a new approach to strategy, which, in 1918, enabled the Entente and its associate, the United States, to cohere better as an alliance and which ensured that the tactical and operational conditions which had hitherto dominated the shape of the war henceforth served strategy and, ultimately, policy.

Before the war, the military had defined strategy in self-referential terms: as the business of generals. Foch, appointed the allied generalissimo on March 26, 1918, said, while lecturing at the Ecole de Guerre in 1901, that strategy sought tactical results and so found its outcome in victory on the battlefield.[4] In doing so, he reflected the presumptions of the nineteenth century, going back to Clausewitz. Strategy, the latter had written in *On War*, is "the use of an engagement for the purpose of war."[5] During the war, it became clear that this was too narrow an understanding of the context in which armies now found themselves. War required national mobilization and had to be fought with allies in three dimensions—sea, land, and air—and on multiple fronts. After the war, Sir William Robertson, chief of the British imperial general staff between December 1915 and February 1918, said that strategy was decided not in a general headquarters but in the nation's capital—at the interface between the waging of the war and the formation of policy. Its formation was a joint civil-military endeavor.[6]

This was a conclusion which one of Foch's former pupils, Henri Mordacq, had reached before 1914.[7] In November 1917, Mordacq was appointed the head of Georges Clemenceau's military cabinet and so placed at the center of the civil-military relationship in France. The new premier, who had made his name as a Dreyfusard at the nadir of the army's relationship with the Third Republic, remobilized France for what Léon Daudet would call "total war" in March 1918.[8] Clemenceau rallied the French nation to the army and committed both to victory. He did not warm to the army's commander-in-chief, Philippe Pétain. Although unable to remove Pétain, who was sanctified in the eyes of the Republic as the savior of Verdun in 1916, he did manage to reduce his power. Foch's elevation to the supreme command made him, not Pétain, France's senior commander at the end of March, and during April and May it became increasingly clear where the premier's favor lay. Back in 1908, during his first stint as prime minister, Clemenceau had resuscitated Foch's career by appointing him director of the Ecole de Guerre.[9] The French army's failure on May 27, 1918, to stem the German offensive in Champagne gave Clemenceau the opportunity to effect six changes in the army command and so to replace those officers around Pétain whom he had distrusted.[10] Foch may have been the allied supreme commander, but Clemenceau reminded him he was still a French officer and in July 1918 cemented the relationship by securing Foch's promotion as a Marshal of France.

In Britain, David Lloyd George had begun his time as prime minister by weakening his own authority with the army and its principal supporters. In February 1917, he subordinated the command of the British Expeditionary Force to the overall direction of France for the duration of the Nivelle offensive without prior consultation with the king or the Conservative cabinet colleagues on whom he depended for his political survival. The attack's failure on April 16, 1917, compounded the sin. However, by the end of the year, Lloyd George had rebounded. The third battle of Ypres, which culminated at Passchendaele in November 1917, dented the confidence in Haig of both Conservatives and the press. In January 1918, two of Haig's principal advisers, his chief of staff and his head of military intelligence, were replaced, and in February, Robertson, the chief of the imperial general staff, was ousted. Although Robertson differed with Haig on the strategy to be pursued on the Western Front in 1917, he had loyally defended him in London. Robertson was succeeded by Sir Henry Wilson, whom Haig distrusted not least because of his political instincts. In the succeeding months, Haig, like Pétain, was increasingly subordinated to Foch.[11] Lloyd George's enthusiasm for Foch grew as the war progressed and, after the armistice with Germany in November 1918, the British prime minister would credit the Frenchman with having won the war.[12]

The Italians resisted the idea that their front should be brought under Foch's command. However, the reassertion of political control over the military had been implemented even sooner on the Isonzo than it was on the Somme or the Marne. The breakthrough of the Central powers at Caporetto in October 1917 led to the dismissal of Luigi Cadorna as the Italian commander-in-chief in November—significantly by the king. Cadorna's successor, Armando Diaz, rebuilt the army. A war council was formed and an effective prime minister,

Vittorio Orlando, was appointed. As one minister, Leonardo Bissolati, put it in January 1918, "At last we are a government because we have a prime minister, that is, a coordinator."[13] According to John Gooch, for the first time, "policy was shaped and timed by military practicalities."[14]

Coordination, both within each of the allied states and across the alliance, enabled the formation of strategy and the delivery of victory. The creation of the Supreme War Council in November 1917 had greater significance than many historians have recognized. The initial plan had been to give it muscle by creating a strategic reserve under its control. One practical problem was the issue of numbers: Where were the men to come from when the armies of both France and Britain had passed their peak strengths and that of the Americans had yet to arrive in Europe? Both Pétain and Haig worked to circumvent the plan for a reserve by pledging each other mutual support in the event of a German attack: a promise which Pétain fulfilled after March 21, 1918, but which Haig proved more reluctant to honor when the Germans' blows fell on the French. In some respects, the formation of the Supreme War Council had looked even further ahead, to the day when the American Expeditionary Force would be the dominant force on the Western Front and would therefore have to coordinate its actions with the French and British. That was expected to occur in mid-1919. As the American buildup strengthened in 1918, so did the role of the Supreme War Council. Its Permanent Military Representatives plotted the distribution of forces and the prioritization of fronts, and from April 1918, when Foch was given "strategic direction of military operations," provided him with a de facto, if small, allied staff.[15]

Unity in civil-military relations delivered success in waging war but then fragmented once again at the moment of victory. On October 3, 1918, Germany requested an armistice. Immediately old worries resurfaced and fresh ones opened. As distrust between statesmen and soldiers grew, the close coordination of policy and strategy, which peacemaking demanded, was increasingly absent. What went wrong?

First, the politicians had not expected to win the war so soon. Allied planning was predicated on victory after the American Expeditionary Force reached its peak strength in June 1919. However, when the Germans' fifth offensive of 1918, launched on July 15, was checked, the balance on the Western Front swung the other way with unexpected rapidity. In what was dubbed the Second Battle of the Marne, the French and Americans counterattacked on July 18, 1918, and regained the ground lost to the south of the river. John Charteris, Haig's erstwhile intelligence chief and now responsible for transport, wrote in his diary on that day that "it brings the end of the war much nearer" and added ten days later, "Things are moving much more rapidly than appears from the published reports, and far more decisively than seemed possible a month ago."[16] The allied generals began to realize that victory might come sooner than they had anticipated. It is important not to overstate these hopes. As autumn arrived and the weather worsened, the allied armies would run out of steam, with their lines of communication lengthening and roads turning to mud. Moreover, the offensive operations of the so-called "hundred days" increased their battle casualties just as the second and most lethal wave of the influenza epidemic hospitalized large numbers. In mid-September, Foch, usually the most optimistic of commanders, told his wife that the war must end in 1919, not in 1918.[17]

The German request for an armistice triggered shorter-term horizons but hopes of a quick end were still tempered. Crucially, the German note contained a political dimension. It was addressed to the American president, Woodrow Wilson, not to the other allies or to the field commander on the Western Front, Foch. It asked for negotiation on the basis of Wilson's Fourteen Points, which the president had enunciated in January. Wilson responded quite properly by consulting his allied partners. They, however, were not yet ready to negotiate the political terms of a peace settlement: this was the sense in which they were "ambushed by victory."[18] Each of them had developed full programs of war aims, but some were still contested domestically and others were more designed to preempt the postwar ambitions of their partners than to punish their enemies. The allies had cobbled together a way to fight a coalition war, but they had not drawn up a collective agreement on their joint goals. Because the German request had come a year early, in 1918, not in 1919, they had been deprived of a whole year of planning and preparation for peace.

Nor did they know how seriously to take the German offer. Almost from the war's outset in 1914, Germany had used offers to negotiate a separate peace—particularly with Russia—to try to peel one ally off from the other: the aim here was not so much to end the war as to enable the Central powers to concentrate their efforts and so wage war more effectively. The armistice offer of October 1918—with its direct appeal to Wilson alone—seemed designed to split the United States from its European partners and so smacked of similar maneuvering. The German army had proved extraordinarily resilient, as evidenced most recently by the sequence of five offensives it had just launched between March and July. It was still fighting well inside the French frontier and the pessimists could not discount its ability to attack once more—if not in the west, then in Italy. Although the statesmen were kept abreast of the generals' rising optimism as the victory of July 18 was followed by the sequence of advances beginning at Amiens on August 8, they had learned through bitter experience to be cautious. Generals, including both Foch and Haig, had told them too often before that the next battle would be decisive.

Victory was more palpable on other fronts. In mid-September, the allies broke through in Macedonia and advanced toward the Danube. The collapse of the Balkan front cut off the Ottoman Empire from Germany and Austria-Hungary and threatened Constantinople with a landward attack from the west. In the same month, the Ottomans lost their hold on Palestine and Syria after suffering a crushing defeat at Megiddo. When Bulgaria requested an armistice at the end of September, Henry Wilson, as Britain's chief of the imperial general staff, asked, "what our Foreign Office is going to do if the Turks follow suit." Arthur Balfour, the Foreign Secretary, responded that he did not know. Britain had made incompatible promises in the Middle East to the Arabs, the French, and the Jews, while also developing its own imperial ambitions. The speed of military events had outstripped the pace of political negotiation.[19]

In France, Foch—like Henry Wilson—saw the need in October to link military effects with political outcomes. He believed that, if the Germans were serious about surrendering, the allies had to exploit the moment of their military success to guarantee France's long-term security. If they did not, the peace would not last. Foch wanted to dismantle Prussia, which he saw as the source of German militarism, to return Alsace-Lorraine to France, and to establish the Franco-German border on the Rhine.[20] Few soldiers, and certainly neither Foch nor any of the Supreme War Council's Permanent Military Representatives, trusted the Germans to keep their word. In 1914, when they had invaded Belgium, they had disregarded their treaty obligations. "Who wants to talk with an adversary," Foch asked, "who tears up treaties as though they were scraps of paper . . . with no respect for sacred rights, who reduces people to slavery, deports them like cattle [?]"[21]

The politicians objected to this conflation of military victory with political outcomes for three reasons. First, they themselves were not only in disagreement on what the peace terms should be but also fearful of the role of the United States and Wilson's potential domination of the outcome. Second, because the evidence that the German army had been defeated on the Western Front was not wholly persuasive, they feared that, if the terms demanded of Germany were too extreme, they would be rejected and the war would continue. Some generals, preeminently Britain's Douglas Haig but on occasion Foch himself, worried that might be the case and so confirmed these fears.[22] Third, the politicians resented soldiers entering a sphere which they saw as their preserve: they had been dancing to the tunes of overmighty warriors for too long.

Clemenceau, in particular, asserted the need for a classic division of powers. Let the war be ended on military terms and then peace could be settled by the civilians. Strategy should cease when the fighting ended and diplomacy should take its place. Foreign ministers had been marginalized during the war by general staffs, and they were anxious to reassert their primacy. Distrust between Clemenceau and Foch grew from October 1918 onwards, before the armistice with Germany was even signed: it was as though Clemenceau the socialist and Dreyfusard stepped forward to replace Clemenceau the organizer of victory.

The trouble with this separation of powers was that the war was not over. It was certainly not over in October, but nor did it end in November, when the last three of the armistices—those with Austria, Germany, and Hungary—were signed. An English legal textbook on the termination of war and treaties of peace, published in 1916, made clear that an armistice was limited in time and could be either the preliminary to a peace negotiation or its product. It quoted article 36 of the 1907 Hague Convention: "An armistice suspends military operations by mutual agreement between the belligerent parties. If its duration is not defined, the belligerents may resume operations at any time, provided always that the enemy is warned within the time agreed upon."[23] The author, Dr. Coleman Phillipson, a barrister at the Inner Temple in London, went on to say that "there are no settled rules with regard to the conclusion of the armistice conventions for the purpose of instituting or carrying on peace negotiations" and added presciently: "Diplomacy is always more effective when supported by victorious arms; but cases are not wanting . . . where the victor in the field was not equal to his adversary's diplomacy in the conference chamber, and eventually derived little or no advantage from his martial success."[24]

The allies were right to be wary. Erich Ludendorff, the First Quartermaster General of the German army, had not seen his impetuous demand for an armistice as necessarily the end of the war. On October 1, he told one of the staff officers at the Oberste Heeresleitung (OHL), the German supreme command, that he did not expect Foch to grant an armistice but that the important thing was to grab a breathing space from the fighting on the Western Front.[25] By imagining that the allied response would rest with Foch, he was treating the matter as narrowly military, but he had then contradicted that interpretation by insisting that Germany's newly appointed chancellor, Max von Baden, not the army's command (and Foch's peers), take responsibility for the negotiations. Max von Baden, like the politicians on the other side of the line, wanted more time to line up his options, not least because he—unlike Ludendorff—recognized that the political implications of such a step would be irreversible.

Throughout the war, Ludendorff had been prone to depression, only then to recover his optimism. On previous occasions, his immediate military superior, Chief of the General Staff Paul von Hindenburg, had managed his mood swings. Now, however, Ludendorff had handed the chancellor that responsibility. Three weeks after insisting that an armistice was essential, Ludendorff changed his mind, arguing that fresh manpower could after all be made available and that the army could fight on. What prompted this *volte-face* was Wilson's third note, sent on October 23, 1918, which emphasized that an armistice would need to make "a renewal of hostilities on the part of Germany impossible" and that one way of ensuring that outcome was that it should be preceded by the full democratization of the German government. Two days later, OHL issued an army order that interpreted the American note as a demand to capitulate. It stated that this was "unacceptable for us soldiers" and that the response must be "to prolong our resistance to the utmost of our power." The next day the Kaiser dismissed Ludendorff at the chancellor's request: Max von Baden still hoped to avoid the Kaiser's abdication and so put the preservation of the Reich ahead of the army command's self-esteem.[26]

Ludendorff's readiness to continue fighting confirmed that nobody in October could conclude that Germany's desire for an armistice would lead inexorably to peace. Moreover, the initial approach to the United States had come from Germany alone and not from the Central powers as a whole. The German-led alliance stopped fighting not with a single instrument of collective surrender but with five separate armistice agreements, of which that with Germany on November 11, 1918, was only the most important. Each constituted part of a continuum, which maintained the pressure on what Ludendorff called the "quadruple alliance," and each formed a step leading to the next. On September 30, Bulgaria agreed terms in Belgrade; on October 29, the Ottomans followed suit at Mudros; on November 4, the Austrians surrendered to the Italians at Villa Giusti; and on November 13—after the Germans—the Hungarians did so last of all. Now it was the Entente that was using separate negotiations to pursue the objective of overall victory. The war ended in October and November 1918 in large part because the alliance of the Central powers imploded.

On three fronts decisive battlefield success led directly to negotiations: the breakthrough in the Balkans and the surrender of Bulgaria, the Italian victory at Vittorio Veneto and the collapse of the Habsburg Empire, and the captures of Damascus and Mosul and the defeat of the Ottomans. The terms of each of the armistices negotiated in the wake of these allied victories were designed to weaken the other Central powers and ultimately to encircle and isolate Germany. They were instruments to continue the war by other means. They required the defeated powers to surrender military equipment and railway rolling stock, so disabling their own forces and reequipping those of the allies. Above all, the terms sought to enable the continuation of the allies' advance and to create opportunities for strategic maneuver: from the Balkans to Belgrade, and thence to Vienna and Berlin; from the Dardanelles to the Black Sea and on to southern Russia; and from northern Italy into Bavaria and then Germany itself.

However, the armistices were not the conclusion of the war, because the making of peace was reserved for the statesmen in Paris. Peace was seen not as a product of strategy, not as the continuation of war by other means, but as the work of diplomacy. From December 1918 onwards, the generals repeatedly sought to impress on the politicians that the war was still not over. Technically, they were right, and they had plenty of evidence to support them. Each armistice was valid for a set period and had to be renewed at its conclusion until the peace treaty was signed or the war resumed. At sea, the blockade continued. The food situation across Central and Eastern Europe in the winter of 1918–19 was dire. The Germans protested that, although soldiers were no longer being killed by the allies, women and children were. Despite sympathy in the United States for the Germans' complaint, the British held their ground. The continuation—and indeed intensification—of economic warfare was a blunt instrument used to ensure that the Germans converted their armistice into a peace treaty. The former was regularly renewed while the negotiations continued. On June 21, 1919, Admiral Ludwig von Reuter broke the armistice when he gave the order to scuttle the German High Seas Fleet interned at Scapa Flow. The ships had been surrendered to the British under the naval terms agreed on November 11, 1918, but their ultimate fate was dependent on the peace negotiations. The latest extension of the armistice, until June 23, was designed to allow the Germans time to respond to the finalized draft of the peace treaty. Reuter pleaded that he did not know of the renewal, although he probably did. He took the decision to scuttle the fleet either because he expected Germany to reject the treaty and to resume fighting, in which case he did not want the Royal Navy to use German ships against Germany, or because he was determined to salve the German navy's honor before its final capitulation. The head of the Admiralty in Germany, Adolf von Trotha, had told Reuter that there was no question of the German ships being surrendered to the enemy. On July 3, 1919, Trotha issued an order to the navy welcoming "the manly act of our crews at Scapa Flow" and hailing it as the final victory of an undefeated fleet.[27]

Many in Britain were genuinely fearful that Germany would opt to fight on. Much to the allies' relief, it did not, and it signed the treaty of Versailles on June 28, 1919. However, even now the war was not over. The final peace treaty was agreed on July 24, 1923, and in Lausanne, not in Paris. The new Turkish Republic overthrew the Treaty of Sèvres, which had been signed by the Sultanate on August 10, 1920, and fought a war of independence, which drove both the Greeks and Italians out of Anatolia, and humiliated the British and French further north at Çannakale. The fighting continued not just because of the lapse of time between the armistices and the finalization of the peace treaties but also because other wars were being fought in the aftermath of the main event. Robert Gerwarth has suggested that possibly four million more lives were lost between 1919 and 1923 in addition to the roughly nine million military dead of the First World War proper.[28] These "wars after the war" can be classified in four different ways, of which the third and fourth were the most significant.

The first were wars that had been ongoing before 1914, which never went away between 1914 and 1918 and which were renewed afterward. Italy's invasion of Libya in 1911 had not resulted in complete conquest by 1912, even if the Ottomans agreed terms. Resistance, supported by the Turks, revived when Italy entered the European war in 1915 and it continued until the 1930s. Greece's wars with the Ottomans in the Balkans in 1912–13 fed the ambition of Eleftherios Venizelos for a greater Greece built on the legacy of Greek colonization two millennia earlier. Lloyd George pandered to these designs and they encouraged Winston Churchill in his hope in late 1914 that the Greeks might contribute the land component to the Gallipoli campaign. The Greeks did not commit themselves in 1915 but, after considerable allied pressure, including blockade and intervention, they did so in the summer of 1917. Venizelos formed a national government and declared war on the Central powers. The immediate efforts of the Greek army were bent on achieving full control of Ottoman territory in the Balkans, but in May 1919 they extended to Asia Minor. Greek troops landed at Izmir in May 1919, partly to preempt the Italians who had also resumed their pre-1914 war with the Turks, and then a year later they plunged deeper into Anatolia. In a campaign characterized on both sides by what would now be called ethnic cleansing, Turkish nationalists under Mustafa Kemal pushed the Greeks back to Izmir and sacked the city in September 1922. Just under a million Greeks were driven from their homes in western Asia and about 400,000 Turks from theirs in southeastern Europe.

The second group of wars which continued after 1918 were the more local conflicts, which had piggybacked on the opportunities created by the outbreak of the greater war in August 1914. The states that entered the war after the initial paroxysm at the end of July had time to weigh their options and think through their aims. They negotiated the terms on which they fought with those to whom they allied themselves, as much as, if not more than, they were impelled by hostility toward those whom they fought. If they had chosen wisely and ended up on the winning side, they expected to see their territorial demands satisfied. Japan was the first to fight on these terms, declaring war on Germany on August 23, 1914. Britain wanted no more than short-term naval support against the German East Asiatic squadron in the Pacific, but Japan had imperial designs on China. On January 18, 1915, Japan's ambassador in Beijing presented the Chinese with twenty-one demands designed to extend its territorial and economic footprint on the Asian mainland. Japan stayed in the war principally in order to consolidate these gains in the peace negotiations, while China entered the war in 1917 to forestall that intention. This was the struggle, albeit between two powers on the same side during the First World War, which would trigger the Second World War as a global conflict in 1937.

In May 1915, Italy, formally speaking the ally of Germany and Austria-Hungary, committed itself to the Entente cause. It did so because its territorial ambitions on its northeastern frontier could only be fulfilled at the expense of Austria-Hungary. When the war on the Italian front ended at Vittorio Veneto in October 1918, Italy's troops were still fighting within its 1915 frontiers and had reached none of its original objectives. For Italian nationalists, the First World War was fought to complete the Risorgimento and the collapse of the Habsburg Empire provided not a reason to halt but the opportunity to press on into Dalmatia. Nor were they alone. Romania had been rapidly overrun by the Central powers after it had entered the war on the Entente side in 1916 and, after the Russians agreed terms at Brest-Litovsk in March 1918, it had accepted similarly humiliating conditions at Bucharest in May. After the allies' breakthrough on the Macedonian front in September, their commander, Franchet d'Esperey, expected Romania to reenter the war on the allied side and so to expedite his advance to the Danube. Romania waited until the last moment, resuming hostilities on November 10, 1918, too late to make any effective military contribution. Its aim was to achieve its territorial objectives in Transylvania and the Bukovina, at the expense, respectively, of Hungary and Bulgaria, in whose pursuit it had originally opted for war in 1916. Italy and Romania were, like Greece, each fighting regional wars for national objectives that ran concurrently with the larger war but which therefore also had the capacity to continue when that greater conflict ended.

More expansive was the third group of wars. These had been provoked by the employment of revolution as a weapon of war to subvert the enemy. Germany had done so in Ireland, North Africa, and across Central Asia to India; Britain had done so in Arabia. In April 1917, after the first Russian revolution of that year, the Germans had smuggled Lenin into Petrograd from Switzerland in a "sealed train." Their action accomplished the end they sought when the Bolsheviks seized power in November and Lenin vowed to take Russia out of the war. In the winter of 1917–18, Russia's erstwhile allies confronted a truly terrible situation in the short term: the Central powers would be able to concentrate their forces to the west and south, free (or so it seemed) of commitments to the east. Britain, France, and the United States, therefore, intervened in Russia in the first instance not so much to crush the revolution as to reopen the Russian front against the Central powers. They supported the counterrevolutionary Whites against the Reds for reasons of strategy more than ideology and that motive persisted until the Germans signed the peace treaty in June 1919.

Even in 1918, however, the fear of Bolshevism began to supplant the hatred of the Boche. The peoples of all the European belligerents, regardless of the side on which they fought, were weary and—after poor harvests from 1916 onwards—hungry. Russia, unlike Romania, was not represented in Paris on the grounds that it had ceased to be an interested party after it agreed terms with the Central powers at Brest-Litovsk. It was therefore excluded from the planning for a new world order and so free to pursue its own revisionist objectives. Following Marxist logic and underpinned by hopes of international working-class solidarity, it sensed the opportunity for revolution beyond its frontiers which the war had created. It supported the Reds against the Whites in the states which sought to establish themselves on its western borders—to the north, those which had been under Russian rule, Finland, Latvia, and Lithuania, and to the south those governed by Austria-Hungary. As the statesmen met in Paris, they feared that Bolshevism would extend further west, taking hold of Austria and Germany too.

The doors to both local national expansion and transnational revolution looked wide open precisely because at the end of 1918, four major and contiguous empires had simultaneously collapsed. The fall of Tsarist Russia in 1917 had been followed by those of the German, Austro-Hungarian, and ultimately Ottoman empires. Nor would the process necessarily end there: Britain faced challenges along the "southern arc" of its empire from Ireland to India, by way of Egypt and Iraq. Woodrow Wilson had poured fuel on the flames of this combustible material when in January 1918 his Fourteen Points had affirmed the principle of national self-determination. That commitment gave immediate substance to the hopes of Czechs and Poles, making Britain, France, and Italy somewhat reluctant partners in the subversion of the Habsburg Empire in 1918, and stoking the hopes for significant gains in the Balkans of allies like the Serbs, Greeks, and Romanians, whose fellow nationals lived under Habsburg or Ottoman rule. The result was civil war across Central and Eastern Europe, from the Baltic to the Balkans and from Cork to the Caucasus. The divisions were not just political, Reds against Whites, but also ethnic, as Slavs fought Teutons. While the peacemakers conferred in Paris, wars were being fought across Europe and Asia. While they drew lines on maps, conflict was changing the situation on the ground.

On Christmas Eve 1918, the chief of the British imperial general staff, Sir Henry Wilson, attended a meeting of the Imperial War Cabinet. That night he wrote in his diary: "They all talked about Peace and the League of Nations, and the whole thing such rubbish that I went away. Why not face the facts, that there are still wars going on in several countries and that until these are crushed out it is no use talking peace?"[29] Throughout 1919, he kept up the refrain that the war was not yet over. By August, he had concluded that Britain faced four "storm centres"—Ireland, Egypt, Mesopotamia, and India.[30] In addition, the country needed soldiers to keep order at home. He thought the situation more dangerous than it had been in 1914, and by November he was writing to Lord Esher that, although one war had ended, "one year and three days after the Armistice we have between 20 and 30 wars ranging in different parts of the world."[31]

Across the Channel, his great friend, Ferdinand Foch, was equally frustrated. On December 4, 1918, Foch noted that "The war is not ended."[32] The two met regularly to commiserate with each other, Wilson increasingly falling back on the vocabulary of contempt for politicians, calling them "frocks." The relationships between the leading statesmen and their principal military advisers collapsed with frightening speed from late 1918, but they did so in different ways and at different tempos.

In both Britain and France, the armistices, even if they were not the end of the war, were greeted as such. In part, this was not the fault of either Lloyd George or Clemenceau, but the response of their nations. The public celebrations precipitated specifically by the German armistice on November 11, 1918, continued for some days, and in France were reechoed in the progressive liberation of towns which had been under German rule—either since 1914 or, in the case of Alsace-Lorraine, since 1871. This felt like the end of the war, even if it was not.

Wives and families expected to welcome their soldiers home for Christmas and exercised immediate pressure for the rapid demobilization of both the British and French armies. Eliane Stern, an eleven-year-old French girl living in Pontarlier, wrote at the end of her journal entry for November, with its excited account of victory and celebration: "I am waiting for Papa. He is never here, but I now know that he will not die fighting on 'the field of honour' as the speeches put it." He had gone to war over four years earlier, in August 1914, but in December she wrote,

> The armistice is signed, the fighting has ceased, but Papa has not come back! I don't understand anything. When is he going to return? The newspapers say nothing about it. Mummy does not know and, as for me, I have a heavy heart. So, as usual each night, I kiss his photo and slip it under my pillow before I go to sleep.[33]

Her father came home on February 10, 1919 and accompanied her to school the following morning, but—in his daughter's judgment—not until the signature of the peace treaty itself did his fear of the war's resumption evaporate and his sense of joy recover. He knew, as his "Lili" could not, that the strain on the French army had not ended in November 1918. In some respects, it was exacerbated, as the United States began to withdraw its troops from Europe and the white soldiers of the British empire from Australia, Canada, and New Zealand, who during the war had been too far from home to be allowed anything other than local leave in Paris or London, followed suit. The soldiers of France and Britain had to occupy the defeated countries, police their own empires, and—if need be—remain ready to resume the war with Germany. Britain retained conscription until 1920 and demobilization was not as fast as either the soldiers or their families expected.

Initially Britain gave priority to the release of those who had the skills necessary for the recovery of the peacetime economy, regardless of the length of service. Unsurprisingly this prioritization of society's needs over those of the individual caused discontent. In January and February 1919, British soldiers on leave refused to return to duty and staged what were called demobilization "strikes."[34] France adopted a different policy: those who had been called up first were also the first to be released. While containing discontent, it did not eliminate it. France's troubles occurred particularly in the Armée d' Orient, whose war in the Balkans ended less neatly than it did on the Western Front and for whose soldiers the journey home was harder to arrange.[35] The Armée d' Orient provided units for the intervention in Russia, and in January 1919, an infantry regiment in Ukraine mutinied. The Black Sea became the epicenter of French military disaffection, which radiated out to the Mediterranean and lasted until October. Its most significant manifestation was the mutiny of a French naval squadron in April. By June, the crews of French patrol boats in the Baltic were demanding leave and demobilization.[36] In northern waters, long periods of inactivity in 1917–18 had generated worries about morale, especially on capital ships. Discipline in the Royal Navy remained generally good until the armistice but fractured in January 1919. The minesweepers of the Grand Fleet refused to put to sea because of low pay and crews on a number of ships, one of which raised the red flag, mutinied. [37]

Both British and French governments met the fear of further disorder in their armed forces with the language of appeasement as much as with the enforcement of discipline. They sought to return their citizen-soldiers more rapidly to civilian life. On June 29, 1919, the British switched to the French model of demobilization by seniority, but mutinies still occurred, most famously in the Connaught Rangers in India in June 1920.[38] The British army mustered 3.8 million men in November 1918 but 890,000 in November 1919 and 430,000 by November 1920.[39] To cut its numbers at that rate and still meet its commitments, it had to be less generous with those who had fewer political rights. Some Indian regiments in the Middle East did not get back home until 1923. When in December 1918, the Black soldiers of the British West Indies Regiment serving in Italy mutinied in Taranto over rates of pay, allowances, and promotion, the sentences looked more severe than those handed out to white troops.[40] France too kept its colonial soldiers under arms for longer, arousing the ire of the Germans by deploying Senegalese in its Army of Occupation, but also growing the proportion of North African troops in the Armée d'Orient to secure its interests outside Europe. The French army, which totaled 900,000 on July 1, 1920, of whom about 650,000 were in France, still stood at 850,000 a year later. These numbers were high enough for the British to worry once more about French domination of Europe and for the Americans to complain that the cost to France was slowing the repayment of its war debt. The French army remained strong enough to deal with Germany militarily, but only because it had effectively cut back on its commitments elsewhere, in the Levant, Poland and Czechoslovakia, and in North Africa and the colonies. As Hubert Lyautey, the former minister of war who was now once again the military governor of Morocco, put it in September 1920, "We have taken on more responsibilities than it is materially possible for this country to shoulder."[41]

Henry Wilson reached the same conclusion. He called for the alignment of means and ends—for Britain to frame its political ambitions according to the size of the army it now possessed. In April 1919, Rear Admiral Walter Cowan, who was commanding the British ships in the Baltic operating in support of the Whites against the Reds, informally asked Wilson if the army could help. Wilson replied that it could only do so if "the Big Four [Woodrow Wilson, Clemenceau, Lloyd George and Orlando] lay down a broad policy. . . . Since November 22 of last year I have been trying to get a policy—trying, trying, trying, and not a shadow of success."[42] He wanted to withdraw British troops from Europe and Russia so that he could concentrate their efforts where he felt they were needed, at home and in Ireland, Egypt, and India.

In other words, Wilson's frustrations with Lloyd George arose from the latter's inability to make choices from which the army could make strategy. In particular, the prime minister's support for the Greeks and contempt for the Turks resulted in the scattering of militarily ineffective detachments of troops around the Black Sea, at Çannakale and in the Caucasus, none of them able to survive if individually attacked. Wilson recorded that on June 17, 1920, he had told Winston Churchill, by then Secretary of War, "that in my opinion we were heading straight for disaster in Constantinople, Dardanelles, Mesopotamia, and Persia. As I had over and over again pointed out, our policy had no relation to the forces at our disposal, and so we were incapable of carrying out our commitments."[43]

Lloyd George had brought Henry Wilson in as chief of the imperial general staff in February 1918 to neutralize his other generals, preeminently Sir William Robertson, who lost his job as a result, and Sir Douglas Haig. Haig did not like Wilson, not least because of his overtly political orchestration of the so-called Curragh mutiny during the Irish home rule crisis in March 1914, and his own leverage was reduced when the fighting ended on the Western Front. By 1919, Wilson was indisputably the government's principal military adviser, but by 1920 he and Lloyd George met with much less frequency. Wilson wrote on February 13, 1921, "If the highest art and form of statesmanship is to reduce an absolutely peaceful, quiet, thinking country into hell then Lloyd George is a master." As in 1914, Ireland again exacerbated a fraught situation. Wilson was an Irish unionist, who in February 1922, on his retirement from the army, was elected as the Member of Parliament for North Down. He pledged himself to devote all his "energies public & private . . . to getting rid of that pack of Cowards: the present Cabinet."[44]

Foch's falling out with Clemenceau began even earlier than Wilson's with Lloyd George. Early in October 1918, with the war not yet over, their relationship "refroze," according to Mordacq.⁴⁵ Clemenceau blamed Foch for not pushing the Americans hard enough in the Argonne. As the head of Clemenceau's military cabinet, Mordacq saw them both regularly. He noted how the harmony in civil-military relations which had brought victory was now breaking down and vitiating the delivery of peace. He attributed the tensions to cumulative misunderstandings, which were then exploited by other powers, especially the United Kingdom and the United States. However, also in play was Clemenceau's deliberate exclusion of Foch from policymaking circles from late 1918 onwards.

The French premier was determined that the army would have no part to play after the armistice. He refused to appoint Foch a French plenipotentiary for the peace negotiations, despite the fact that Foch was meeting the Germans regularly when the politicians were not. Foch had to renegotiate and reaffirm the armistice terms every thirty-plus days. Clemenceau saw Foch's efforts to lay down the conditions for France's future security and for an enduring peace in Western Europe as a military intrusion into the political space. "The right to speak [la parole] was no longer with the soldiers," he said on October 19, 1918.⁴⁶ As the allied advance forced Foch to move east and away from Paris, the problem was compounded by physical separation. By November 11, Mordacq averred, the trust between Foch and Clemenceau had collapsed.⁴⁷

On April 28, 1919, Foch, "who is more maddened than ever by the Frocks," told Wilson "that the Tiger [Clemenceau] never sees him or tells him anything."⁴⁸ As a result, the plans for the military occupation of Germany were drawn up by the "Big Four" without their consulting Foch or any other soldier. Throughout 1919, Foch's efforts to ensure France's—and by implication Europe's—future security, at the point when that security could have been delivered because Germany was at its lowest ebb, were frustrated. He was defeated on the settlement of Germany's western frontier and the Rhineland. When neither Lloyd George nor Woodrow Wilson would support the French proposals, Clemenceau caved in and accepted the guarantee of American and British military aid if it were required. The Foch-Clemenceau relationship was irretrievably fractured. In Foch's view, France was left as exposed as it had been in August 1914.

Behind Lloyd George and Clemenceau loomed the leverage of Woodrow Wilson, a president educated in the orthodoxy of American civil-military relations and unschooled in the realities of continental strategy. The American president sought a settlement based on universal principles of law and democracy, not on the balance of power. Generals were subordinates, not colleagues. His own principal military adviser was Tasker Bliss. Like Foch and Wilson, Bliss recognized the need to marry military means to political ends in ending the war, but unlike them he lacked assertiveness in stating his views.[49] Bliss had been the US Army's chief of staff in the second half of 1917, but Woodrow Wilson rarely consulted him. At one level that was surprising: Bliss was the bookish and multilingual son of a classics professor who ought to have appealed to the former president of Princeton. However, Wilson was in awe of John J. Pershing, the commander-in-chief of the American Expeditionary Force, who thought Bliss an introvert and pedant.[50] In November 1917, Bliss accompanied a mission to France led by Edward House, the president's closest adviser, and so was on the spot when the Supreme War Council was formed. He was duly appointed America's Permanent Military Representative. As the United States was not regularly represented at the political level on the council, Bliss enjoyed a more enhanced role than those of his peers, gaining traction in allied councils in Europe and an attentive readership for his reports back in Washington. At the war's end, he was appointed as an American plenipotentiary to the Peace Conference, so potentially acquiring an influence greater than that of either Foch or Henry Wilson. However, his views now merely echoed Woodrow Wilson's thinking, rather than supplemented it: he called for a rapid conclusion to the peace settlement and swift disarmament, not for the elevation of strategy in peacemaking. The president spoke to him only five times during the conference and much of Bliss' time in Paris seems to have been spent in sorting out hotel bookings for his country's delegation.[51]

The tendency has been to see the ruptures in civil-military relations after 1918 in traditional terms and to cast Henry Wilson and Foch as "men on horseback." The pre-1914 histories of both Britain and France confirmed the trajectory of soldiers who did not limit their aspirations in conformity with democratic norms. Wilson's central role in the Ulster crisis of 1914 found its reflection in April 1920, when Sir William Tyrell of the Foreign Office likened him to Ludendorff.[52] In 1921–2 the question of Ireland again undermined the British government's dealings with its general staff. Bernard Ash called his biography of Wilson, published in 1968, *The Lost Dictator*. Eight years earlier, in *Foch vs Clemenceau*, American academic J. C. King studied the breakdown of their relationship in 1918–19 and presented Foch as a direct military challenge to the predominance of the civil power. However, for all his frustrations, Foch never orchestrated a coup. Like Wilson, he saw his insubordination as an expression of strategic wisdom rather than of political impropriety. It was Clemenceau, the Dreyfusard, the socialist schooled in the threat which the army posed to the Third Republic, who saw Foch as a potential Boulanger.

The breakdown in civil-military relations after November 1918 was catastrophic for the peacemakers. They lacked the military instrument with which to impose the terms which they planned on maps in Paris or negotiated in smoke-filled rooms distant from the realities on the ground. By contrast, those who united civil and military power were able to settle the frontiers of Eastern and Central Europe on their own terms. Ataturk, the former Mustafa Kemal, embodied this success, creating a form of victory for Turkey from the embers of Ottoman defeat. There were others: Pilsudski in Poland, Mannerheim in Finland, and Trotsky in Russia. They were also to be found among the allies: Gabriele d'Annunzio succeeded in fulfilling Italians' ambitions in Fiume with the support of the army and the complicity of Armando Diaz, Italy's chief of staff.[53]

Ending the First World War proved harder than beginning it, but the difficulties and complexities were in many respects self-imposed. By 1918, the "Big Four" knew how to integrate civil and military effects in order to shape strategy. By 1919, in their wish to celebrate the peace before they had made it, they forgot the need to use the tools of strategy, preferring the diplomacy of peace when there was too little opportunity for peace to work.

That this happened was not due to any narrowing of the conception of strategy. The events of 1918–23 only served to reinforce the idea that strategy was the use of war for the purposes of policy, as both Sir William Robertson and Henri Mordacq among others stressed. Nor was it necessarily the consequence of the collapse of the institutions which had worked so effectively to coordinate allied strategy in 1917–18. The Supreme War Council continued to exist until at least February 1921, with the Permanent Military Representatives meeting on a regular basis. Instead what occurred shows the power of individuals to undermine good concepts and sound institutions. The fashion was then, and has been since, to blame Foch and Henry Wilson; in reality we should look to Clemenceau, Lloyd George, and the man Henry Wilson called "his cousin," Woodrow Wilson. The president's long-term vision for a new international order, based on the League of Nations, discounted the role of war before peace had been secured, and Wilsonian idealism was never tempered by the realism or realities of European politics.

In 1943, Major General Sir Frederick Maurice, who had been the director of Military Operations at the War Office in 1917–18, wrote a short book titled *The Armistices of 1918* for the Royal Institute of International Affairs at Chatham House in London. Among his conclusions was the following: "Since armistices are suspensions of hostilities and peace does not come until treaties of peace are ratified, the Allies must maintain for an indefinite period the power to enforce their will on their enemies." He went on: "If disturbance and unrest are to be avoided on the conclusion of hostilities, the fact should be made clear to the public and to the men and women serving in the forces of the several allies."[54] Two years later, the allies did not repeat the mistakes of 1918.

Notes

1   Dallas D. Irvine, "The Origins of Capital Staffs," *Journal of Modern History* 10 (1938): 161–79.
2   Arden Bucholz, *Moltke, Schlieffen and Prussian War Planning* (New York: Berg, 1991), draws out these implications.
3   Peter E. Wright, *At the Supreme War Council* (London: Eveleigh Nash Co., 1921), 95, 100–5, as adapted by Walter Lippmann, *Public Opinion* (New York: Harcourt, Brace & Co., 1922), 152.
4   Ferdinand Foch, *The Principles of War*, trans. H. Belloc (London: Chapman and Hall, 1918), 43.
5   Carl von Clausewitz, *On War*, ed. and trans. Michael Howard and Peter Paret (Princeton: Princeton University Press, 1976), 177.
6   William Robertson, *Soldiers and Statesmen 1914–1918,* vol. 2 (London: Cassell, 1926), 300–1.
7   Henri Mordacq, *La Stratégie historique, évolution* (Paris: Fournier, 1912); Mordacq, *Politique et stratégie dans une démocratie* (Paris: Plon-Nourrit, 1912).
8   Léon Daudet, *La guerre totale* (Paris: Nouvelle Librairie Nationale, 1918); Daudet dated his conclusion March 27, 1918, and the book was published in April.
9   Jean-Christophe Notin, *Foch* (Paris: Perrin, 2008), 57–60.
10 Jean-Baptiste Duroselle, *Clemenceau* (Paris: Fayard, 1988), 690–2.
11 David Woodward, *Lloyd George and the Generals* (East Brunswick: Associated University Presses, 1983), esp. 145–53; 231–2; on the erosion of Haig's power, see too John P. Harris, *Douglas Haig and the First World War* (Cambridge: Cambridge University Press, 2008), for example, 461–4.
12 Henri Mordacq, *Le ministère Clemenceau: le journal d'un témoin*, 4 vols. (Paris: Plon, 1930–1), vol. 3, 29.
13 John Whittam, *The Politics of the Italian Army* (London: Croom Helm, 1977), 206.
14 John Gooch, *The Italian Army and the First World War* (Cambridge: Cambridge University Press, 2014), 247; see also John R. Schneider, *Isonzo: The Forgotten Sacrifice of the Great War* (Westport: Praeger, 2001), 261–2.
15 Meighen McCrae, *Coalition Strategy and the End of the First World War: The Supreme War Council and War Planning, 1917-1918* (Cambridge: Cambridge University Press, 2019).

16 John Charteris, *At G.H.Q.* (London: Cassell Ltd., 1931), 317.

17 Elizabeth Greenhalgh, *Foch in Command; The Forging of a First War General* (Cambridge: Cambridge University Press, 2011), 465.

18 Meighen McCrae, "'Ambushed by victory': Britain, France and American Plans to Defeat France in 1919," *War in History* 38, no. 4 (2019): 320–33.

19 David Fromkin, *A Peace to End All Peace: The Fall of the Ottoman Empire and the Creation of the Modern Middle East* (New York: Avon Books, 1990), 364.

20 Greenhalgh, *Foch*, 466.

21 Ibid., 468.

22 Harry D. Rudin, *Armistice 1918* (New Haven: Yale University Press, 1944), 168, 177, 182, 288–9, 397.

23 Coleman Phillipson, *Termination of War and Treaties of Peace* (London: T. Fisher Unwin, 1916), 62.

24 Ibid., 74.

25 Albrecht von Thaer, *Generalstabsdienst an der Front und in der O.H.L.*, ed. Siegfried A. Kaehler (Göttingen: Vandenhoeck & Ruprecht, 1958), 235–6.

26 Max von Baden, *Erinnerungen und Dokumente*, ed. Golo Mann and Andreas Burckhardt (Stuttgart: Ernst Klett, 1968), 463, 470.

27 Nicolas Wolz, *From Imperial Splendour to Internment: The German Navy in the First World War* (Barnsley: Seaforth Publishing, 2015), 200–10.

28 Robert Gerwarth, *The Vanquished: Why the First World War Failed to End 1917–1923* (London: Allen Lane, 2016), 7. There may well be double counting here: for example, the British counted all those service personnel who died up until 1921 as First World War dead.

29 Charles E. Callwell, *Field Marshal Sir Henry Wilson, Bart., GCB, DSO: His Life and Diaries*, 2 vols. (London: Cassell and Company Ltd., 1927), vol. 2, 157.

30 Keith Jeffery, *Field Marshal Sir Henry Wilson: A Political Soldier* (Oxford: Oxford University Press, 2008), 244.

31 Keith Jeffery, *The Military Correspondence of Field Marshal Sir Henry Wilson, 1918-1922* (London: The Bodley Head, 1985), 133.

32 Greenhalgh, *Foch*, 495.

33 Eliane Stern and Viviane Koenig, *L' étoile: le journal d'une petite fille pendant la grande guerre* (Paris: Oskar, 2014), 52–4; see also 68. Eliane Stern died in Auschwitz in 1942, followed, in 1943, by her parents, her husband, and her own children.

34 William Butler, "'The British soldier is no Bolshevik': The British Army, Discipline, and the Demobilization Strikes of 1919," *Twentieth-Century British History* 30, no. 3 (2019): 321–46.

35 Bruno Cabannes, *La victoire endeuillée: la sortie de guerre des soldats français (1918-1920)* (Paris: Seuil, 2004), 284–95, 327–34.

36 Matt Perry, *Mutinous Memories: A Subjective History of French Military Protest in 1919* (Manchester: Manchester University Press, 2019), 3–8, provides a chronology;

for the navy specifically, see Philippe Masson, *La marine française et la mer noire (1918–1919)* (Paris: Publications de la Sorbonne, 1982).

37 Laura Rowe, *Morale and Discipline in the Royal Navy during the First World War* (Cambridge: Cambridge University Press, 2018), 238.

38 Mario Draper, "Mutiny under the Sun: The Connaught Rangers, India, 1920," *War in History* 27, no. 2 (2020): 202–23.

39 Jeffery, *Wilson*, 231.

40 Sneha Reddy Tumu, "North African and Indian soldiers in the First World War in Palestine and Syria, 1917-1923" (PhD Thesis, University of St Andrews, 2020); Glenford Howe, *Race, War and Nationalism: A Social History of West Indians in the First World War* (Kingston: Ian Randle Publishers, 2002), 164–7; Richard Smith, *Jamaican Volunteers in the First World War: Race, Masculinity and the Development of National Consciousness* (Manchester: Manchester University Press, 2004), 130–5.

41 Jean Doise and Maurice Vaïsse, *Diplomatie et outil militaire: politique étrangère de la France, 1871-1969* (Paris: Imprimerie nationale, 1987), 263–8.

42 Callwell, *Wilson*, vol. 2, 182; see also Geoffrey Bennett, *Cowan's War: The Story of British Naval Operations in the Baltic, 1918-1920* (London: Collins, 1964).

43 Callwell, *Wilson*, vol. 2, 244.

44 Jeffery, *Wilson*, 278–9.

45 Mordacq, *Le ministère Clemenceau*, vol. 2, 268–9.

46 Ibid., 284.

47 Ibid., 313.

48 Callwell, *Wilson*, vol. 2, 182; see also 185.

49 See his warnings about Japanese intervention in Russia in March 1918: Carol Willcox Melton, *Between War and Peace: Woodrow Wilson and the American Expeditionary Force in Siberia, 1918–1921* (Macon: Mercer University Press, 2001), 5.

50 David R. Woodward, *Trial by Friendship: Anglo-American Relations 1917-1918* (Lexington: University Press of Kentucky, 1993), 31–2, 56, 155; Geoffrey Wawro, *Sons of Freedom: The Forgotten American Soldiers who Defeated Germany in World War I* (New York: Basic Books, 2018), 71–2, 94, 101.

51 Margaret MacMillan, *Paris 1919: Six Months That Changed the World* (New York: Random House, 2002), 5–6.

52 Peter J. Yearwood, *Guarantee of Peace: The League of Nations in British Policy 1914-1925* (Oxford: Oxford University Press, 2009), 155.

53 Lucy Hughes-Hallett, *The Pike: Gabriele d'Annunzio: Poet, Seducer and Preacher of War* (London: Fourth Estate, 2013), 491–3.

54 Frederick Maurice, *The Armistices of 1918* (London: Oxford University Press, 1943), 80.

3

The Post–Cold War US Army and Debates over Peacekeeping Operations

David Fitzgerald

In October 1995, American soldiers from 1/15 Infantry, 3rd Infantry Division formed up in their barracks in Schweinfurt, Germany, in preparation for a peacekeeping deployment to the Former Yugoslav Republic of Macedonia. On the morning of October 10, the 550 troops scheduled to deploy as part of Task Force Able Sentry were arrayed on the parade square, awaiting a uniform inspection. One soldier, 22-year-old Specialist Michael New, stood out in the ranks as he was the only one not wearing the blue beret and the UN insignia. New was immediately dismissed from the parade and subsequently charged with disobeying a lawful order. His chain of command had been anticipating this disobedience, as he had penned a letter to his commander explaining his stance once he heard in August 1995 that the unit was deployed to Macedonia, and, more significantly, given an interview to the far-right publication, *The New American,* that had been published on October 2.[1] His father had also posted about the situation on an internet bulletin board back in the United States, prompting a flood of mail from conservative activists supporting New's actions.[2]

New ultimately received a dishonorable discharge from the military, which made his case a conservative *cause celebré.*[3] The incident provided fuel for talk radio hosts who believed that the UN was undermining US sovereignty, while candidates running in the 1996 Republican Presidential primary repeatedly referenced the young soldier's plight in their campaign speeches.[4] In total, 100 members of Congress cosponsored legislation that would prohibit a president from ordering US soldiers to wear UN insignia. Republican House Majority Whip Republican Tom DeLay argued that "forcing soldiers to wear the uniform of the United Nations effectively asks the soldier to serve another power. No American soldier should be put in Michael New's position—forced to choose allegiances between the United States and the United Nations."[5]

This wave of support allowed New to pursue a series of legal appeals against his dismissal, which ran for well over a decade and only ended in 2007 when the US Supreme Court refused to hear the case, the final defeat in a streak of unsuccessful suits against the army. New's defense rested on a series of assertions about the army's uniform regulations but also on the more consequential issue of whether or not the president had the authority to put soldiers under the operational control of foreign officers (or, in the defense team's telling, in a non-American chain of command).[6] At the heart of the issue lay questions of sovereignty but also questions surrounding the ambiguity of these missions. If captured by armed actors, would New be a prisoner of war, and thus entitled to Geneva convention protections, or something else? New argued that President Clinton was effectively ordering him into a situation that might end in combat without following the correct legal procedures that should pertain to such risky missions.[7] His legal team's arguments found no purchase with the various judges that they appeared before, but they did capture a segment of the public imagination, revealing a deep-seated unease with the nature of such deployments.

The New case was very straightforward as a matter of law, but the outsized attention it received from politicians, media figures, activists, and members of the public demonstrates that peacekeeping missions were the site of fierce political contestation in the 1990s United States. That decade marked the first, and to date only, time that the US military participated in such missions on a large scale. Soldiers were deployed to places like Northern Iraq, Somalia, Bosnia, Haiti, and Kosovo and encountered wildly varying levels of complexity, ambiguity, and violence. The sheer number of deployments, coupled with a sense of uncertainty about the future of combat and the role of land forces in a post–Cold War environment, made them a topic of conversation for Americans interested in foreign policy and national security. Liberals, neoconservatives, and anti-interventionist conservatives alike projected their anxieties about, and ambitions for, the place of the United States in the world and the future of the US military onto these missions, which provided endless fodder for opinion columns and Congressional hearings.

This political debate mirrored a more restrained, but no less anxious, discussion within the US military as to what attitude the institution should take toward peacekeeping. This was most acute within the army as, more than the other services, it was in the throes of an identity crisis after the ending of the Cold War deprived it of the mission for which it had prepared for more than forty years. Peacekeeping missions were a far cry from defending the Fulda Gap, and extensive army participation in these deployments called into question the relevance of its training, doctrine, education, and even force structure. From senior leaders to the junior enlisted ranks, soldiers wrestled with these issues as they tried to make sense of their new operational environment.

For all involved in the debate—from army leaders and civilian policymakers to ordinary soldiers, academics, and political commentators—these discussions all circled around a central question: in an era with seemingly very little prospect of conventional war, what were soldiers for? At stake was the issue of whether or not American soldiers should be violent warfighters or armed humanitarians, professional warriors, or citizen-soldiers. Thus, beyond discussions of whether or not peacekeeping was an appropriate role for the army lay deeper concerns about the identity and purpose of the American soldier. This chapter will sketch out the contours of these discussions and examine how post-Cold War anxieties over peacekeeping operations related to more fundamental questions about the role of the US Army and its place in American society.

To read the professional journals of the US Army in the early 1990s is to get a sense of the unease caused by the end of the Cold War. Strategists, planners, and theorists struggled to understand how to best reposition the American military for this new world. Despite the recent overwhelming victory in the Persian Gulf, journals published article after article warning that what the army had accomplished there was a one-off and not a harbinger of the decade to come. Writing in *Parameters*, the journal of the US Army War College, Daniel Bolger drew historical parallels with the pre–First World War British army:

> Just as Omdurman rang with the last stirrings of the Scots Greys' headlong dash at Waterloo, so the American Army's brilliantly successful Gulf War is a final echo of the Third Army's great wheel across France. The British soon found Boers out there as well as Dervishes, and Americans will shortly find Boers of their own to confront in El Salvador, the Philippines, or a dozen other hot, grimy flashpoints.[8]

Bolger warned that the US Army "must turn from the warm and well-deserved glow of its Persian Gulf victory and embrace, once more, the real business of regulars, the stinking gray shadow world of 'savage wars of peace,' as Rudyard Kipling called them."[9] There was a sense that what had worked so well in Kuwait and southern Iraq was already irrelevant.

Certainly, the operational tempo of the post-1991 military suggested that their day-to-day reality overseas would be different than it had been during the Cold War. Between January 1989 and December 1993, the army deployed no fewer than forty-eight "named" operations, ranging from hurricane relief to peacekeeping and peace enforcement operations.[10] Enthusiasm for these operations was initially bipartisan, with both major party candidates in the 1992 presidential election proclaiming optimism about prospects for US involvement in peacekeeping missions. President George H. W. Bush spelled out his ambition for future US participation in UN peacekeeping operations in a September 1992 address to the General Assembly of the United Nations, noting that he had "directed the establishment of a permanent peacekeeping curriculum in US military schools."[11] His opponent, Governor Bill Clinton of Arkansas, found little to disagree with on that front and in his own campaign speeches he offered to commit American troops to a mooted standing UN rapid deployment force.[12]

Despite political enthusiasm for peacekeeping, many within the military were skeptical of the merits of such operations. Chairman of the Joint Chiefs of Staff General Colin Powell told reporters at a press briefing that he was "going to give them a little bit of a tutorial about what an armed force is all about." Powell argued that "notwithstanding all of the changes that have taken place in the world, notwithstanding the new emphasis on peacekeeping, peace enforcement, peace engagement, preventive diplomacy, we have a value system and a culture system within the armed forces of the United States. We have this mission: to fight and win the nation's wars."[13]

For Powell, missions like Haiti, Somalia, and Bosnia were traps to be avoided. Reflecting on the US intervention in Haiti, Powell's successor as chairman of the joint chiefs, General John Shalikashvili, cautioned that "we need to remember that the primary mission of the armed forces of the United States is to fight and win on the battlefield, and we ought not to get in the habit of this sort of thing."[14] That he felt the need to remind his audience of the US military's prime mission even in the aftermath of a successful (from an American perspective) peacekeeping operation demonstrates not only the antipathy of many senior leaders toward these missions but the anxiety they felt about them as well.

Part of the reason for Shalikashvili's reticence was that the United States had recently experienced a less than successful peacekeeping operation in Somalia, where peacekeepers had been drawn into conflict with one of the armed factions, and American soldiers had engaged in a days-long running battle in Mogadishu that led to the death of nineteen Americans and hundreds of Somalis. Somalia caused the Clinton administration to back away from its commitment to peacekeeping operations, and Clinton's May 1994 Presidential

Decision Directive "PDD 25: Reforming Multilateral Peace Operations" affirmed that US forces would only be committed to peace operations when participation would advance US interests, the risk to US forces was considered acceptable, US participation was considered necessary for the mission's success, a clear endpoint for that participation could be identified, and other nations were willing to commit sufficient forces to achieve clearly defined objectives.[15]

This sort of policy, which both accepted the inevitability of participation in peace operations and then attempted to attach a string of caveats to it, was typical of how most senior army leaders talked about peacekeeping. Writing in *Military Review*, one group of officers acknowledged that "reading the tea leaves . . . the Army will participate in peacekeeping and peace enforcement (like it or not)"; in general, speeches from army leaders emphasized that preparing for such missions could not be avoided.[16] In the wake of intervention in Somalia, Army Chief of Staff General Gordon R. Sullivan noted that the army must resist the urge to focus solely on conventional operations, as "we will no longer be able to understand war simply as the armies of one nation-state or group of nation-states fighting one another. Somalia again demonstrates that this understanding is too narrow—it always has been." Sullivan recognized that "we must learn to deal with reality as it is, not as we want it to be . . . in not facing reality as it is, we could prepare the Army for the wrong war."[17] General George Joulwan, head of US European Command, went further and argued that "one might say that the US military is returning to normal at the conclusion of the anomalous Cold War era because, historically, 'normal' operations for US Forces are operations other than war."[18] Joulwan believed that US forces must be ready to fight a conventional war if required, but that securing the peace would be more important in a post–Cold War world.

In order to prepare itself for these new missions, the army commissioned several surveys to examine how peacekeeping missions affected readiness, how army personnel felt about such missions, and to ask what type of soldiers were needed for these deployments.[19] These surveys provide us with valuable evidence as to the views of rank-and-file soldiers and demonstrate that those serving on such missions had a more nuanced view of peacekeeping than critics had allowed. Peacekeeping looked different to those deployed than it did to senior army leadership. Soldiers found these missions challenging in different ways, but they felt that peacekeeping missions did not degrade readiness for conventional war. Their biggest difficulty was in making sense of army policies on the use of force and force protection, issues that provoked complaints on virtually every deployment.

Northwestern University sociologist Charles Moskos carried out several of these studies for the army, seeking to determine whether peacekeeping deployments affected readiness for combat missions. Based on surveys and interviews with soldiers in Haiti, Somali, Bosnia, Kosovo, and Macedonia, he concluded that while there was some loss of skills on things like crew-served weapons, soldiers thought that "these skills can be quickly relearned upon returning to home station."[20] Further, soldiers welcomed the opportunity to put some of their other skills into practice. Moskos argued that "nowhere else in the Army do mid-level NCOs organize patrols, record border incursions, and take care of the health, welfare, and discipline of soldiers in isolated areas."[21]

Surveys also found that soldiers often struggled to make sense of these operations. Infantry units in Haiti, Bosnia, and Macedonia expressed frustration that "they didn't come in shooting," and in places like Somalia, where there was shooting, soldiers complained about the American public's lack of appreciation for the dangers they faced and the lack of clarity from army leadership about the nature of the mission. Many of those deployed to Somalia had come straight from the humanitarian relief effort for Hurricane Andrew and were surprised to find that Somalia involved more combat than humanitarian action.[22] Several thought their experience similar to Operation Desert Storm; one veteran of that operation declared that "Saudi was Disneyland compared to this. There we were never shot at."[23]

This ambiguity led to a divide among soldiers. According to Charles Moskos and Laura Miller, a stark divide emerged between two different groups of soldiers in Somalia—the "warriors" and the "humanitarians." Based on a survey of just under 800 soldiers in Somalia and a series of interviews, Moskos and Miller found that a large subset of soldiers held very negative views of the Somalis, seeing the locals as lazy, uncivilized, and "ungrateful bastards."[24] One interviewee reported of his colleagues: "I've noticed that some of the women over here have been very gentle with the society around them and are putting too much trust in the (Somalis) they associate with. Men are far better suited to adjust to harsh situations . . . I have become a real "asshole" to the people in this country."[25]

By contrast, the "humanitarians" were much more sympathetic to the plight of Somalis, whom they saw as simply unfortunate and were reluctant to use force unless they felt it strictly necessary for self-preservation. One interview participant reported that "sometimes it's hard to feel sorry for the people over here. I mean when they are throwing rocks at you, but when you see the little children on the road so happy that we are here, it changes your mind."[26] There were clear demographic correlations for both the warriors and humanitarians, with Black and female soldiers, along with support troops, all far more likely to be "humanitarian" than whites, males. and combat troops. The US contingent in Somalia was quite unusual in that it was relatively gender-integrated and very multiracial: 12 percent of those deployed were female and over one-third were Black. Most other contingents were all-male and tended to be all of a single racial type (i.e., all-white European contingents, all-brown Pakistani contingents, etc.).[27] For Moskos and Miller then, the very demographic diversity of US forces in Somalia was a tactical asset.

After Somalia, neither the "warriors" nor the "humanitarians" would be satisfied, as US policy shifted toward a more conservative approach. American troops stood ready to use violence if necessary, but they would accept far less risk in their day-to-day operations, and soldiers often had to limit their contact with civilians due to security concerns. The American experience in Bosnia neatly encapsulated those dilemmas, with troops rarely allowed to leave their compounds, in contrast to their British colleagues, who were allowed to socialize in Sarajevo in civilian attire. American soldiers were also required to wear body armor at all times, which aggravated complaints about being micromanaged. US soldiers serving under the British-led Allied Rapid Response Corps (ARRC) in Sarajevo were not required to wear body armor, while their V Corps colleagues serving in the same location but under a different chain of command were, resulting in a force protection policy that looked "schizophrenic" to the US Army soldiers who endured it.[28]

For the senior officers who dealt with complaints from allies and junior ranks about these policies, American force protection measures were not a sign of excess caution but of discipline and toughness. Army Chief of Staff General Denis Reimer noted that during the initial American deployment into Bosnia, "they watched how we came across. They knew we lead with the tanks. They knew we lead with the soldiers who had their flak vests on and their Kevlars buckled and it was a new way of doing business." Reimer related that colleagues in the Hungarian military had told him: "'there's a lot of forces in Bosnia, but there's only one Army, the US Army' . . . and that is terribly important and the way you deter war is you remain strong."[29] Brigadier General Stanley Cherrie reported that a Bosnian corps commander told him that "all my men out there are fighters, not yet soldiers. You Americans are soldiers. You all dress alike, you all have discipline, you have clean weapons at the ready, you always travel in four vehicle convoys, even your helicopters fly in formation. Soldiers do that and we notice it."[30] For the US military leadership, being an effective soldier meant adhering to traditional martial virtues like discipline, virtues in tune with the self-image they had before the army became involved in these operations.

For some conservative critics of the late twentieth-century military though, this approach was deeply worrying. Ralph Peters, a recently retired lieutenant colonel and a neoconservative media commentator, had supported intervention in the Balkans and welcomed the US deployment to Bosnia because he felt these sorts of conflicts were the wave of the future, and the US military needed to adapt to these missions sooner rather than later. Peters argued that "an Army's peacetime mission is to acquire the skills and knowledge that enable it to win in war," and Bosnia was an ideal learning environment. He argued that US leaders in Bosnia were interested in bringing their troops home without taking any casualties and that all other priorities were a distant second; the shadow of Vietnam still hung over army generals. For Peters, this was a sign not only of a caution borne of bitter experience in Indochina and Somalia but a sign of a larger moral decay. He wrote: "Most Americans today—including soldiers— have lived incredibly sheltered lives by global or historical standards. We must expose them to foreign reality . . . the notion of sheltering our soldiers from the big, bad world is a politically correct absurdism."[31] He complained that "we have the vision of spoiled children" and that "since we have entered a new age of an American expeditionary military, I suggest that, if we leave the Balkans without any broad, deep understanding of the place, we will have failed as a military."[32]

While most conservatives may have shared Peters' concerns about American society, they were less supportive of peacekeeping missions.[33] Charles Krauthammer—hardly a dove, as the author of a *Foreign Affairs* article that had proclaimed the "unipolar moment"—noted that the ultimate objective of US peacekeepers in Haiti was not getting shot.[34] For Krauthammer, this was "as insane a purpose as sending American Marines in 1982 to sit in Beirut airport. If we are not sending the military to pacify, control and remake countries, as we did after the Second World War, why in God's name are we there? If 'force protection is job one,' it is a job best done at Fort Dix, New Jersey."[35]

Like Peters, he thought the peacekeeping status quo of the late 1990s was an absurdity but, unlike Peters, Krauthammer thought withdrawal, not deeper engagement, was the best solution. The key concern for Krauthammer and other critics and, indeed, for senior army leaders, was the extent to which such missions atrophied warfighting skills. During the 2000 presidential campaign, Republican George W. Bush ran on a platform of global retrenchment and disengagement from peacekeeping while his foreign policy adviser, Condoleezza Rice, argued that "carrying out civil administration and police functions is simply going to degrade the American capability to do the things America has to do. We don't need to have the 82nd Airborne escorting kids to kindergarten."[36]

In a similar vein, Krauthammer decried "Clintonian do-goodism" in his *Washington Post* column and claimed that "the world's sole superpower has no business squandering its resources and diluting its military doing police work and hand-holding in places like Haiti, Bosnia and Kosovo." For Krauthammer, "Americans make lousy peacekeepers—not because they are not great soldiers but precisely because they are. . . . Many nations can do police work; only we can drop thousand-pound bombs with the precision of a medieval archer."[37] Echoing fellow neoconservative Robert Kagan's argument that there had been a sharp divergence between the United States and Europe in recent years, Krauthammer closed by declaring, "We fight the wars. Our friends should patrol the peace."[38] In this vision of contemporary operations, soldiering and peacekeeping were inherently antithetical activities.

This critique was taken further in the writing of Air Force colonel Charles Dunlap, who repeatedly disparaged peacekeeping missions in a variety of publications. In a satirical article entitled "The Last American Warrior: Non-Traditional Missions and the Decline of the US Armed Forces," Dunlap imagined a world in which the United States had been resoundingly defeated by a competitor who hadn't forgotten how to fight wars. Written in the form of a report to the "glorious leader" of a group simply known as "the Victors," Dunlap attempted to offer a warning from the future. He referenced an incident in which US Marines deployed on a border patrol in Arizona had fired warning shots at drug smugglers and imagined this event as a symbol of the decay of American warfighting skills. The fictitious report writer gloats: "When our troops attacked American positions during the war, you can be assured, Glorious Leader, that our soldiers had not been trained to shoot over heads!"[39] Dunlap was also deeply concerned that US forces on peacekeeping operations were not promoting US ideals abroad but promoting dubious concepts in the minds of people in the developing world, most notably, "the socialist notion that only government—not private enterprise—can better their lot."[40]

Dunlap saw a negative feedback loop where a more isolated military was taking on more and more nontraditional missions that took it further and further away from its proper role. Dunlap argued that the increased number of nontraditional missions was a threat to democracy. Counter-drug operations, hurricane relief, civil affairs operations, and peacekeeping missions were all things the military should not be doing. In Dunlap's eyes, the only reason the

US military was given these tasks was because of the high esteem in which it was held.[41] The military's perceived ability to solve any problem thrown at it meant that the army was not only losing combat skills but becoming more and more of a politicized organization.

Other observers recognized that the need for proficiency in both peacekeeping and conventional warfare posed challenges for army capabilities, even if they understood the problem in less drastic terms. However, unlike Dunlap, they saw peacekeeping operations not as a threat to civil-military relations but as an opportunity to remake the All-Volunteer Force. Crucial to this effort was the question of who should serve on such operations. Not only did most US soldiers surveyed by military sociologists agree that the job was one better suited to military police than infantry, but many felt that reserve forces, with their mix of civilian skillsets and a mentality that was often less aggressive than that of their active component counterparts, would be ideal for peacekeeping operations. Senior officers tended to prefer reserve forces for such missions too, although not necessarily due to any perceived suitability for peacekeeping. Rather, the army had been greatly reduced in size since the end of the Cold War and a stretched force leaned more and more on its reserve component as the tempo of deployments increased. By 1998, one-third of the US force in Bosnia were reservists or National Guardsmen, most of them on a compulsory deployment. Deputy Commander of Army Forces Command, Brig. Gen. Pat O'Neal told the *New York Times* that, unlike the Cold War years, "everyone is in the pool . . . they are all eligible to go. That's the change."[42]

Indeed, even as the large-scale deployment of US forces on peacekeeping missions was in its early days, the army experimented with deploying reserve forces on a large scale by sending a battalion of reservist volunteers to serve as military observers in the peacekeeping mission in the Sinai that started in the 1980s.[43] Writing to Army Chief of Staff General Gordon R. Sullivan, Charles Moskos argued that there was a strong political as well as military rationale for such a force. For Moskos, this "rainbow battalion" would connect the mission to a broader cross section of the American people, it would increase political support for such missions because it enhanced the role of the National Guard (an organization beloved of many Congressmen), and, perhaps most importantly, "in the event of casualties, the political fallout will be less for a dedicated battalion of "double volunteers" than for a standard . . . unit."[44] For proponents of such missions, the more diverse the unit deployed on peacekeeping operations, the more operationally effective and politically viable these missions would be.

Moskos also argued that these missions were suited not only to reservists but also to people interested in joining the army on a short enlistment, a proposed scheme that was dear to his heart. Since the advent of the All-Volunteer Force, Moskos had worried about the changing demographics of the army, with fewer and fewer urban, middle-class college students interested in joining, and the burden of service falling more and more on the rural and urban working class and those who already came from military families. Moskos argued that peacekeeping missions were ideal ways to attract college graduates in search of adventure, as these deployments didn't necessarily require the sort of skills that would necessitate lengthy technical training. The ideal enlistment was eighteen months to two years in length, with basic and mission training followed by a six-month deployment overseas before a return to the United States and civilian life. In the absence of any realistic hope of reinstituting the draft, Moskos made the case for a short-service enlistment repeatedly throughout the decade (and indeed up until his death in 2008) in correspondence with politicians and generals, and in op-eds for national newspapers where he published articles with such titles such as "From College to Kosovo."[45]

Thus, questions about the makeup of American peacekeeping forces were connected to a broader project aimed at remaking the All-Volunteer Force. Moskos worked with centrist Democrats from the Democratic Leadership Council, such as Sam Nunn, Al Gore, Paul Tsongas, and Bill Clinton, to publicly make the case for some form of national service. All recognized that the draft would not return, but all were uncomfortable with the idea of a military drifting away from civilian society.[46] These efforts—which were ultimately unsuccessful—to use the needs of peacekeeping and similar missions to change the makeup of the armed forces were part of what Gary Gerstle has identified as a liberal nationalist project to reclaim war from conservatives. Gerstle points out that in films like *Saving Private Ryan*, documentary series like Ken Burns' *The Civil War*, and in Stephen Ambrose's series of immensely popular histories of the Second World War, we see not only an attempt to make the case that there is such a thing as a good war but a repeated celebration and elevation of the citizen-soldier as an ideal for the Republic.[47] For Moskos and the DLC, some return to a more democratic form of soldiering would be welcome and the increased tempo of deployments and particular requirements of peacekeeping missions made the need for this transformation more urgent than ever.

Moskos' enthusiasm for using the needs of peacekeeping missions to undertake a fundamental transformation of the army's recruiting process and its demographic makeup, although unsuccessful, speaks to the potential these operations had for unsettling basic assumptions about the army's purpose. While this campaign was far removed politically from Specialist Michael New's refusal to wear the UN's blue beret, both Moskos and New shared the sense that something was changing, even if they didn't quite know what it was. Similarly, politicians, military leaders and commentators projected anxieties about the future of the army and its soldiers onto peacekeeping missions, exposing deep fissures within the army about what sort of attributes its soldiers would need in the twenty-first century. Army leaders and personnel deployed on peacekeeping operations struggled to articulate which martial values best applied to peacekeeping. Did being tough mean wearing body armor and having an alert posture on patrols, or an inclination to take risks and engage with locals? Did it mean restraint or a willingness to use violence when the situation called for it?

Ultimately, no one offered a convincing and coherent response to these questions, and the army essentially sought to get through these missions as best they could, while relying heavily on the adaptability of their soldiers, who would be left to figure out the answers for themselves. Thus, policymakers would ask a lot of these soldiers throughout a decade of deployments, and the soldiers themselves had a variety of views about the missions they participated in and about the qualities that they would need to develop in order to succeed at them. Not all views were as extreme as those held by Specialist New—after all, 549 other soldiers donned their UN berets without complaint on that October morning in Schweinfurt—but these debates had an urgency that belied the US military's relatively comfortable position in the decade between the Cold War and the war on terror. The questions posed by peacekeeping operations were ones that the army would have to face again as it encountered new problems in Iraq, Afghanistan, and beyond in the years to come.

Notes

1 "I Am Not a UN Soldier," *The New American*, October 2, 1995. The case had also been the subject of an article in a local North Carolina newspaper in mid-September. Dennis Cuddy, "The Case for Army Specialist New," *Fayetteville Observer-Times*, September 14, 1995.

2 Alan Cowell, "G.I. Gets Support for Shunning UN Insignia," *The New York Times*, November 24, 1995, https://www.nytimes.com/1995/11/24/world/gi-gets-support-for-shunning-un-insignia.html.

3   "US Convicts G.I. Who Refused to Serve Under UN in Balkans," *The New York Times*, January 25, 1996, https://www.nytimes.com/1996/01/25/world/us-convicts-gi-who-refused-to-serve-under-un-in-balkans.html.

4   Marc Fisher, "War and Peacekeeping," *Washington Post*, March 4, 1996, https://www.washingtonpost.com/archive/lifestyle/1996/03/04/war-and-peacekeeping/adfd68e7-9be7-4e16-94fb-ea566ec3fd03/.

5   Imre Karacs, "US Medic Who Would Not Wear the Blue Beret Goes on Trial," *The Independent* (London), November 18, 1995, https://www.independent.co.uk/news/world/us-medic-who-would-not-wear-the-blue-beret-goes-on-trial-1582468.html.

6   Robert S. Winner, "Spc. Michael New v. William Perry, Secretary of Defense: The Constitutionality of US Forces Serving under UN Command," *DePaul Digest of International Law* 30, no. 3 (Spring 1997), http://www.kentlaw.edu/academics/courses/admin-perritt/winner.htm.

7   New maintains a website that includes court documents giving an extensive account of the case. "United States v. Michael G. New: Legal Documents," *MikeNew.com*, accessed December 8, 2020, https://www.mikenew.com/courtdocs.html.

8   Daniel P. Bolger, "The Ghosts of Omdurman," *Parameters* 21, no. 3 (1991): 31.

9   Bolger, "Ghosts of Omdurman," 32.

10 Francis M. Doyle, Karen J. Lewis, and Leslie A. Williams, *Named Military Operations from January 1989 to December 1993* (Fort Monroe: US Army Training and Doctrine Command, April 1994).

11 George H. W. Bush, "Address before the General Assembly of the United Nations," September 21, 1992, Online by Gerhard Peters and John T. Woolley, *The American Presidency Project*, https://www.presidency.ucsb.edu/node/267788.

12 Reuters, "The 1992 Campaign: Excerpts from Clinton's Speech on Foreign Policy Leadership," *The New York Times*, August 14, 1992, https://www.nytimes.com/1992/08/14/us/the-1992-campaign-excerpts-from-clinton-s-speech-on-foreign-policy-leadership.html.

13 William J. Durch, *UN Peacekeeping, American Politics, and the Uncivil Wars of the 1990s* (New York: Palgrave Macmillan, 1996), 41. For more on the Powell Doctrine, see Colin L. Powell, "U.S. Forces: The Challenges Ahead," *Foreign Affairs*, 1992; Colin L. Powell and Joseph E. Persico, *My American Journey: An Autobiography* (New York: Random House, 1995); Gail E. S. Yoshitani, *Reagan on War: A Reappraisal of the Weinberger Doctrine, 1980–1984* (College Station: Texas A&M University Press, 2011).

14 Harry G. Summers, "Military Strategy: Conversations with Harry G. Summers," interview by Harry Kreisler and Thomas G. Barnes, March 6, 1996, *Conversations with History*, Institute of International Studies, UC Berkeley, http://globetrotter.berkeley.edu/conversations/Summers/summers4.html.

15 "Presidential Decision Directive/NSC 25: Reforming Multilateral Peace Operations" (Washington, DC: The White House, 1994), https://fas.org/irp/offdocs/pdd/pdd-25.pdf.

16 William W. Allen, Antione D. Johnson, and John T. Nelsen, "Peacekeeping and Peace Enforcement Operations," *Military Review* 73, no. 10 (1993): 59.

17 Gordon Sullivan and James Dubik, *Envisioning Future Warfare* (Fort Leavenworth: US Army Command and General Staff College Press, 1995), 52.

18 George A. Joulwan, "Operations Other Than War: A CINC's Perspective," *Military Review* 74, no. 2 (February 1994): 5.

19 David R. Segal and Dana P. Eyre, *The US Army in Peace Operations at the Dawning of the Twenty-First Century, US Army in Peace Operations at the Dawning of the Twenty-First Century* (Alexandria: US Army Research Institute for the Behavioral and Social Sciences, 1996); Beatrice J. Farr and Ruth H. Phelps, *Reserve Component Soldiers as Peacekeepers* (Alexandria: US Army Research Institute for the Behavioral and Social Sciences, 1996).

20 Charles C. Moskos, "Memo to Gordon R. Sullivan: Soldiers and OOTW," February 12, 1995, Charles C. Moskos Papers, Northwestern University Archives (hereafter Moskos Papers).

21 Ibid.

22 Ibid.; Laura Miller and Charles C. Moskos, "Sociological Survey of US Army Soldiers Serving in Bosnia in 1996 and 1998: Questionnaire Results," n.d., Moskos Papers.

23 Laura L. Miller and Charles Moskos, "Humanitarians or Warriors?: Race, Gender, and Combat Status in Operation Restore Hope," *Armed Forces & Society* 21, no. 4 (July 1, 1995): 615–37.

24 Ibid.

25 Ibid., 627.

26 Ibid., 630.

27 Ibid., 616.

28 Walter E. Kretchik, "Force Protection Disparities," *Military Review* 77, no. 4 (August 1997): 75.

29 Denis J. Reimer, "Address to the Adjutant General Association. U.S.," September 8, 1998, Denis J. Reimer Papers: 870-51 CSA, United States Army Heritage and Education Center, Carlisle, PA.

30 Stanley F. Cherrie, "Task Force Eagle," *Military Review* 77, no. 4 (August 1997): 72.

31 Ralph Peters to Charles Moskos, "Your Task Force Eagle Report," December 1998, Moskos Papers.

32 Peters to Moskos, December 1998, Moskos Papers.

33 For a detailed discussion of neoconservative debates on US involvement in peacekeeping missions, especially in the Balkans, see Maria Ryan, *Neo-conservatism and the New American Century* (New York: Palgrave Macmillan, 2010).

34 Charles Krauthammer, "The Unipolar Moment," *Foreign Affairs* 70, no. 1 (1990): 23–33.

35 Charles Krauthammer, "The Short, Unhappy Life of Humanitarian War," *The National Interest* (Fall 1999): 8.

36 Michael R. Gordon, "The 2000 Campaign: The Military; Bush Would Stop U.S. Peacekeeping In Balkan Fights," *The New York Times*, October 21, 2000, http://query .nytimes.com/gst/fullpage.html?res=9C07E4DE1E3EF932A15753C1A9669C8B63 &sec=&spon=&pagewanted=1.

37 Charles Krauthammer, "We Don't Peacekeep," *The Washington Post*, December 18, 2001, https://www.washingtonpost.com/archive/opinions/2001/12/18/we-dont -peacekeep/45dd2154-c2ac-474a-a9ca-03499d0a0c0e/.

38 Robert Kagan, *Of Paradise and Power: America and Europe in the New World Order* (New York: Vintage, 2004), 3–11; Krauthammer, "We Don't Peacekeep."

39 Charles J. Dunlap, "The Last American Warrior-Non-Traditional Missions and the Decline of the U.S. Armed Force," *Fletcher Forum of World Affairs* 18 (1994): 70.

40 Ibid., 74.

41 For more on the issue of esteem, see David Fitzgerald, "Support the Troops: Gulf War Homecomings and a New Politics of Military Celebration," *Modern American History* 2, no. 1 (March 2019): 1–22.

42 Mike O'Connor, "A Downsized Army Leans on Reserves for Duty in Bosnia," *The New York Times*, May 25, 1998, sec. World, http://www.nytimes.com/1998/05/25/ world/a-downsized-army-leans-on-reserves-for-duty-in-bosnia.html.

43 For more on the Sinai peacekeeping battalion, see David R. Segal, "Is a Peacekeeping Culture Emerging Among American Infantry in the Sinai MFO?" *Journal of Contemporary Ethnography* 30, no. 5 (2001): 607–36; David R. Segal, Theodore P. Furukawa, and Jerry C. Lindh, "Light Infantry as Peacekeepers in the Sinai," *Armed Forces & Society* 16, no. 3 (1990): 385–403.

44 Charles C. Moskos, "Memorandum for Gordon R. Sullivan: Dedicated 'Rainbow' Battalion for Peacekeeping Missions," November 2, 1993, Moskos Papers.

45 Charles Moskos, "From College to Kosovo," *Wall Street Journal*, August 25, 2000.

46 Moskos' papers are full of correspondence relating to national service. For a representative sample of correspondence with DLC figures on the topic, see Charles C. Moskos, "Letter to Sam Nunn," April 17, 1993, Charles C. Moskos Papers, Northwestern University Archives; Charles C. Moskos, "Memorandum to Vice President Al Gore: Your Enlisted Army Days, Military Recruitment and National Service," August 14, 1999, Moskos Papers.

47 Gary Gerstle, "In the Shadow of War: Liberal Nationalism and the Problem of War," in *Americanism: New Perspectives on the History of an Ideal*, ed. Michael Kazin and Joseph A. McCartin (Chapel Hill: The University of North Carolina Press, 2006), 128–52.

4

Soldier or Diplomat?

The Gray Area of UN Peacekeeping in Cambodia

Wietse Stam

Cambodia's "sortie de guerre" was a long process. On October 23, 1991, after more than four years of international peacemaking efforts, representatives of the four Cambodian factions and eighteen other nations gathered in Paris to sign a peace agreement that aimed to end the civil war that had ravaged the small Southeast Asian country for more than two decades. At this second Paris Peace Conference on Cambodia (the first, in 1989, failed to lead to an agreement), it was decided to entrust the responsibility for implementing the transition from conflict to peace and national reconciliation to the United Nations Transitional Authority in Cambodia (UNTAC). The end of the Cold War generated a certain optimism about the potential of the United Nations to manage conflicts and assist countries on the path to peace and liberal democracy.[1] But the Paris Peace Agreements were a fragile compromise and reflected more the will of the great powers to improve their relations and find a solution to the Cambodian problem than the genuine commitment to peace among the Cambodian factions themselves. As soon as UN troops arrived in Cambodia, one of the signatories to the peace agreements, the notorious Khmer Rouge, declined to cooperate.

This chapter investigates how the leading military officers in Cambodia perceived and defined their role as peacekeepers and how they determined the balance between the military and diplomatic aspects of their mission when the cooperation of one party, in particular, was eroding. A UN peacekeeping operation is in essence a hybrid form of diplomatic and military activity. Several scholars have characterized the sending of blue-helmeted soldiers under the UN flag to conflict areas in those terms. Jocelyn Coulon described peacekeepers as "soldiers of diplomacy" and Marie-Claude Smouts portrayed their activities as *la diplomatie en kaki*.[2] The famous adage that "peacekeeping is not a soldier's job, but only a soldier can do it" also deserves to be mentioned because it illustrates the paradoxical identity of the peacekeeper.[3] The founding principles of UN peacekeeping were established after lightly armed soldiers from different UN member states were dispatched to the Sinai desert to act as an interposition force during the Suez crisis in 1956. The guidelines that were written down in the aftermath of this improvised emergency measure determined that a UN force needed the consent of the parties involved, was to remain impartial, and could use force only in self-defense. Although UN operations were generally deployed under chapter VI of the Charter of the United Nations, the then UN Secretary-General Dag Hammarskjöld already pointed out that the activity actually fell somewhere between chapter VI "the pacific settlement of disputes" and chapter VII "action with respect to threats to the peace, breaches of peace and acts of aggression." Despite the hypothetical "chapter six and a half" character of UN peacekeeping, the operations involving blue-helmeted soldiers monitoring ceasefires were clearly distinguished from "green-helmeted" enforcement actions, such as the 1991 Operation Desert Storm in Kuwait and Iraq.[4]

In the 1990s, UN peacekeeping hit a rocky road as peacekeepers were deployed with ambitious mandates in challenging intrastate conflicts. By the end of 1993, political scientist John Ruggie argued that the problem was that the UN distinguished between peacekeeping and enforcement operations, while in reality peacekeepers found themselves wandering in a gray area lying somewhere between the two.[5] UN Secretary-General Boutros Boutros-Ghali had contributed to the conceptual confusion himself through the publication of *An Agenda for Peace* in June 1992, a document in which he proposed the creation of peace enforcement units and also seemed to argue that consent from all the parties was no longer an absolute precondition for the deployment of a peacekeeping operation.[6]

Ruggie and other scholars primarily focused their analyses on the UN operations in the former Yugoslavia, Somalia, and Rwanda. The operation in Cambodia—which was at the time of its creation the largest UN operation since the Congo in the early 1960s—has received much less academic attention, not in the last place because it was eventually overshadowed by the aforementioned traumatic UN experiences. UNTAC is generally considered as a partial success because it succeeded in some parts of its mandate, such as the repatriation of Cambodian refugees and the organization of free and fair elections, but it failed in the task that was specifically entrusted to the military component of the multidimensional mission: the disarmament and demobilization of the Cambodian factions' armies. With the Khmer Rouge's cooperation and consent waning, military and civilian leaders were confronted with the dilemma to what extent they could induce this faction to respect its obligations under the peace accords. Scholars have generally argued that UNTAC's mandate was restricted to chapter VI peacekeeping, giving it no other choice than to opt for a diplomatic approach.[7] But this assumption takes the legal and rather theoretical distinction between peacekeeping and enforcement as a starting point and ignores the gray area between the two as well as the hybrid diplomatic-military identity which are both inherent parts of peacekeeping operations.

Two Generals, Different Visions

Even before UN troops were fully deployed in Cambodia, it became clear that the Khmer Rouge was not genuinely cooperating with the implementation of the peace agreements. The UN operation started in November 1991 with the United Nations Advance Mission in Cambodia (UNAMIC), which was tasked with maintaining the ceasefire and making preparations for the arrival of the main UN force, UNTAC. Both objectives were hindered when fighting broke out in the strategically important province of Kompong Thom, 125 kilometers north of the capital Phnom Penh. UNAMIC's force commander, French Brigadier General Michel Loridon, held endless meetings with the representatives of the armies of the Cambodian factions in an effort to keep the peace, but on February 6, 1992, the Khmer Rouge leadership secretly decided to stop its cooperation with the UN and merely use the peace agreements "as a weapon" to gain time and weaken the government in Phnom Penh.[8] This immediately became clear when a relatively cooperative Khmer Rouge general was suddenly replaced by a hardliner. But the alarm calls Loridon sent to New York did not receive serious attention at UN headquarters, which was in the middle of a reorganization ordered by the newly appointed Boutros-Ghali.[9] This reorganization, incidentally, led to the creation of the Department of Peacekeeping Operations (DPKO).

On March 15, 1992, UNAMIC transitioned into UNTAC, which was placed under the leadership of Japanese UN official Yasushi Akashi, who had been appointed Special Representative of the Secretary-General (SRSG). Australian Lieutenant General John Sanderson took over the military command from Loridon, who became his deputy. But the working relationship between the two generals was tense from the beginning as they had very different ideas about how the peacekeeping operation ought to be conducted. When the first units of UNTAC's military component arrived in Cambodia, Khmer Rouge commander-in-chief Son Sen announced that he was willing to accept a ceasefire in Kompong Thom if UNTAC would send a battalion of peacekeepers to the disputed province. Loridon, therefore, recommended to immediately deploy the freshly arrived Indonesian troops between the belligerent parties.[10] Sanderson, however, was cautious and did not want to send his troops into the area before the fighting had stopped, ceasefire lines had been drawn, and a detailed plan for their supervision had been made. "I don't want UN troops stumbling blind around the countryside," the force commander told a journalist. "We are in Cambodia as peacekeepers, not peace enforcers. I will not put UN forces in the middle of a confused environment and no ceasefire where the roads are mined."[11]

After two weeks, an agreement was finally reached in Phnom Penh to pick up two Khmer Rouge generals from the jungle with a UN helicopter and bring them to Kompong Thom where Loridon and UN military observers succeeded in convincing the parties to accept a local ceasefire agreement.[12] But this success was short-lived because of further delays in the deployment of peacekeepers to the province, which meant that a positive momentum in the early phase of the operation could not be exploited.[13] This allowed the Khmer Rouge to launch a new offensive and raise the price for its cooperation.

The guerrillas increased their intransigent behavior further by refusing to allow a battalion of Dutch peacekeepers to set up headquarters in the Khmer Rouge-controlled town of Pailin, in the extreme west of the country.[14] Although Khmer Rouge leaders in Phnom Penh made vague promises of cooperation, UNTAC was never given the required freedom of movement on the ground. Akashi and Sanderson experienced this obstruction themselves when they traveled to Pailin and attempted to drive to the Thai border to meet with the Dutch battalion commander. They didn't get far, because less than a kilometer outside of Pailin, the convoy of UN vehicles was halted by a couple of Khmer Rouge soldiers who blocked the road with a flimsy bamboo pole. The two highest-ranking UN officials in the country were unable to persuade the Khmer Rouge soldiers to let them pass and decided to turn around.[15] A group of journalists who were present in the convoy witnessed what came to be known as "the bamboo pole incident": a moment that symbolized the UN's powerlessness in Cambodia. Defending their decision to turn back, Sanderson later wrote to Akashi: "To attempt to push through the barrier with our unarmed party might have made a good story for the press but it would have achieved nothing except to place you and the rest of the party at risk."[16]

On the day of the bamboo pole incident, deputy force commander Loridon sat down with a group of French journalists and expressed his skepticism about the UN's ability to succeed in Cambodia. The general, who was not of the *grande muette*-type, argued that, in his view, the UN should show firmness and determination by moving into the zones controlled by the Khmer Rouge and pushing them to cooperate. He also predicted that the plan to disarm and demobilize the factions' armies by inviting their soldiers into regrouping areas and cantonments would not work and expressed his disappointment that his alternative proposal to disarm the factions on the spot by using small mobile units had not been taken into consideration.[17] The articles that appeared in the French newspapers about Loridon's cri de cœur were a cause of concern to the French government's diplomatic agenda. By openly questioning the UN strategy in Cambodia—and indirectly criticizing his superiors—Loridon had exceeded his authority, and the French Minister of Defense, Pierre Joxe,[18] decided to call the outspoken general back to France.[19] Before his departure from Cambodia, Loridon told the *Far Eastern Economic Review* that he was leaving frustrated because of UNTAC's inability to succeed in its mission and argued that "courage and a willingness" were needed to push the Khmer Rouge into respecting the terms of the peace accords instead of "just sitting and waiting for the Khmer Rouge leaders to agree to disarm their troops."[20] The article further quoted Loridon as saying, "It is possible at some point they will try to block the UN move by force. If it comes to that one may lose 200 men—and that could include myself—but the Khmer Rouge problem would be solved for good."[21] Despite the fact that Loridon later regretted his "provocative" remarks,[22] this single quote resurfaced in many news reports and subsequently led scholars to conclude, erroneously, that Loridon was a loose cannon proposing "a swift war against the Khmer Rouge" with the aim of putting them out of business with a "one-shot civil war victory."[23] Other analysts, however, believed that Loridon was right in demanding that UNTAC should have at least tried to make the Khmer Rouge honor the blue helmets' freedom of movement.[24]

From a legal perspective, both generals could claim that their interpretation of the mandate was the right one. UNTAC's standard operating procedures stipulated that military personnel were authorized to use force not only in self-defense but also in "resisting forceful attempts to prevent UNTAC from accomplishing its mission."[25] It had become standard practice since 1973 to include the provision that UN peacekeepers were allowed to use force "in defense of the mandate," but this principle was open to a wide range of interpretations.

In order to understand why the two generals maintained these diverging visions, it is important to look beyond legal explanations and be aware of their different backgrounds and mindsets. The calm and gentlemanly Sanderson was an army engineer and an experienced military planner who had previously been Director of Plans of the Australian Army.[26] In Cambodia, the Australian general continuously emphasized the importance of "detailed planning" in the conduct of UNTAC's operations. "You are all military officers," Sanderson said to the Cambodian generals during a meeting in Phnom Penh,

> and you know that you should make a plan before you commit your troops to an operation. Before I put UN soldiers in villages in the Kompong Thom area I must know what arrangements we have agreed there, who we are going to meet, what roads we are going to use, who is going to guarantee the opening of those roads.[27]

The head of DPKO in New York, Marrack Goulding, remembered Sanderson as "rather conventional" and "very cautious."[28] Political scientist Janet Heininger has described Sanderson as "a model diplomat-general."[29] Loridon, on the other hand, was a vigorous and dynamic paratrooper with much operational experience in Africa, which made him more familiar with quick deployments and adapting to changing circumstances on the ground.

Risk

After the end of their mission, both Sanderson and Loridon published articles in which they reflected on their command in Cambodia and on the conduct of UN peacekeeping operations in general. Although these writings serve in part as ex post facto justifications for their decisions in Cambodia, they also provide an interesting amplification of their visions. Although their analyses are very different, the returning theme in both their reflections is the issue of risk. Sanderson defends his diplomatic approach by emphasizing the diplomatic character of the mission, arguing that peacekeepers are "instruments of diplomacy—not of war."[30] He develops the idea that there is a great risk for peacekeeping operations to "dabble into war" if control is lost.[31] Where Sanderson warns for "the incalculable dynamic of force,"[32] Loridon observes that the unwillingness to take any risks paralyzed the UN in Cambodia.[33] Although acknowledging that military leaders always have the responsibility to protect the lives of their soldiers, he identifies the concern with a "zero mortality rate" as the central factor that prevents peacekeepers from achieving their mission.[34]

It must also be noted that both generals propose a different interpretation of the peacekeeping principles. With regard to "the minimum use of force,"

Sanderson emphasizes that UNTAC had no legitimate authority to use force against any party in Cambodia because this was contrary to the pacific nature of chapter VI of the UN Charter.[35] Loridon, however, argues that his proposal came down more to the demonstration of firmness rather than immediately resorting to the actual use of armed force.[36] This distinction between a show of strength and the use of force has also been made by Sir Brian Urquhart, the UN official who was in charge of peacekeeping operations for the larger part of the Cold War.[37] Concerning the principle of "impartiality," Sanderson emphasizes the importance of absolute impartiality for peacekeepers in order to protect their credibility as honest brokers in a peace process, not in the last place for their own protection.[38] Loridon explicitly challenges the notion of impartiality as a peacekeeping principle, arguing that it should be replaced by "active neutrality," meaning a neutral posture but with the ability to be firm with parties that do not respect their obligations.[39]

The doctrines for peacekeeping operations that were later developed by Australia and France can be seen as conceptualizations of the conflicting visions of Sanderson and Loridon in Cambodia. The Australian peacekeeping doctrine defined peacekeeping as "a non-coercive instrument of diplomacy,"[40] whereas the French developed the term *restauration de la paix* (restoration of peace) to underpin the idea that there is a continuum between peacekeeping and peace enforcement.[41] It seems likely that the origins of these national peacekeeping doctrines can be partly found in the Cambodian experience.

Besides the differences in military culture between France and Australia, an appreciation of the different political contexts in these countries during their involvement in Cambodia is required to understand how the different mindsets of the force commander and his deputy were shaped. For Australia, the Cambodian peace process presented a major opportunity to demonstrate its commitment to becoming an influential regional player and to show its—in the words of Foreign Minister Gareth Evans—"middle power creative problem-solving capacity."[42] From early 1989, when the Australian government began discussing options for a contribution to a peacekeeping operation in Cambodia, a political debate emerged around the nature of the mission and the dangers to which Australian personnel might be exposed.[43] Evans recalled the "less-than-happy" role Australia had played two decades earlier in Indochina through its participation in the Vietnam War. "This time round," he stated, "we want any contribution we might make to be wholly peaceful and constructive," and further emphasized that Australia would not send troops into a "shooting war."[44] The Australian government eventually decided to contribute a communication unit of 527. In order to reassure the very critical opposition, Prime Minister Paul Keating underlined the peacekeeping character of the operation by stating in parliament that "UNTAC most definitely will <u>not</u> have a role enforcing or imposing the peace if hostilities break out."[45] In his speech, given two weeks after Sanderson's arrival in Cambodia, Keating also made it clear that Australia could not sustain its presence if the situation would escalate: "if we conclude that there is no longer a peace to keep in Cambodia, the Australian and other UN forces will have to be withdrawn."[46] This domestic political climate conditioned a risk-averse command of the operation.

Although relations between France and Australia were improving after two decades of tensions around nuclear tests in the South Pacific and French actions in New Caledonia, some friction between the two countries remained as the UN operation in Cambodia allowed both France and Australia to regain influence in a part of the world they had left on less peaceful terms. Nevertheless, the context in which the two generals operated was very different. Sanderson had been involved in planning Australia's contribution to a future peacekeeping operation in Cambodia since 1989 when he was responsible for Australia's international military-strategic policy.[47] By contrast, the French government, primarily preoccupied with the crisis in the former Yugoslavia, rather randomly appointed Loridon only a few weeks before sending him to Cambodia, without any specific instructions. Moreover, there was no public debate in France about the country's contribution to the operation in Cambodia, let alone the safety of its military personnel. Indeed, as Brigitte Stern has pointed out, in France the possibility of casualties in peace operations is considered as "the price France is prepared to pay to retain its rank as a permanent member of the Security Council and a defender of the fundamental values of international society, respect for human rights, humanitarian law, democracy, and peace."[48]

Carrots and Sticks

Besides the different visions among UNTAC military leaders, the civilian leadership did not agree either on the question to what extent peacekeepers should be used to pressure the Khmer Rouge into cooperation. Scholars have often portrayed Akashi as a cautious and risk-averse diplomat, but new archival evidence reveals that in Cambodia the SRSG was actually in favor of using the military in support of a tougher approach vis-à-vis the Khmer Rouge. As it became clear that the Khmer Rouge would not hand in their weapons to the

UN, Akashi requested the Secretary-General to bring the Security Council into play. Despite the fact that Boutros-Ghali had expressed the view in *An Agenda for Peace* that the use of force by the UN was essential to maintain its credibility when peaceful means had failed, he made a different analysis with regard to the situation in Cambodia.[49] Believing that Khmer Rouge leader Khieu Samphan—with whom he maintained a personal correspondence—might be persuaded with the force of intellectual arguments, he requested Akashi to pursue a policy of "quiet diplomacy" and work out "an acceptable compromise" with the Khmer Rouge "in a friendly and constructive spirit."[50] Akashi, however, did not share Boutros-Ghali's optimism and objected to the instructions from New York which, in his view, miscomprehended the reality of the situation on the ground in Cambodia.[51] He pointed out to DPKO-chief Goulding that he had been using mostly "carrots" in his efforts to obtain the Khmer Rouge's cooperation and emphasized the need to shift the balance to the use of more "sticks" in order to break the deadlock. Akashi did not wish to invoke chapter VII of the UN Charter and move into enforcement but nonetheless felt that getting the Khmer Rouge to comply required "a certain firmness and resolve, as well as a willingness to press them very hard when we can."[52]

To Goulding's frustration, the Secretary-General allowed Akashi to run UNTAC relatively independently.[53] The SRSG, pressured from different sides to act more assertively, requested Sanderson to make a plan to use UN troops to close off the border between Thailand and the Khmer Rouge-controlled zones in order to put a stop to the Khmer Rouge's lucrative trade in gems and logs with Thai businesses, which provided the guerrillas with a vital source of income and supplies.[54] Besides pressuring the Khmer Rouge economically, Akashi felt that such an operation would have an important symbolic value by demonstrating UNTAC's determination in asserting its freedom of movement.[55] But Goulding opposed the implementation of these measures because he did not think that UNTAC had the military capacity to mount the necessary border checkpoints in the Khmer Rouge's zone and doubted whether it could count on the cooperation by the Thai military. Goulding feared that if UNTAC failed in the operation, it would mean "a major blow to its credibility."[56] Sanderson also believed that there were too many risks involved in such an operation and presented an operational plan, codenamed "Dovetail," which was essentially designed to persuade Akashi that it would be ill-advised.[57] While Dutch peacekeepers prepared themselves for a forceful move into Khmer Rouge territory, Akashi was talked out of the idea.[58] Eventually, on November 30, 1992, Akashi's plan was nonetheless unofficially supported with the adoption of a Security Council Resolution that explicitly requested UNTAC to mount border checkpoints in order to enforce a ban on the export of logs. But the decision had already been made not to take any action that could provoke the Khmer Rouge and increase the risk of an escalation.[59]

In Defense of the Mission

From December 1992 onward, the situation in Cambodia deteriorated further. The Khmer Rouge showed an increasingly aggressive attitude by first detaining and later killing UN peacekeepers. With the reputation of the UN on the line, the Secretary-General and the Security Council decided to push through with the elections, despite the fact that the armies of the two largest Cambodian factions remained almost fully intact. With the Khmer Rouge threatening to violently disrupt the elections and endanger the much-needed success for the UN, the diplomatic approach was clearly abandoned and a more liberal interpretation of the mandate adopted. Tasked with protecting the elections, UNTAC troops changed their posture into a more robust one and were instructed that force was allowed in defense of the mission. Eventually, the elections were a great success with high voter turnouts and only minor security incidents. Yet UNTAC was only able to protect the electoral process against the Khmer Rouge threat by signing an agreement of cooperation with the other factions, return some of their weapons, and especially allow the army of the Phnom Penh government to undertake preemptive attacks against the Khmer Rouge, measures that jeopardized the UN's impartiality and the peacekeeping objectives of the mission.[60]

Conclusion

A closer look at the peacekeeping operation in Cambodia demonstrates that an analysis focused on the black-and-white distinction between peacekeeping and enforcement is insufficient to understand the complexity of the reasons for military leaders to emphasize either diplomatic or military measures in fulfilling their peacekeeping mission. In Cambodia, these considerations were influenced by many factors, such as the personal and political context in which they operated, but mainly revolved around the issue of risk: a concept that soldiers accept as part of their profession and diplomats generally try to avoid in achieving their goals. Sanderson clearly defined his role as peacekeeper more as a diplomat than as a soldier. Loridon, on the other hand, believed that a certain military dynamic was required to save the peace. Despite plans by the civilian leader of the mission to use the peacekeepers' military capabilities to pressure the Khmer Rouge into cooperation, the force commander adhered to the diplomatic

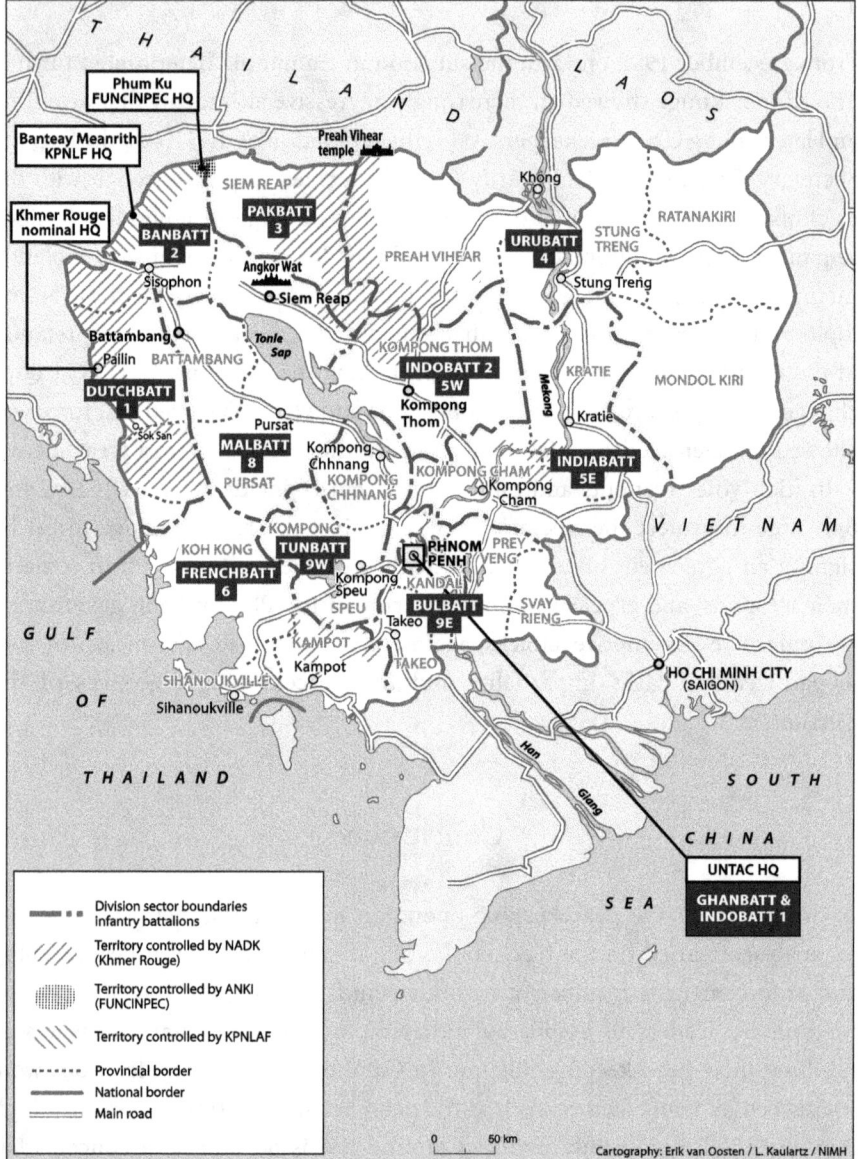

Figure 4.1 UNTAC's deployment in Cambodia, 1992. Netherlands Institute for Military History, The Hague.

approach. This analysis of the peacekeeping operation in Cambodia reminds us that peacekeeping strategies are not necessarily determined by considerations about doctrines and mandates and that it is important to understand how peacekeepers themselves define their role in the search for a balance in their diplomatic-military task. These insights are of relevance in understanding the gray area between conceptual theory and the reality in the field that still characterizes UN peacekeeping operations today.[61]

Notes

1 Between 1988 and 1993, twenty new UN operations were deployed in the field, whereas only thirteen had been set up between 1948 and 1988.

2 Jocelyn Coulon, *Soldiers of Diplomacy: The United Nations, Peacekeeping, and the New World Order* (Toronto: University of Toronto Press, 1998); Marie-Claude Smouts (ed.), *L'ONU et la guerre: la diplomatie en kaki* (Brussels: Éditions Complexe, 1994).

3 A quote that is often attributed to the second Secretary-General of the United Nations Dag Hammarskjöld (1953–1961).

4 Ronald Hatto, *Le maintien de la paix: L'ONU en action* (Paris: Armand Colin, 2015), 78.

5 John Gerard Ruggie, "Wandering in the Void: Charting the U.N.'s New Strategic Role," *Foreign Affairs* 72, no. 5 (November/December 1993): 26–31, 26; John Gerard Ruggie, "The UN and the collective Use of Force: Whither or Whether?" in *The UN, Peace and Force,* ed. Michael Pugh (London: Frank Cass, 1996), 1–20, 4.

6 Boutros Boutros-Ghali, *An Agenda for Peace: Preventive Diplomacy, Peacemaking and Peace-Keeping* (New York: United Nations, 1992), 11.

7 Mats Berdal and Michael Leifer, "Cambodia," in *The New Interventionism, 1991–1994: United Nations Experience in Cambodia, Former Yugoslavia, and Somalia,* ed. James Mayall (Cambridge: Cambridge University Press, 1996), 25–57, 25; MacAlister Brown and Joseph J. Zasloff, *Cambodia Confounds the Peacemakers, 1979-1998* (Ithaca: Cornell University Press, 1998), 104; Trevor Findlay, *Cambodia: The Legacy and Lessons of UNTAC* (Oxford: Oxford University Press, 1997), 129; Janet E. Heininger, *Peacekeeping in Transition: The United Nations in Cambodia* (New York: The Twentieth Century Fund Press, 1994), 136.

8 "Clarification of Certain Principles Views to Act as de Basis of Our Views and Stance," February 6, 1992, S-0794-0049-0001, United Nations Archives New York, New York, USA (UNANY).

9 Cable Loridon to Goulding, "Situation au Cambodge," February 17, 1992, S-0995-0001-0004, UNANY; Cable Goulding to Akashi, "Planning for UNTAC," February 24, 1992, S-0794-0012-0001, UNANY.

10 Cable Loridon to Goulding, "Situation au Cambodge," March 15, 1992, S-0995-0001-0004, UNANY.

11 Nate Thayer, "Phnom Penh Launches Offensive as Cease-fire Efforts Stall," *Associated Press*, March 29, 1992; Sheri Prasso, "Generals Refuse to Halt Fighting in Central Cambodia," *Agence France Presse (AFP)*, March 27, 1992.

12 Cable Sanderson to Goulding, "Kampong Thom Ceasefire Negotiations," April 1, 1992, S-0794-0046-0004, UNANY; "Le retour à la paix Cambodge: timide progrès sur le terrain," *Le Figaro*, April 1, 1992; Colette Braeckman, "La drôle de paix de Kompong Thom," *Le Soir*, April 14, 1992.

13 Cable Goulding to Sanderson, "Indonesian Contingent," April 23, 1992, S-0997-0006-0003, UNANY.

14 Message Lt Col. Dukers to UNTAC HQ, "Deployment NL Bat into Sector 1," May 23, 1992, box 1226, file 7, Marnstaf Cambodja, Semi Statisch Archief Ministerie van Defensie (SSAMD), The Hague, The Netherlands.

15 Sean O'Meara, "Keeping the Peace a Cambodian Diary Dec. 1991–June 1993," *An Cosantóir—The Defence Forces Magazine* 52, no. 10 (October 1992): 34–6, 36; Fax Lt Col. Malik to UNTAC HQ, "Visit of Mr Akashi and Lt Gen Sanderson," May 30, 1992 S-1854-0060-0004, UNANY; Cable French Ambassador Phnom Penh to Paris, "Montée de la tension avec les Khmers Rouges," June 1, 1992, 10 POI/1 1309, Archives Diplomatiques Nantes (ADN), Nantes, France.

16 Internal memorandum Sanderson to Akashi, "The Bamboo Pole incident," March 12, 1993, S-0796-0056-0002, UNANY.

17 Patrice de Beer, "Le scepticisme tempéré du général Loridon," *Le Monde*, June 2, 1992; Dominique Artus, "Colère française au Cambodge," *Le Journal du Dimanche*, May 31, 1992; "Inquiétude au Cambodge," *L'Humanité*, June 1, 1992; Frédéric Pons, "Le syndrome du buffle," *Valeurs Actuelles*, June 22, 1992; François Luizet, "Cambodge: la paix en panne, les Khmers rouges bloquent l'ONU," *Le Figaro*, June 11, 1992.

18 Pierre Joxe is the son of Louis Joxe (1901–91) who was Minister for Algerian Affairs in President De Gaulle's government and designated to lead the negotiations with the Algerian independence movement FLN. In reaction, a group of high-ranking French generals committed a putsch in Algiers in April 1961. This key event has shaped the idea among the French political class that senior military officers should refrain from commenting on political-strategic issues.

19 Cable French PR New York to Paris, "APRONUC Remplacement du général Loridon," July 2, 1992, 10POI/1 1309, ADN.

20 Nyan Chanda, "UN Divisions: Signs of Growing Franco-Australian Rivalry within Peacekeeping Force," *Far Eastern Economic Review* (July 23, 1992): 8–9, 9.

21 Ibid., 9.

22 "Message from Phnom Penh," July 29, 1992, *AFP*, accessed via Dow Jones Factiva database; Author's interview with M. Loridon, July 23, 2018, France.

23 Berdal and Leifer, "Cambodia," 42; David Horner and John Connor, *The Good International Citizen Australian Peacekeeping in Asia, Africa and Europe, 1991–1993* (New York: Cambridge University Press, 2014), 119; Sorpong Peou, *Conflict Neutralization in the Cambodian War From Battlefield to Ballot Box* (Oxford: Oxford University Press, 1997), 229, 249; Brown and Zasloff, *Cambodia Confounds the Peacemakers*, 284.

24 Andrzej Sitkowski, *UN Peacekeeping Myth and Reality* (Westport: Praeger Security International, 2006), 93; Raoul M. Jennar, *Croniques Cambodgiennes 1990-1994: Rapports au Forum International des ONG au Cambodge* (Paris: Éditions l'Harmattan, 1995), 299, 348, 349.

25 "UNTAC Standard Operating Procedures, Section 4 Use of Force," file 22, UNTAC-099, Netherlands Institute for Military History (NIMH), The Hague, The Netherlands.

26 "CV Lieutenant General John Sanderson," BZ-00391, Archief Ministerie van Buitenlandse Zaken (ABZ), The Hague, The Netherlands.

27 "Minutes of the 11th meeting of the Mixed Military Working Group," March 27, 1992, S-1854-0080-0006, UNANY.

28 Interview by James S. Sutterlin with Sir Marrack Goulding, June 30, 1998, Oxford, United Kingdom, Yale United Nations Oral History Project (YUNOP).

29 Heininger, *Peacekeeping in Transition*, 123.

30 John M. Sanderson, "UNTAC: The Military Component View," in *The United Nations Transitional Authority in Cambodia: Debriefing and Lessons, International Conference UNTAC: Debriefing and Lessons Singapore—August 3, 1994*, ed. The Institute of Policy Studies Singapore and UNITAR (London: Kluwer Law International, 1995), 125–38, 130.

31 John Sanderson, "Dabbling into War: The Dilemma of the Use of Force in United Nations Intervention," in *Peacemaking and Peacekeeping for the New Century*, ed. Olara A. Atunnu and Michael W. Doyle (Oxford: Rowman & Littlefield publishers, 1998), 145–68, 150.

32 John M. Sanderson, "The Incalculable Dynamic of Force," in *UN Peacekeeping in Trouble: Lessons Learned from the Former Yugoslavia Peacekeeper's Views on the Limits and Possibilities of the United Nations in a Civil War-like Conflict*, ed. Wolfgang Biermann and Martin Vadset (Aldershot: Ashgate Publishing, 1998), 203–17.

33 Michel Loridon, "Le rôle des casques bleus," *Le Casoar* (July 1993): 86–8, 87.

34 Michel Loridon, "The U.N. Intervention in Cambodia 1991/1993," unpublished paper given at the RUSI-Swedish War College seminar, April 23–24, 1996.

35 John M. Sanderson, "Peacekeeping or Peace Enforcement? Global Flux and the Dilemmas of UN Intervention," in *The United Nations at Fifty: Retrospect and Prospect*, ed. Ramesh Thakur (Dunedin: University of Otago Press, 1996), 179–200, 183.

36 Michel Loridon, "Cambodge, les raisons d'un échec," in *Opérations des Nations unies, leçons de terrain: Cambodge, Somalie, Rwanda, ex-Yougoslavie*, ed. Jean Pierre

Cot and Franck Debié (Paris: La Documentation française, 1995), 107–10, 108; Michel Loridon, "La fermeté: un droit et un devoir pour l'ONU," in *Les interventions extérieures de l'armée française,* ed. Pierre Pascallon (Brussels: Bruylant Bruxelles, 1997), 241–8, 246.

37 Erwin A. Schmidl, "Speak Softly and Carry a Big Stick: The Use of Force in Peace Operations, Past and Present," in *Peacekeeping with Muscle: The Use of Force in International Conflict Resolution,* ed. Alex Morrison, Douglas A. Fraser, and James D. Kiras (Clementsport: Canadian Peacekeeping Press, 1997), 83–90, 85.

38 Sanderson, "Peacekeeping or Peace Enforcement?" 186.

39 Loridon, "The U.N. Intervention in Cambodia." In 1995, the French Chief of Defence Staff Admiral Lanxade equally referred to "active impartiality." See: Shaun Gregory, "France and missions de paix," *The RUSI Journal* 145, no. 4 (2000): 58–63, 62.

40 Trevor Findlay, *The Use of Force in Peace Operations* (Oxford: Oxford University Press-SIPRI, 2002), 406.

41 Thierry Tardy, "The Reluctant Peacekeeper: France and the Use of Force in Peace Operations," *The Journal of Strategic Studies* 37, no. 5 (2014): 770–92, 776.

42 Ken Berry, *Cambodia—from Red to Blue: Australia's Initiative for Peace* (St. Leonards: Allen & Unwin in association with the Department of International Relations, RSPAS, ANU, 1997); Gareth Evans, *Incorrigible Optimist: A Political Memoir* (Melbourne: Melbourne University Press, 2017), 152.

43 Horner and Connor, *The Good International Citizen*, 82.

44 "No Shooting War for Us in Cambodia, Evans Says," *The Canberra Times*, August 25, 1989.

45 "Statement by the Prime Minister, the Hon P. J. Keating MP Cambodia Peacekeeping," April 1, 1992, 00168, ABZ (emphasis in original document).

46 Ibid.

47 John Sanderson, "Command at the Operational Level," presentation to the Australian Command and Staff College, unpublished paper given at Queensclif on June 26, 2000.

48 Brigitte Stern, "Conclusion," in *United Nations Peace-Keeping Operations: A Guide to French Policies,* ed. Brigitte Stern, Yves Daudet, Philippe Morillon, and Marie-Claude Smouts (Tokyo: UN University Press, 1998), 124–5.

49 Boutros-Ghali, *An Agenda for Peace*, 25.

50 Letter Boutros-Ghali to Akashi, July 7, 1992, S-1829-0314-0003, UNANY; Cable Goulding to Akashi, "Implementation of the Paris Agreements," July 24, 1992, S-0794-0043-0001, UNANY.

51 Cable Goulding to Akashi, "Khmer Rouge / UNTAC Radio Station," June 30, 1992, S-0794-0043-0001 UNANY; Cable Goulding to Akashi, "Implementation of the Paris Agreements," July 24, 1992, S-0794-0043-0001, UNANY.

52 Cable Akashi to Goulding, "Reply Mr. Khieu Samphan to the Secretary-General," July 10, 1992, S-0794-0047-0003, UNANY; Cable Akashi to Goulding, "Implementation of Paris Agreements," July 31, 1992, S-0794-0047-0003, UNANY.

53 Interview by James S. Sutterlin with Sir Marrack Goulding, YUNOP.

54 Cable French Ambassador Phnom Penh to Paris, "Analyses et suggestions sur le Cambodge (II—l'hypothèse des sanctions)," June 17, 1992, 10POI/1 1309, ADN; Letter U.S. Ambassador Phnom Penh to Akashi, June 3, 1992, S-0997-0006-0003, UNANY; Cable Akashi to Goulding, June 10, 1992, S-0795-0045-0003, UNANY; Cable Akashi to Goulding, "Military Options," August 12, 1992, S-0794-0020-0001, UNANY.

55 Cable Akashi to Goulding, "The First Six Months 15 March–15 September 1992," September 17, 1992, S-0794-0047-0004, UNANY.

56 Cable Goulding to Akashi, "Khmer Rouge," June 1, 1992, S-1829-0314-0003, UNANY; Cable Goulding to Akashi, "Implementation of the Paris Agreements," July 24, 1992, S-0795-0043-0005, UNANY.

57 Cable Akashi and Sanderson to UN New York, "Draft Document Deployment of Checkpoint in Western Cambodia," September 28, 1992, S-0794-0048-0002, UNANY; "Operation Order 3/92, Operation Dovetail," UNTAC-099, file 56, NIMH.

58 Cable Akashi to Goulding, "Report on UNTAC's Activities," September 26, 1992, S-0794-0048-0002, UNANY; Karolien Bais, *Het mijnenveld van een vredesmacht Nederlandse blauwhelmen in Cambodja* (The Hague: SDU Uitgeverij, 1994), 54.

59 Cable Akashi to Goulding, "Implementation of Resolution 792," December 4, 1992, S-0794-0011-0001, UNANY.

60 This element is elaborated further in the author's PhD Thesis.

61 Mateja Peter, "Between Doctrine and Practice: The UN Peacekeeping Dilemma," *Global Governance* 21 (2015): 351–70.

5

United Nations Military Observers in Former Yugoslavia

Strategic Influencers or Sitting Ducks?

Dion Landstra and Thomas Wijnaendts van Resandt

Introduction

Sarajevo, May 26, 1995: Major Jos Gelissen and several of his UNMO colleagues find themselves trapped in the lion's den. For days they have been hunkering down in their supposedly safe UN house. Bosnian-Serb forces have sabotaged their telephone line and cut off their access to running water. Completely isolated, all the men can do is anxiously await their fate. Instead of receiving instructions from UNMO headquarters, all they hear on their radio are cries for help from other observers pinned down by Serbian small-arms fire. Soon the situation devolves into a veritable nightmare as two black SUVs pull up in front of the house and a heavily armed Serbian arrest team gags and abducts the unfortunate military observers.

Gelissen and his colleagues are among dozens of other UN peacekeepers to be taken hostage by Serbian forces in retaliation for NATO airstrikes. Forced to live in poor conditions, the dismayed observers are routinely interrogated under threat of death and are used as human shields to deter any further airstrikes. Feelings of anxiety, depression, and helplessness abound. Their imprisonment is nothing less than a direct attack on the UN and, consequently, on the very tenets of international law. Only after three harrowing weeks would the last of the hostages be released. Gelissen and his fellow UNMOs would thankfully survive the ordeal, but the experience had scarred them for life.[1]

The hostage crisis brought the accountability of the United Nations into the limelight. If anything, it signified the impotence of the international community in former Yugoslavia, where it appeared to be little more than a toothless tiger desperately attempting to maintain a veneer of security and peace in a country increasingly torn apart by war and genocide. Moreover, the UN's flailing efforts demonstrated the complexity of peacemaking and brought into question the subsequent role of military observers. How responsible was it to use this traditional peacekeeping instrument in a highly dangerous area based on little more than a precarious "symbolic inviolability" and the goodwill of the belligerent parties?

Before we can venture any further into this question, a brief historical overview of the observer instrument is in order. The deployment of military observers to conflict areas is nearly as old as the international community itself. The first budding attempts at collective peace and security crystallized with the establishment of the Concert of Europe after Napoleon's defeat in 1815. Although its influence and effectiveness remained marginal, the Concert marked the inception of humanitarian and peacekeeping missions. Its successor, the League of Nations, rose out of the ashes of the First World War in 1919. Under the auspices of President Woodrow Wilson's "Fourteen Points," member states conformed to a covenant in the service of collective security. This covenant opened the door to collective military action on a lawful basis. The deployment of military observers to conflict zones became the instrument of choice. After ceasefire agreements had been made between the belligerent parties, observers were deployed and tasked with monitoring the peace.[2] The efforts of the League, however, ultimately faltered in the face of surging authoritarian ideologies in the 1930s, and it would take another global conflict to finally convince world leaders that international cooperation was paramount.

The United Nations, established in 1945, followed in the footsteps of the failed League of Nations and marked a renewed attempt at collective peace and security. Its principal organ, the Security Council, was permanently seated by the main victorious powers: Great Britain, the United States, the Soviet Union, France, and China.[3] The realities of the Cold War, with its East-West divide, however severely inhibited the role of the UN on the world stage. Of a total of only seventeen peacekeeping operations undertaken during the Cold War, ten were traditional observation or verification missions conducted entirely by military observers. During missions in Yemen, India, Pakistan, Georgia, Afghanistan, and elsewhere, a total of 1,840 unarmed officers surveyed armistices and the implementation of peace accords.[4] The oldest and longest-running of these missions is the United Nations Truce Supervision Organization (UNTSO), which began in May 1948 and saw the deployment of hundreds of military observers to the borders of Israel. The Cold War era was also significant because it laid the foundations for modern-day peacekeeping, basing its deployments around three principles: the consent of the belligerent parties, neutrality, and the use of force in self-defense.

The observers' main area of operations during this time was along state borders and in demilitarized zones. Accordingly, their tasks were executed either from static observation posts or through patrols.[5] Even so, the UNMOs of these "traditional" missions at times found themselves having to go beyond their formal observation and verification tasks. During missions in Indonesia (UNGOC), India-Pakistan (UNMIGOP), and Iran-Iraq (UNIIMOG), monitors acted as mediators in local disputes and as makeshift diplomats assisting local civil and military authorities with the implementation of ceasefires, the withdrawal of troops, and other arrangements. On top of that, observers facilitated humanitarian operations and prisoner-of-war exchanges. By executing these additional tasks, UNMOs hoped to prevent a renewal of hostilities and to build mutual trust.[6]

The end of the Cold War marked a sudden and drastic change in the geopolitical landscape. No longer held back by superpower conflict, the UN was finally in a position to act more often and more decisively as a true neutral arbiter in conflict zones.[7] This change coincided with an increasing demand for peacekeeping missions, after the breakdown of the relative "stability" provided by the Cold War triggered age-old ethnic, intrastate conflicts.[8] Between 1989 and 1991, the UN, in cooperation with other international organizations, launched seven peacekeeping missions (five of which could be typified as traditional observer missions) and deployed a total of 1,888 unarmed military observers.[9]

The changing character of armed conflict also forced the UN to adopt a more integrated political-military approach to peacekeeping. The protection of human rights, humanitarian aid, and the development of democratic institutions turned out to be necessary components in resolving conflicts in places like Angola (MONUA/UNAVEM II), El Salvador (ONUSAL), Mozambique (ONUMOZ), and Guatemala (MINUGUA).[10] In practice, this meant that the mandate of the peacekeeping forces had to be expanded and diversified, which included a broader mandate on the use of force as conflicts grew more violent.[11] The traumatizing experiences of missions in Angola, Rwanda, and Somalia taught the UN the hard way that *peacekeeping* did not suffice in these types of conflicts; peace now also had to be *enforced*.[12] However, due to a general lack of political will to pick sides and take risks, the international community was often hesitant to do so. Accordingly, the demand for unarmed military observers remained unchanged.

As part of multifunctional peacekeeping forces, observers were deployed to such volatile places as Cambodia, Somalia, and former Yugoslavia. During the latter effort, the UNMOs quickly discovered that it proved extremely difficult to deal with the rapidly escalating intrastate conflict. As the violence spread from Croatia into Bosnia and Herzegovina, they were faced with an increasing number of tasks and risks to their personal safety. In essence, military observers in former Yugoslavia acted as chameleons, constantly having to react and adapt to the dynamic situation on the ground. At times—as the opening anecdote illustrated—observers could do little more than survive. Handcuffed both literally and figuratively, the effectiveness of their work was often left to the good graces of the belligerent parties. The question was whether the benefits had been worth the risks? Could the international community, in good conscience, send unarmed men to a highly dangerous area with little more to protect them than "symbolic inviolability"?

Adding to the larger discussion on the complexity of peacemaking, this chapter evaluates the underexamined role UN military observers played within the peacemaking process during their deployment to former Yugoslavia between 1991 and 1995. In doing so, it aims to answer several pivotal questions: What were the observer's tasks and how did they develop over time? What were the day-to-day risks observers had to face and how did these impact their experience? What can be said about the benefits, costs, and overall effectiveness of this traditional peacekeeping instrument? Were observers, in the final analysis, merely "sitting ducks" or were they pivotal strategic influencers?

UNMOs Formal and Informal Tasks

The fragmentation of the Yugoslav state and the subsequent eruption of violence were direct results of the end of the Cold War, yet ethnic tensions had been brewing for decades. Since its establishment in 1945, the Socialist Federal Republic of Yugoslavia consisted of six constituent republics: Slovenia, Croatia, Bosnia and Herzegovina, Macedonia, Serbia (including the independent provinces of Vojvodina and Kosovo), and Montenegro. With the death of its leader Josip Tito in 1980, the bond that had held these disparate peoples together began a process of disintegration, which would culminate with the fall of the Eastern Bloc about a decade later.

The first step toward Yugoslavia's fateful breakdown occurred on June 25, 1991. After nationalist parties from Slovenia and Croatia won their respective elections, both states declared their independence from Belgrade. Unwilling to recognize the validity of these proclamations, the federal government deployed units of the Federal Yugoslav Army (JNA) to Slovenia on June 27. However, tough Slovenian resistance and deserting Slovenian and Croatian JNA soldiers put an early halt to the offensive. After the international community condemned Belgrade's aggression, the federal government folded. Slovenia secured its independence after only ten days of skirmishing. Besides, the country had been of little importance to the Serbian government from the outset as only very few ethnic Serbs lived within its borders. On July 7, the European Community mediated the signing of the Brioni Agreement, which implemented a ceasefire between Slovenia and the JNA. Additionally, both Slovenia and Croatia agreed to postpone their respective declarations of independence for three months. This provided a window of opportunity to initiate the European Community Monitoring Mission (ECMM), which deployed forty-eight monitors from twelve Community partners and five OCSE nations to Slovenia and Croatia to verify compliance with the agreement.

The Croatian puzzle proved tougher to solve. Still affected by the traumas inflicted upon them by the Croatian collaborationist state during the Second World War, the large Serbian minority decided to revolt against Franjo Tudjman's nationalist government. After countless failed international mediation attempts, Croatia descended into months of bitter fighting between the Serbian secessionists aided by the JNA and the Croatian National Guard.[13] In the meantime, similar storm clouds were starting to gather over neighboring Bosnia and Herzegovina. Bitter ethnic divisions between Bosnian-Serbs, Bosnian-Muslims, and Bosnian-Croats reached a boiling point following the announcement of the republic's declaration of independence. While Bosnian-Croats and Bosnian-Muslims favored secession, pro-Belgrade Bosnian-Serbs responded in mid-September by setting up their own respective autonomous regions. The situation escalated further when it became clear that the Bosnian-Serbs intended to expand these regions by force with the help of the federal government.[14] After Slovenia and Croatia, Bosnia and Herzegovina would be the third former Yugoslavian republic to be dragged into civil war.

In response, the European Community scrambled to expand their mandate and move the operational center of gravity toward Croatia and Bosnia. Meanwhile, calls for the deployment of a UN peacekeeping force were growing louder. On November 23, Lord Carrington (the Community's peace negotiator) and Cyrus Vance (the UN Secretary-General's special envoy) managed to broker a tenuous ceasefire agreement between the Serbian and Croatian presidents, Slobodan

Milosevic and Franjo Tudjman, and the federal Minister of Defense, Veljko Kadijevic.[15] The Vance Plan was ratified by the Security Council a month later with the passing of Resolution 724, which opened the door for the deployment of a UN peacekeeping force.[16] Unfortunately, a series of geopolitical blunders lead to a renewal of hostilities and the proclamations of both the autonomous *Republika Srepska Krajina* (RSK) in Croatia and the *Republika Serpska* (RS) in Bosnia and Herzegovina.[17] More than a month would pass before another hard-earned ceasefire was agreed upon in Sarajevo on January 2, 1992.[18]

Two months later, the United Nations Protection Force (UNPROFOR) was finally began to deploy. Besides constituting a regular peacekeeping force, UNPROFOR also included a United Nations Military Observer (UNMO) contingent, staffed by 100 officers from 29 countries.[19] Although initially set up in Sarajevo, the UNMO organization was eventually forced to move its main headquarters to the Croatian capital, Zagreb, in the spring of 1992. Additionally, several constituent sector HQs were established across the country. After UNPROFOR expanded into Bosnia and Herzegovina, UNMOs also set up a Regional HQ in Kiseljak, which was subsequently moved to Sarajevo in early 1994. This HQ was in turn supported by several constituent sector HQs.

Although formally under the operational control of UNPROFOR's main peacekeeping force, in practice UNMOs operated on a more or less autonomous basis.[20] The UNMOs' primary objective was to observe and report on the implementation of the ceasefire and verify compliance with the agreed demilitarization of the Serb-dominated areas (UNPAs) in Croatia, the withdrawal of troops, and the lifting of blockades. Second, UNMOs were expected to mediate between the belligerent parties, encourage compliance with the agreed terms, and assist in maintaining peace and stability.[21] Monitors mediated in volatile situations on multiple occasions and were instrumental in opening a space for dialogue between the combatants. Additional liaison activities included setting up local networks of the authorities of the various ethnic communities, facilitating UN convoy frontline crossings, and escorting JNA convoys through Croatia and Bosnia and Herzegovina.[22] As Dutch UNMO major Bert van Kaathoven put it: "In principle, the UNMOs were involved with everything that could calm the situation."[23]

Despite these considerable efforts, violence continued to spread, forcing UNPROFOR and the UNMO organization to send in reinforcements and expand their mandate. The first of these expansions was the signing of the Sarajevo Airport agreement in June 1992, which reopened the airstrip for humanitarian aid deliveries and put it under UNPROFOR's control.[24] With the adoption of

Resolutions 758 and 761, the Security Council authorized sixty UNMOs to verify this agreement.[25] Subsequent Resolutions 762 and 776 expanded both the mandate and the size of the UN mission and authorized another 140 military observers whose area of operations would be the demilitarized Pink Zones (60) and Bosnia and Herzegovina (80).[26] Two additional Resolutions followed a few months later. Resolution 779 mandated monitors to observe the demilitarization of the Prevlaka peninsula,[27] and Resolution 786 prohibited the belligerent parties from flying military sorties in the newly established No-Fly Zone (NFZ). To help enforce the NFZ, seventy-nine UNMOs were deployed to keep a permanent watch over the air traffic of fifteen airports in three countries.[28] On December 11, a further thirty-five UNMOs were ordered to take part in the UN's preventive deployment to Macedonia after the Security Council signed off on Resolution 795. Their principal task was to operate along the border region between Macedonia and Albania.[29]

In the meantime, ongoing hostilities between the Bosnian-Serbs and the Bosnian-Muslims were leading toward a humanitarian disaster in Bosnia and Herzegovina, as Serbian units lay siege to the Muslim enclaves of Srebrenica, Zepa, Gorazde, Bihac, Tuzla, and Sarajevo. The situation deteriorated to such an extent that the UN "promoted" the enclaves to so-called "safe areas," with the adoption of Resolutions 821 and 824. Having theoretically been immunized from any kind of outside attack, a group of fifty UNMOs were the first to be deployed to monitor the situation in these open-air prisons. Observers were primarily present to keep an eye on the deteriorating humanitarian circumstances.[30]

The final expansion of UNPROFOR took place between February and April 1994 in response to the signing of two large-scale ceasefires, namely the Sarajevo ceasefire and the Washington Accords. With open conflict officially called to a halt in Croatia and the peacemaking process slowly making headway in Bosnia and Herzegovina, observers were tasked to implement the armistices and observe the demilitarized zones around the cities of Sarajevo and Gorazde.[31] To perform this task, the Security Council authorized the deployment of a final 170 UNMOs with Resolutions 908 and 914. In sum, the UN observer mission had expanded exponentially; within two years, the UNMO organization had grown from 100 to 748 observers and had developed from a "traditional" observer mission with a limited number of tasks to a dynamic and multifarious effort spread out over an expansive area of operations.

However, as the situation deteriorated, fulfilling this mandate became extremely difficult. With the main peacekeeping force spread thin, monitors, aided by their unique role and extensive knowledge of their local communities, increasingly began to conduct several additional informal tasks. As the main peacekeeping force was spread thin, UNMOs were at times the only evidence of the international community's presence in an area. As such, "showing the flag" became a task in itself. The monitors' physical presence in restricted and remote regions showed the resolve of the international community and was utilized in hopes of tempering violence in volatile areas. Dozens of observers were deployed to Mostar and Sarajevo for this specific reason. Their presence also served to prevent volatile situations from escalating in places like Neum, Derventa, Brcko, and the Bosnian-Muslim enclaves.[32]

Additionally, the independent third-party status of the UNMOs, combined with their military expertise, enabled observers to work as on-the-ground subject matter experts (SMEs). Their familiarity with the specific geographic and ethnographic layouts of their assigned areas made them ideally suited to reconnoiter potential areas of operation for regular peacekeeping forces and take part in the subsequent deployment decision-making process.[33] Their frequent participation in various research committees also gave them exclusive access to regions beyond their formal mandate. On top of that, monitors were on the scene to investigate attacks on civilian targets on multiple occasions.[34]

Besides these additional military tasks, UNMOs provided humanitarian assistance to local communities. Due to their integration into these communities, observers were able to supplement and guide existing NGO efforts; Monitors, often in collaboration with the International Red Cross (ICRC), participated in the taking in of refugees, facilitated prisoner exchanges, distributed food and medicine, and helped improve housing and access to medical care. UNMOs would increasingly find themselves taking up this additional responsibility as existing humanitarian efforts buckled under the weight of the escalating conflict.[35]

In sum, although the formal tasks of the military observers in former Yugoslavia were initially limited, the UNMO organization gradually expanded in both size and scope. But as the situation continued to deteriorate, monitors were forced to take up an increasing number of informal tasks. This, however, proved to be a precarious endeavor; the escalating violence severely restricted the UNMOs freedom of movement while also seriously increasing the risks to their personal safety.

Risks

Restriction of movement was one of the principal factors impeding the effectiveness of the UNMOs. In former Yugoslavia, belligerent parties not only regularly barred observers access to certain areas because they could not guarantee their safety but also seriously complicated the observers' work in various other ways. Intimidation, harassment, and vehicle searches at gunpoint by often highly inebriated soldiers occurred on a systematic basis and resulted in unpredictable and dangerous situations. These holdups at times made it impossible for observers to conduct patrols or to assist in the delivery of humanitarian aid in closed off areas.[36] At other times, monitors would be held back for hours or were interrogated at local headquarters.[37] Hijackings and robberies were equally common. A Dutch UNMO vividly remembered how his vehicle was stolen by a Croatian soldier, leaving him and his team stranded on the road for hours. Worse still, UNMOs risked being abducted, abused, and utilized as human shields by Serbian forces.[38]

The escalation of violence in Croatia and Bosnia and Herzegovina also meant that the unarmed observers ran the risk of getting caught in the crossfire.[39] Mine incidents during patrols—at times deliberately placed on UNPROFOR routes—occurred regularly.[40] Depending on the area of operations, artillery and mortar shelling posed a constant threat. Similarly, monitors in urban areas such as Sarajevo, Bihac, Gorazde, and Mostar had to brave heavy firefights and deadly sniper fire on a near-daily basis.[41] Even UNMO sector HQs were not completely safe. In May 1992, shrapnel from a mortar explosion in Mostar seriously wounded Finnish major Mikko Rahikkala, making him the first UNMO casualty of the war.[42] Around the same time, Belgian ECMM monitor Bertrand Borrey was shot and killed near Cula by JNA troops after a futile attempt to identify his team's European Community status.[43] In Sarajevo, the situation eventually deteriorated to such an extent that peacekeepers were only able to traverse the city in armored vehicles.[44] In short, being a military observer in former Yugoslavia was a highly risky endeavor. From 1991 to October 1994, the UNMO organization suffered thirty-three casualties, twenty-four of whom were wounded and nine of whom were killed in action.[45]

Those who otherwise returned physically unscathed nonetheless often brought home mental trauma that affected their personal as well as the lives of their families. Research has indicated that individually deployed servicemen tend to run a higher risk of developing psychological and relational problems after their deployment.[46] The potentially lasting psychological consequences of the UNMOs' deployment thus constituted a final risk. Post hoc evaluations revealed that many former observers suffered from chronic and severe headaches and amnesia. For some, these issues reemerged years after their deployment when asked to share their experiences or after being called to testify in front of the ICTY. Others struggled with alcoholism, marital issues, and PTSD. One observer lamented a full twenty-three years after his deployment that he had "become an embittered man; the deployment controls my entire life and that of my children. I just think it's terrible."[47]

But the prevalence of mental issues was not merely restricted to those UNMOs returning from their deployment. "Acute Peacekeeping Stress" is a term used to signify outbursts of anger due to high levels of stress experienced while on mission.[48] A tragic consequence of this phenomenon occurred on February 1, 1995, when Finnish captain Heikki Voutilainen was bludgeoned to death by his "mentally disturbed" colleague, the Nigerian Major Lamikanra.[49]

In sum, continuing violence seriously hampered the UNMOs' freedom of movement and forced them to contend with considerable risks to their personal safety and mental well-being, all of which hampered their ability to perform their tasks. Nevertheless, observers were rarely recalled and continued to operate throughout former Yugoslavia for the duration of the mission. At first glance, this may seem somewhat surprising considering the peacekeepers' reputation for avoiding overt risks. To sufficiently explain this incongruity, we have to take a closer look at the UNMO organization's value and effectiveness in the field.

Value and Effectiveness

The question which this leaves us with is to what extent the monitors were able to fulfill their mandate and contribute to the broader goals of conflict resolution, despite these considerable impeding factors. If "impotence" is the one-word takeaway of the UNPROFOR mission, what exactly was the specific value of its most vulnerable assets to the international community? Notwithstanding the extreme difficulty of their mission, military observers did in fact contribute to the improvement of the situation in several notable ways.

As stated before, the UNMOs' access to key players and their up-to-date knowledge of their designated area of operations perfectly positioned them to report valuable information to UNPROFOR commanders and NGOs. This information consisted primarily of local and regional military developments. Additionally, these reports contained early warning signs about rising tensions in both Croatia and Bosnia and Herzegovina, long and detailed descriptions of their mediation efforts, and updates on political and humanitarian developments in their area of operations. The latter included investigations into forced ethnic evacuations of several cities and visits to prisoner-of-war camps. In brief, monitors provided a substantial contribution to the situational awareness of the force commander, a contribution that went well beyond the confines of formal military situation reports.[50]

This information consequently also reached key policymakers such as the president of the European Commission in Brussels and the Under-Secretary-General (USG) for Special Political Affairs (the predecessor of the Department of Peacekeeping Operations or DPKO) of the UN in New York.[51] Significantly, monitor dispatches were put to good use in negotiations with the leaders of the warring factions by special envoys like Henry Wijnaendts, Lord Carrington, Cyrus Vance, Lord David Owen, and Thorvald Stoltenberg.[52] In the summer of 1993, Jens Stoltenberg—co-chairman of the steering committee of the International Conference on the Former Yugoslavia—personally commended the efforts of the UNMOs: "I have been impressed by the manner in which United Nations Military Observers in UNPROFOR have accurately and rapidly reported their observations on the ground. This assistance has been of great value to Lord Owen's and my efforts."[53]

UNMO information also proved of utmost importance to the decision-making process of the European Council and the Security Council. Observer reports by Dutch captain Josh Zoutendijk and Canadian captain Dan Flynn, for instance, led directly to the adoption of Resolution 816, which enabled the UN to enforce the NFZ with NATO fighter aircraft.[54] Monitors thus contributed both directly and indirectly to the political negotiation process.

Furthermore, observers regularly participated in direct negotiations themselves. In some instances, these talks had an immediate operational effect. This was the case when CMO John Wilson negotiated the reopening of Sarajevo Airport in June 1992, which resulted in the adoption of Security Council Resolutions 757 and 758 and led to the expansion of the mandate and the size of UNPROFOR.[55] Some successes were also achieved on the tactical level, as monitors managed to mediate several local ceasefires in Croatia and Bosnia and Herzegovina. In one instance, on September 15, 1993, Chief Military Observer (CMO) B. Pellnas and Senior Military Observer of the Southern Sector Lieutenant-Colonel O. Nielsen successfully mediated a ceasefire agreement between the Serb and Croat authorities, resulting in the withdrawal of the Croat army around Medak.[56] Other notable examples include the crucial mediation efforts by Nielsen, Pellnas, and the Chief Operations Officer (COO) of UNMO HQ, A. M. H. Joscelyne, in the implementation of ceasefire agreements in Erdut and Mostar.[57] In short, due to their expanding liaison activities and neutral, unarmed status, UNMOs found themselves in a position to successfully participate in negotiations.

However, notwithstanding their essential value to the international community, these local successes ultimately proved insufficient to stem the general escalation of violence. Ceasefire agreements like those signed in Dubrovnik and Osijek ultimately did not last. The ethnic tensions were frequently too overbearing for lone observers to enact lasting change without structural societal or governmental support. As such, the UNMOs' mediation efforts often only had a temporary effect.[58]

Relatively more success was to be achieved on the humanitarian front. As discussed earlier, the humanitarian role of the UNMOs proved a vital supplement to existing NGO efforts. Organizations such as the International Red Cross, Doctors Without Borders, and the UNCHR were generally understaffed. Help from monitors was therefore dearly appreciated, although both sides remained careful not to compromise their neutrality. These humanitarian contributions mainly consisted of escorting humanitarian convoys, evacuating citizens, and monitoring living conditions in prisoner-of-war camps. One of the exemplary successes achieved during this collaborative effort took place in Mostar in May 1992. After having mediated three brief ceasefires on May 3, 9, and 13, UNMOs, together with the Red Cross, succeeded in evacuating three convoys of, respectively, 1,900, 1,500, and 1,300 women and children out of the warzone.[59] Moreover, monitors were on the scene to reconstruct houses, participate in the ICRC vaccination program in Mostar, and initiate a shelter project in the former safe area Zepa.[60] The observers were also tasked to investigate alleged violations of human rights and the Geneva Conventions. A multitude of worrisome reports of widespread murder, pillaging, and other excesses of violence were shared with policymakers in Brussels, the OSCE, the ICTY, and NGOs such as the ICRC.[61]

Yet UNMOs were often powerless to avert the spread of violence. In practice, observer deployments were more symbolic and diplomatic than truly preventive in nature. As stated before, monitors were unable to prevent the conflict from escalating in Sarajevo, Mostar, Bihac, Gorazde, and the southern Krajina in Croatia. Even so, many felt that their presence did make a difference. As a Dutch major stated, "If we hadn't been there then the city [Sarajevo, DL] would have been completely eradicated and the Serbs would probably have carried out a ground assault."[62] His colleague, a Regional Senior Military Observer (RSMO) and commander of the UNMOs in Bosnia and Herzegovina, shared in this sentiment: "Although the presence of UNMOs does not by definition rule out the use of violence, you can be certain that if we're not there, aggression will without a doubt erupt."[63] This belief in the preventive power of observers was put to the test again in late 1992 and early 1993, as UNPROFOR and ECMM expanded their area of operations to the border regions of Macedonia, Hungary, Bulgaria, Albania, and the former Yugoslavia, in hopes of containing the spread of violence there.[64]

Furthermore, the UNMOs' presence in sometimes remote and desperate areas like the Pink Zones and the Prevlaka peninsula was the only link between UNPROFOR and the situation on the ground. The same was true for some of the safe areas where UNMOs would at times be the sole peacekeepers present for several weeks or even months. In these situations, observers inadvertently came to be seen as the only sign of hope for the frightened local population. Significant evidence of this sentiment was palpable in Mostar in 1992, where disappointment, sorrow, and despair descended on the local population after the UNMOs were forced to leave the city.[65]

Finally, observers played a key role as SMEs in the preparation and deployment of UNPROFOR and the establishment of UNPROFOR HQ. On several occasions, UNMOs were used to augment UNPROFOR's situational awareness of a potential area of operations. In early 1992, monitors reconnoitered Mostar, Bihac, Sarajevo, and Macedonia, as well as several drop zones for the airlift of humanitarian supplies in remote regions.[66] Furthermore, observers at times prepared local authorities for the coming arrival of the main bulk of the peacekeeping force, manned so-called crossing points on the confrontation lines to facilitate the movement of UN units, and were utilized as trailblazers during the deployment of forces in the safe areas of Srebrenica, Gorazde, and Zepa.[67]

Last, their military expertise and experience enabled monitors to investigate and analyze evidence of war crimes. In one such instance, Dutch lieutenant-colonel Harry Konings led the UNMO team responsible for conducting the crater analysis of the deadly mortar attack on Markale market in Sarajevo on August 28, 1995.[68] Similarly, observers were also able to capture evidence of arbitrary harassment of civilians by Bosnian-Serb forces in Sarajevo. Findings like these were later utilized to testify against war criminals during the ICTY trials and subsequently proved vital for the effective prosecution of high-level Serbian leaders such as Radovan Karadzic, Ratko Mladic, and Tihomir Blaskic.[69]

Conclusion

In the final analysis, it is clear that military observers deployed to former Yugoslavia between 1991 and 1995 were faced with a highly complex and multifarious set of tasks. It would therefore be mistaken to attempt to draw one single conclusion regarding their efforts. At times, UNMOs were neither "sitting ducks" nor highly effective strategic influencers, while at other times, they were both. Their difficult-to-define experience reflects the complexity and multifaceted nature of the broader peacemaking process.

Military observers were seriously debilitated by the rapidly changing and dynamic nature of the conflict. Achieving their primary observation and mediation tasks proved more difficult than expected for a multitude of reasons. Principal among these were the restriction of movement and the ongoing violence, which posed great risks to the safety of the unarmed observers. Liaison and mediation efforts usually resulted in local, temporary ceasefires, and citizen evacuations, but proved insufficient to stem the overall tide of the conflict. Despite their formal neutrality and "symbolic inviolability," the UNMO organization endured significant casualties. Those who weren't scarred physically returned home with invisible but often lasting mental complications or moral injuries.

On the other hand, it would be equally untrue to claim that observers were therefore largely ineffective. The responsibilities and tasks of monitors grew concurrently with the escalation of violence in Croatia and Bosnia and Herzegovina. First and foremost, monitor reports formed a crucial source of information for both commanders and policymakers. These were especially valuable when observers constituted the sole presence in a region. Their efforts contributed greatly to the situational awareness of the UN, which gratefully utilized their reports in the decision-making process. Furthermore, UNMOs played a role in the drafting of various resolutions regarding places like Sarajevo, the Pink Zones, and the Prevlaka peninsula. Additionally, the increasing violence and the consequent displacement of people increasingly shifted monitor activities toward delivering sorely needed humanitarian aid. At times, the mere physical presence of the observers was seen as a marker of hope by the local populace. Finally, the observers' role as SMEs proved essential to the effective investigation of war crimes.

In sum, the overall value and effectiveness of the UNMO organization in former Yugoslavia was a mixed bag, and one could rightfully ask whether the benefits outweighed the risks and the costs. Notwithstanding the relative powerlessness of UNPROFOR to keep the peace in the Balkans, military observers nonetheless provided vital assistance in a number of key areas, not the least of which was their contribution to bringing several high-level war criminals to justice. These benefits proved sufficiently important for both operational commanders and policymakers to reluctantly accept the high costs. Although in their minds these costs may have been high, they would have ultimately paled in comparison to the even greater tragedy which might have unfolded had the international community decided to look the other way.

Notes

1   Jos Gelissen, *De Gijzeling en de gevolgen* (Netherlands: Brave New Books, 2015); Jos Gelissen, interviewed by Dion Landstra, February 10, 2018.

2   Paul F. Diehl, *International Peacekeeping* (Baltimore: Johns Hopkins University Press, 1993), 14–20; David W. Wainhouse, *International Peace Observation; A History and Forecast* (Baltimore: Johns Hopkins Press, 1966), 7; Alex J. Bellamy and Paul D. Williams, *Understanding Peacekeeping* (Cambridge: Polity Press, 2010), 71–81.

3   Diehl, *International Peacekeeping*, 20–6.

4   UN Publication, *Blue Helmets: A Review of United Nations Peacekeeping* (New York: UN Reproduction Section, 1996, third edition), v–vi, 672, 691–773; UN document, *A/521* (January 9, 1948), 32; Joachim A. Koops et al., *The Oxford Handbook of United Nations Peacekeeping Operations* (Oxford: Oxford University Press, 2013), 31–2.

5   Frederik H. Fleitz Jr, *Peacekeeping Fiascoes of the 1990s: Causes, Solutions and U.S. Interests* (Westport: Praeger Publishers, 2002), 12; Jaïr van der Lijn, *Walking the Tightrope: Do UN Peacekeeping Operations Actually Contribute to Durable Peace?* (Amsterdam: Rozenberg Publishers, 2006), 1, 15; Christ Klep and Richard J. A. van Gils, *Van Korea tot Kabul: De Nederlandse militaire deelname aan vredesoperaties sinds 1945* (Netherlands: Sdu uitgevers, 2005), 18.

6   Walter Dorn, *Keeping Watch: Monitoring, Technology and Innovation in UN Peace Operations* (New York: UN University Press, 2011), 10; Arthur ten Cate, *Waarnemers op heilige grond Nederlandse officieren bij UNTSO 1956-2003* (Den Haag: NIMH, 2003), 12, 32–43 86, 195; Rhys Crowley et al., *The Long Search for Peace: Observer Missions and Beyond 1947-2006* (Cambridge: University Printing House, 2019), 77–8, 85–6, 99–100, 125–6, 132, 190–1, 201–3; Pauline Dawson, *The Peacekeepers of Kashmir* (New York: St. Martins Press, 1994), 65–73; Koops et al., *The Oxford Handbook*, 157–8, 184, 275–81.

7   Bellamy and Williams, *Understanding Peacekeeping*, 90, 95, 98; L. Harbom and P. Wallensteen, "Armed Conflict, 1989-2006," *Journal of Peace and Research* 44, no. 5 (2007): 623–34.

8   Van der Lijn, *Walking the Tightrope*, 1.

9   The peacekeeping missions deployed by the UN between 1989 and 1991 were UNAVEM I, UNTAG, ONUCA, UNIKOM, UNAVEM II, ONUSAL and MINORSO; UN Publication, *Blue Helmets*, 214, 272, 282, 711–75.

10 Ronald Hatto, "From Peacekeeping to Peacebuilding: The Evolution of the Role of the United Nations in Peace Operations," *International Review of the Red Cross* 95, no. 891/892 (2013): 506, 512; Koops et al., *The Oxford Handbook*, 338–48, 351–60, 416–26, 555–61.

11 Mats Berdal and David H. Ucko, "The Use of Force in UN Peacekeeping Operations," *The RUSI Journal* 160, no. 1 (2015): 6; Hatto, "From Peacekeeping," 495–500, 506–8; Marrack Goulding, edited text of *The Evolution of United Nations and NATO in Former Yugoslavia* ('s Gravenhage: Netherlands Atlantic Commission, 1994), 1–7.

12 Bellamy and Williams, *Understanding Peacekeeping*, 119–20.

13 Colm Doyle, *Witness to War Crimes: The Memoirs of a Peacekeeper in Bosnia* (Yorkshire: Pen & Sword Books, 2018), 17; Brendan O'shea, *The Modern Yugoslav Conflict 1991-1995: Perception, Deception, Dishonesty* (New York: Frank Cass, 2005), 21–5.

14 Arthur ten Cate, *Sterven voor Bosnië?* (Amsterdam: Boom uitgeverij, 2007), 48–9, 66.

15 NIOD, *Srebrenica (band I)* (Amsterdam: Boom uitgeverij, 2002), 385–94.

16 UN document SCR 721, November 27, 1991.

17 On December 16, the EC decided to recognize the independence of Slovenia and Croatia after January 15, 1992, if the Badinter Arbitration Committee ruled that the countries met the necessary criteria; see also O'shea, *The Modern Yugoslav Conflict*, 25–6.

18 Marrack Goulding, *Peacemonger* (Houston: Johns Hopkins University Press, 2002), 300, 307; David Horner and John Connor, *The Good International Citizen: Australian Peacekeeping in Asia, Africa and Europe 1991–1993* (New York: Cambridge University Press, 2014), 341.

19 UN document SCR 743, February 21, 1992; UN document SCR 749, April 7, 1992; Lewis Mackenzie, *Peacekeeper: The Road to Sarajevo* (Vancouver: Douglas & McIntyre, 1993), 99–110; NIOD, *Srebrenica*, 497.

20 Col S. T. Harders, chief operations officer, "Orders for Advance Party UNPROFOR," March 11, 1992, S-1838-0192-0007, UNANY; Col S. T. Harders, chief operations officer, "Deployment of Recce & HQ Teams," March 14–16, 1992, S-1838-0192-0007, UNANY; Confidential interviews with ex-CMOs and UNMOs, interviewed by Dion Landstra, January 11, 2018, January 18, 2018, February 15, 2018, and March 15, 2018.

21 "Command directive from USG Marrack Goulding to SMLO Col. John Wilson," January 10, 1992, S1828-0003-0005, UNANY; UN document S/23513 ANNEX II, February 4, 1992; UN document S/23280, December 11, 1991, ANNEX III, Par 13, 18.

22 "Implementing Accord 2 January 1992, Par II Liaison and Monitoring Arrangements," January 1992, S-1830-0009-0004, UNANY; "Ik zie ik zie wat jij niet ziet deel 1, ervaringen," W. J. Posthumus, Collectie vredesoperaties UNPROFOR-

UNMO, dossier Posthumus, NIMH; "Report of Proceedings," Gwyn Rees, May–June 1992, Collectie vredesoperaties UNPROFOR-UNMO dossier van Knijff, NIMH; Confidential interviews with ex-UNMOs, interviewed by Dion Landstra, May 7, 2018 and May 15, 2018.

23 L. L. G. M. van Kaathoven, "Het werk van de United Nations Military Observer in het voormalig Joegoslavië," *Komma* 14, no. 3 (1992): 22–4.

24 Goulding, *Peacemonger*, 315; Mackenzie, *Peacekeeper*, 198–200.

25 UN document S/24075, June 6, 1992, par 5; UN document SCR 758, June 8, 1992, par 1, 2, 3; UN document SCR 761, June 29, 1992.

26 UN document S/24188, June 26, 1992, par 16, 17, 26; UN document S/24600, September 28, 1992, par 25; "Mandate of UNPROFOR," Collectie vredesoperaties UNPROFOR-UNMO, dossier Posthumus, NIMH.

27 Memorandum of MIO branch UNMO HQ to COO, "Update on Situation in Dubrovnik/Prevlaka Peninsula," August 9, 1993, S-1837-0030-0001, UNANY; Fax from FC to USG Goulding, "Prevlaka Situation Summary," October 22, 1992, S-1837-0030-0001, UNANY; Fax from police headquarters in Dubrovnik, October 24, 1992, S-1837-0030-0001, UNANY.

28 "Operation Order No-fly Zone," November 4, 1992, UNMO HQ, S-1838-0177-0005, UNANY; "Memo from C-MCCC to DFC, MCCC no Fly Zone Operations," November 19, 1992, S-1837-0127-0001, UNANY; UN document S/24767, November 5, 1992; UN document S/24783, November 9, 1992; UN document S/24810, November 13, 1992; UN document, S/24840, November 24, 1992; UN document S/24870, November 30, 1992; UN document S/24900, December 7, 1992.

29 UN document SCR 795, December 11, 1992.

30 UN document SCR 821, April 16, 1993; UN document SCR 824, May 6, 1993.

31 "UNMO in UNPROFOR/UNPF Post Mission Report, 5," S-1829-0185-0006, DPKO, UNANY; UN document SCR 908, March 31, 1994; UN document SCR 914, April 27, 1994; UN document S/1994/291, March 11, 1994; UN document S/1994/300, March 16, 1994; UN document S/1994/333, March 24, 1994.

32 Sean M. Maloney, "Operation Bolster: Canada and the European Community Monitoring Mission in Former Yugoslavia," *International Peacekeeping* 4, no. 1 (1993): 38; Wolfgang Biermann and Martin Vadset, eds., "UN Military Observers' Role in De-escalation of Local Conflict: Lessons Learned from a Soldiers Perspective," in *UN Peacekeeping in Trouble: Lessons Learned from the Former Yugoslavia* (Aldershot: Ashgate publishing, 1998), 324–8.

33 Crypto fax from SMLO Wilson to USG Goulding, "UNMLOY recce team Banja Luka," March 1992, S-1830-0009-0005, UNANY; Col S. T. Harders, chief operations officer, "Deployment of Recce & HQ Teams," March 16, March 14, 1992, S-1838-0192-0007, UNANY; Philippe Morillon, *Croire et Oser Chronique de Sarajevo* (Paris: Editions Grasset & Fasquelle, 1993), 21; Mackenzie, *Peacekeeper,* 113.

34 Confidential interviews with ex-UNMOs, interviewed by Dion Landstra, April 11, 2018, May 7, 2019, October 27, 2020.

35 Opplan sector south, July 19, 1994, S-1838-0079-0002, UNANY; Briefing sheet UNMO BiH command, 1993, UNMO dossier Pastoor, Collectie Vredesoperaties, NIMH, Netherlands; Wim H. Lutgert and Rolf de Winter, *Check the Horizon: de Koninklijke Luchtmacht en het conflict in voormalig Joegoslavië 1991-1995* (Sdu Uitgevers, 2001), 355; Biermann and Vadset, eds, "UN Military Observers," 324–8; Confidential interview with ex-UNMO by Dion Landstra, March 27, 2018.

36 Fax from UNMO HQ Zagreb to all SHQ's on vehicle security, November 3–4, 1994, S-1838-0206-0004, UNANY; Press release, joint declaration with respect to freedom of movement, November 30, 1993, S-1837-0129-0005, UNANY; Message of the Secretary-General, November 18, 1993, S-1837-0129-0004, UNANY; Message from BiHC to SRSG, FC and DFC, "Freedom of Movement UNPROFOR in Bosnia," November 7, 1993, S-1837-0129-0004, UNANY; Confidential interviews with ex-UNMOs, interviewed by Dion Landstra, May 7, 2018, May 15, 2018, February 19, 2019, February 21, 2019, March 7, 2019.

37 Restriction of movement report in UNPA East, from SMO Eastern Sector to Sector Commander East, June 11, 1992, S-1837-0122-0001, UNANY; Daily sitrep UNMO Bihac to HQ UNROFOR Sarajevo, June 21, 1992, S-1837-0122-0001, UNANY; Fax from UNMO sector south Knin to CMO daily sitrep, June 22, 1992, S-1837-0122-0001, UNANY.

38 Confidential interviews with ex-UNMOs, interviewed by Dion Landstra, August 27, 2019, April 11, 2018, February 5, 2018, April 6, 2018.

39 L. Buurman and P. Poharnok, "Het vervolg van de ervaringen van onze UNMOs in Sarajevo," *Achterbanier* 14, no. 8 (1992): 6; Lutgert and De Winter, *Check the Horizon*, 348–66; Confidential interviews with ex-UNMOs, interviewed by Dion Landstra March 28, 2019, May 22, 2019, June 6, 2019, August 23, 2019.

40 Report of proceedings, NZ-UNMO Gwyn Rees, May-June-July 1992; Report of proceedings, NZ-UNMO Gwyn Rees, April–May 1992, UNMO dossier van Knijff, Collectie Vredesoperaties UNPROFOR, NIMH; Fax from UNMO HQ SN to UNMO HQ Zagreb on mine accident, including investigation report mine accident, September 19, 1994, S-1838-0183-0005, UNANY; Confidential interviews with ex-UNMOs, interviewed by Dion Landstra, February 7, 2019, March 4, 2019.

41 Daily military activity, March 25, 1992, Box 54, 10, ECMM-archive, EEAS Archive, Brussels; Buurman and Poharnok, "Het vervolg van," 6; Lutgert and De Winter, *Check the Horizon*, 83–7; Confidential interviews with ex-UNMOs, interviewed by Dion Landstra, January 16, 2018, February 7, 2018, February 13, 2018, March 27, 2018, March 21, 2019, March 28, 2019, April 4, 2019.

42 Memoires Jacques Brinkhof, "militair waarnemer voor de Verenigde Naties in het voormalig Joegoslavie," May 4, 1992, UNMO dossier Brinkhof, Collectie

Vredesoperaties UNPROFOR, NIMH; Confidential interviews with ex-UNMO, interviewed by Dion Landstra, May 7 and 18, 2018.

43 Report board of inquiry, death of ECMM monitor Bertrand Borrey, June 24, 1992, ECMM 50.16A, Monitor Mission, January 1992–June 1993, Archive European Council (AEUR), Brussels, Belgium.

44 UN document S/24075, June 6, 1992; NIOD, *Srebrenica (part I)*, 548; Mackenzie, *Peacekeeper*, 185, 191; Morillon, *Croire et Oser*, 87–8.

45 *UNMO casualties in UNPROFOR*. UNMO dossier Bastiaans, Collectie Vredesoperaties UNPROFOR, NIMH, NL; UNMO in UNPROFOR/UNPF Post mission report, 47, S-1829-0185-0006, DPKO, UNANY.

46 Onderzoek van de Gezondheidszorg Dienst KL ten aanzien van Individueel uitgezondenen met de Status van Waarnemer, uitzendperiode 1991–1997, July 2000, dossier UNMOs in voormalig Joegoslavië, 1, 6, Collectie Vredesoperaties UNPROFOR, NIMH.

47 Confidential interviews with ex-UNMOs, interviewed by Dion Landstra, February 8, 2018, May 16, 2019, June 12, 2019.

48 Claes R. Johansson, Gerry Larsson, and Curt R. Wallenius, "Military Observers' Reactions and Performance when Facing Danger," *Military Psychology* 16, no. 4 (2004): 212, 222, 226–7.

49 Confidential interviews with ex-UNMOs, interviewed by Dion Landstra, May 21, 2019, June 6, 2019, August 23, 2019; Fax from Ralph Zacklin to Shashi Tharoor on the death of Finnish UNMO serving within UNPROFOR, March 10, 1995, S-1829-0332-0004, DPKO, UNANY.

50 Periodic report from SMLO to USG Goulding, February 10–11, 1992, S-1838-0194-0005, UNANY; Message from FC Wahlgren Zagreb to SG Annan NY, situation Mostar, May 8–9, 1993, S-1837-0136-0001, UNANY; Memo from SRSG Stoltenberg to FC Wahlgren and others, Monitoring Humanitarian Situation in safe areas, May 26, 1993, S-1837-0158-0001, UNANY; Daily sitrep from SMLO Wilson UNMLOY to HQ UN NY, January 26–March 29, 1992, S-1829-0181-0005 and 0006, UNANY; Visit to Yugoslavia by Mr. Goulding, flag E statistics, January 1992, S-1830-0009-0006, UNANY; *Periodic report from SMLO Wilson to UN NY*, February 10–17, 18–24, 1992, S-1834-0053-0006, UN Archive, NY, USA; Daily sitrep from SMLO Wilson UNMLOY to HQ UN NY, January 15–24, 1992, S-1829-0182-0001, UNANY; Daily sitrep from SMLO Wilson UNMLOY to HQ UN NY, January 25–31, 1992, S-1829-0181-0006, UNANY.

51 End of mission report, UNMO in UNPROFOR, June 26, 1992, S-1829-0185-0006, P6-7, UNANY; UN document S/24188, June 26, 1992, par 3.

52 Memo from SRSG Stoltenberg to FC Wahlgren, HOM ECMM, ICRC-Sommaruga, UNHCR—ms Ogata, T. Mazowiecki, M. Goulding: "Monitoring Humanitarian Situation in Safe Areas," May 26, 1993, S-1837-0158-0001, UNPROFOR, UNANY; Message from FC Wahlgren Zagreb to SG Annan NY, situation Mostar, May 8–9,

1993, S-1837-0136-0001, UNANY; Memo from SRSG Stoltenberg to FC Wahlgren and others, Monitoring Humanitarian Situation in safe areas, May 26, 1993, S-1837-0158-0001, UNANY; UN document S/23280, December 11, 1991, par 4, 5, 6; UN document S/23900, May 12, 1992, par 5, 7, 9; UN document S/23777, April 2, 1992, par 7, 16.

53 Fax from Thorvald Stoltenberg to CMO HQ UNPROFOR on UNMO cooperation, August 4, 1993, S-1835-0040-0005, UNANY.

54 J. Zoutendijk, interviewed by Dion Landstra, January 29, 2018; UN document SCR 816, March 31, 1993.

55 Goulding, *Peacemonger*, 315; Mackenzie, *Peacekeeper*, 198, 200.

56 Fax from SMO sector south to HQ UNPROFOR, meeting with CA officials at Gospic, September 18, 1993, S-1838-0076-0003, UNANY; Oporder 18/93 from Force Commander, General J. Cot, September 14, 1993, S-1838-0076-0003, UNANY; Press and information, chronology of the Croatian Army incursion into the Medak pocket, September 1993, S-1837-0195-0004, UNANY.

57 Loose minute from COO UNMO to CMO, "Meeting held to discuss withdrawal arrangements with Croatian Army in step with Erdut Agreement," August 1993, S-1838-0161-0001, UNANY; Memo from CMO B. Pellnas to FC Wahlgren, "CMO activities in Mostar," April 18–22, 1993, April 23, 1993, S-1837-0129-0002, UNANY; Memo from J.P. Thebaut to HQ ECMM, "central Bosnia peace negotiations," April 18, 1993, S-1837-0129-0002, UNANY; (CMO) B. Pellnas, interviewed by Dion Landstra, September 18, 2018.

58 UNMO Mostar sector final report by Lcol. J. Lundgren, SMO sector Mostar, May 20, 1992, S-1837-0122-0001, UNANY; Confidential interviews with ex-UNMOs, interviewed by Dion Landstra, March 15, 2018, May 7, 2018; UN document, S/23900, May 1992, par 9, 12.

59 UNMO Mostar sector final report by Lcol J. Lundgren, SMO sector Mostar, May 20, 1992, S-1837-0122-0001, UNANY; UN document S/24000, May 26, 1992, par 8, 9, 10.

60 Confidential interviews with ex-UNMOs, interviewed by Dion Landstra, July 22, 2019, March 27, 2018.

61 Fax from humanitarian section to HQ ECMM, ICRC and Mazowiecki Commission: report on interethnic violence in Vitez, Busovaca, and Zenica, May 17, 1993, ECMM box 5, A030.2-030, EEAS Archive, Brussels, Belgium; Confidential interviews with ex-UNMOs, interviewed by Dion Landstra, 3 and June 2020, May 7, 2019, October 27, 2020.

62 Confidential interview with ex-UNMO, interviewed by Dion Landstra, January 16 and February 13, 2018.

63 Confidential interview with ex-UNMO, interviewed by Dion Landstra, February 15 and December 4, 2018.

64 Memoranda of Understanding Hungary (December 9, 1992), Bulgaria (September 18, 1992), Albania (December 21, 1992), box 21, Archive ECMM, Semi Statisch

Informatie Beheer (SSIB), Rijswijk, The Netherlands; UN document SCR 795, December 11, 1992; Arie Bloed, *The Conference on Security and Co-operation in Europe, Basic Documents 1993–1995* ('s Gravenhage: Martinus Nijhoff Publishers/ Kluwer Law International, 1997), 8, 9, 31, 32, 66.

65 UNMO Mostar sector final report by Lkol J. Lundgren, SMO sector Mostar, May 20, 1992, S-1837-0122-0001, UNANY; Fax van major Brinkhof aan OCKLU, kort verslag inzet VN waarnemers in Kroatië en Bosnië-Hercegovina, March 25–May 25, 1992, UNMO dossier Brinkhof, Collectie Vredesoperaties UNPROFOR, NIMH; Confidential interview with ex-UNMO, interviewed by Dion Landstra, March 15, 2018.

66 Report on recce of Mostar / Bihac area from mission HQ Belgrade to SMLO, February 21–27, 1992, February 29, 1992, S-1838-0192-0007, UNANY; Fax from UNMO HQ Zagreb to all UNMO Sector HQ's airdrop coordination SOP, October 12, 1994, S-1838-0205-0002, UNANY; Fax from DFC to UNPROFOR HQ—Joint Planning Team for the implementation of SCR 770–776 incl. ANNEX A & B, September 15, 1992, S-1837-0092-0006, UNANY; Crypto fax van SMLO Wilson to USG Goulding, UNMLOY recce team Banja Luka, March 1992, S-1830-0009-0005, UNANY; Periodic report from SMLO Wilson to USG Goulding, February 25–March 2, 1992, S-1834-0009-0006, UNANY; Confidential interviews with ex-UNMOs, interviewed by Dion Landstra, February 18, 2019, March 21, 2019; UN document S/24923, December 9, 1992, ANNEX I, par 19 t/m 25; UN document SCR 794, December 11, 1992.

67 Orders for Advance Party UNPROFOR, Col S. T. Harders, chief operations officer, March 11, 1992, S-1838-0192-0007, UNANY; Deployment of recce & HQ teams 16 March, Col S.T. Harders, chief operations officer, March 14, 1992, S-1838-0192-0007, UNANY; Preliminary recon for B-H humanitarian escort operation, September 1992, S-1838-0188-0003, UNANY; Timings for deployment of teams to sectors. Memo from CMO Col. J.B. Wilson to Chief Operations Officer (COO) in Belgrade, May 23, 1992, S-1837-0122-0001, UNANY; van Kaathoven, "Het werk van de United Nations Military Observer in het voormalig Joegoslavië," 22; W. A. M. van Dijk, "UNMO actie naar Zepa," *Carré* 7/8 (1993): 22; Confidential interviews with ex-UNMOs, interviewed by Dion Landstra, January 29 and February 19, 2018, March 28, 2019.

68 Harry Konings, interviewed by Dion Landstra, October 27, 2020.

69 Confidential interviews with ex-UNMOs, interviewed by Dion Landstra, April 11, 2018, May 7, 2019, October 27, 2020, https://www.icty.org/case/mladic, witness list; https://www.icty.org/case/karadzic.

Part II

The Military and the Population

6

Turning "Enemies" into "Friends"

The Role of the Military in Peacemaking in France after Napoleon (1815–18)

Christine Haynes

To illustrate my contribution to this collection on the role of the military in peacemaking, I begin with a print from 1815, during the occupation of France after the defeat of Napoleon, entitled "La Russe, ou les Alliés à Tivoli" (Figure 6.1).

Depicting Russian officers mixing with French women at the Tivoli leisure garden in Paris, this print illustrates a function not usually associated with the military: dancing. Yet in this occupation, dancing was actually an important tool among a repertoire of strategies for peacemaking between the Allied troops who had defeated Napoleon and their former enemies, the now-occupied French. Throughout the occupation, which lasted for three years until November 1818, Allied (especially Russian) officers organized balls, at which their troops mingled with local women and foreign steps alternated with French, often by official ordinance.[1] As a result of these balls, one French bourgeois in the Russian sector remembered, "There were no more enemies; / there were neither victors / nor vanquished, but only / liberators and good friends!"[2] While this memory may be overly rose-colored, sociability between occupiers and occupied certainly did help to transform former enemies into something like "friends," or at least to restore peace between the Allies and the French.

The role of such fraternization in peacemaking between enemy nations has long been recognized with regard to the world wars of the twentieth century.[3] However, it originated at the beginning of the previous century, in what was arguably the first modern peacekeeping operation, the so-called "occupation of guarantee" against revolution in northeastern France from 1815 to 1818. This occupation was part of a whole complex of measures to restore peace and order to the Continent—what the team of scholars led by Beatrice de Graaf has termed

Figure 6.1 La Russe, ou les Alliés à Tivoli. Print, *c.* 1815. Musée Marmottan, Paris/
Bridgeman Images.

"security culture"—after the Revolutionary and Napoleonic Wars.[4] In comparison
to the contemporaneous Congress of Vienna, however, this occupation has until
recently received little scholarly attention.[5] Those who mention it usually focus
on the negotiation over the occupation by political and diplomatic leaders, from
above, or on one particular Allied contingent or French region.[6] Only recently
has the occupation been discussed by Beatrice de Graaf and others in a trend
toward a more transnational, pan-European approach to the "Allied machine"
that arose to counter a perceived threat of revolutionary terror after 1815.[7]
Based on research from my own book in this vein, *Our Friends the Enemies:
The Occupation of France after Napoleon*, this chapter instead examines how this
seminal peacekeeping mission was implemented on the ground in northeastern
France, by military forces from across Europe.[8]

Designed by a military commander, Sir Arthur Wellesley, the Duke of
Wellington, this peacekeeping occupation depended upon a number of "military
modalities," including a multinational force with a unified command structure;
distinct zones for national contingents, surrounded by a demilitarized zone
between the occupying force and the French national army; joint exercises
and reviews; and the reconstruction of defensive fortresses outside the border
of France. Ultimately, however, the success of the operation hinged upon the

thousands of individual experienced officers and ordinary soldiers who worked for months in localities across the occupied zone to enforce peace in France. To make peace with the occupied French, Allied forces relied heavily on local military and civilian authorities, with whom they cultivated relations, often (as during the Congress of Vienna) via institutions and practices of sociability.[9] While such sociability had long been central to peacemaking between aristocratic officers, statesmen, and diplomats, now it was employed among the bourgeois and even popular classes, to reconcile not just sovereign states but also whole nations in the aftermath of ideologically motivated "total" war.

To show how military forces facilitated peace between former enemies, I will highlight two cases in particular: first, that of the Austrian headquarters in Colmar, where the commander, Baron Maria-Philippe von Frimont, developed close relations with the local prefect, André de Biaudos, Count de Castéja; and second, that of the Russian occupation zone around Maubeuge, where the commander Count Mikhail Semenovich Vorontsov and subordinate officers such as Baron V. I. Löwenstern imposed tight discipline on their troops but also devoted considerable time to socializing with French elites—in Masonic lodges, hunts, salons, banquets, and balls—in the interest of ensuring "harmony" with local civilians. While the leadership of such officers was essential, this peacekeeping operation also depended heavily on the attitudes and actions of ordinary soldiers, throughout all of the occupation zones. To illustrate this point, I will briefly discuss the case of the small occupation force from Denmark (5,000) in and around Bouchain. Through these examples, I will argue that, in the aftermath of the Revolutionary and Napoleonic Wars, Allied officers and their soldiers implemented a new approach to military occupation, not for conquering territory but for ensuring peace.

*   *   *

The occupation of guarantee was the brainchild of a military general, Sir Arthur Wellesley, Duke of Wellington. Following his victory over Napoleon at the Battle of Waterloo, Wellington, along with Prussian Field Marshal Gebhard Leberecht von Blücher, led a massive invasion of France by 1.2 million troops from all across Europe. Within a month, these troops covered two-thirds of French territory, in a quite brutal military occupation. Rather than agreeing quickly on a peace settlement as they had the year before following the first defeat of Napoleon and restoration of the monarchy, now the Allies spent months debating how to handle a French nation that, by supporting the returned emperor, had forced them to remobilize. Some members of the coalition, particularly Prussia and

Austria but also British prime minister Lord Liverpool, thought the French should be punished severely, via financial exactions and territorial concessions. However, this punitive approach was resisted by other Allied leaders, including the Russian Tsar Alexander, the British foreign minister Lord Castlereagh, and especially the British commander the Duke of Wellington. Concerned not to destabilize France (and Europe) but to pacify it, Wellington proposed a more moderate settlement, centered on a temporary occupation of the defeated nation, to help the monarchy secure a stable government and loyal army and to enable the Allies to obtain financial compensation for their troubles. Informed by past experiences with the British army in India and Spain, the duke argued, in a letter to Castlereagh in August 1815: "These measures will not only give us, during the period of occupation, all the military security which could be expected from the permanent cession [of territory], but, if carried into execution in the spirit in which they are conceived, they are in themselves the bond of peace."[10]

Heeding Wellington's advice, the Allies ultimately endorsed this novel approach to peacemaking in the Second Treaty of Paris, dated November 20, 1815. According to this treaty, 150,000 troops from all of the Allied countries (including not just the four major powers but also the minor German states) would be stationed in national zones around eighteen garrisons along the northeastern frontier, under the command of the Duke of Wellington (Figure 6.2). Financed by the French government (at the rate of 150 million francs per year for food, equipment, and pay), this occupation was due to last up to five years, until the defeated nation had indemnified the Allied powers for the damages caused by the return of Napoleon, to the tune of 700 million francs. In addition to these very modern war reparations, the treaty of 1815 also introduced a number of relatively progressive institutional mechanisms for peacemaking, including the Council of Allied Ambassadors, in which Wellington himself was an active participant.[11] Conceived by a military general with extensive experience in pacifying hostile populations, the peace settlement of 1815 and particularly the occupation of guarantee aimed not to punish but to reconstruct the defeated nation. Ultimately lasting three years, until November 1818, it helped France— and, by extension, the rest of Europe—to transition from war to peace.

Once it was finalized, this treaty's implementation depended largely on Allied military forces, on the ground in northeastern France. Under the leadership of Wellington, Allied officers developed a new, positivist system for administering occupied territory, including significant cooperation between military and civilian authorities on discipline, policing, and justice. As the Allies transitioned from the military occupation of 1815 to the peacekeeping one of 1815–18, they

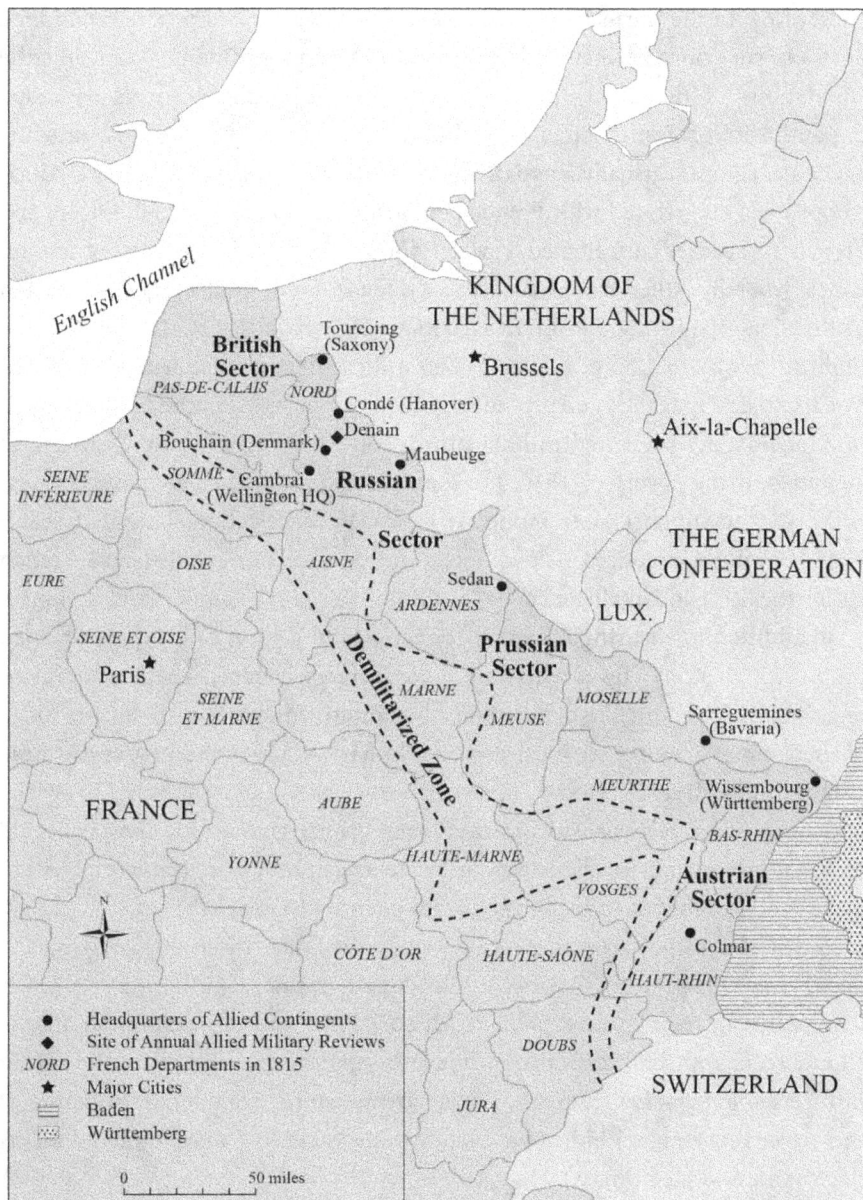

Figure 6.2 Occupation of guarantee, November 1815–18. Allied sectors and demilitarized zones overlaid on French departments. Copyright Christine Haynes.

systematized the requisitioning process and moved as many soldiers as possible out of private billets into barracks, to minimize conflict with local civilians. To defuse tensions, Allied officers throughout the occupation zones imposed tight discipline on their troops, strictly regulating drinking, dancing, smoking, and curfew in the towns where they were stationed. Violators were sanctioned by their superiors severely, often with corporal punishment. Following the stipulations of the Treaty of November 20, 1815, Allied officers defended the authority of French officials, including in policing and customs. In some occupation zones (usually Russian and Austrian vs. British or German), Allied troops even cooperated with French gendarmes in policing. Allied officers and French authorities coordinated a system for judging offenses in the occupation zones, whereby Allied troops accused of offenses were tried by a court-martial of their national army and French civilians by a royal court. To facilitate the political reconstruction of France, Allied military leaders also worked to check Bonapartist propaganda and promote moderate policies. After the Allied Council of Ambassadors pressured the king to dissolve the Ultraroyalist Chamber of Deputies in the spring of 1816, for example, Allied officers encouraged local authorities to support more moderate candidates in elections later that year.[12] Together, these practices helped meet the goal of both Allied and French authorities of "good intelligence" or "harmony" between occupiers and occupied.

In addition to ensuring discipline, policing, and justice, Allied troops helped promote "harmony" by providing aid to French civilians, whether moral or material. Throughout the occupation, they often worked (usually at the order of their officers) alongside local peasants to harvest grain and grapes. In some communities, they also worked to repair infrastructure or fight fires. On special occasions or in response to disasters such as fire or famine, they collected monetary donations for the communities in which they were stationed.[13] All of these practices helped to reconcile former enemies to each other.

But perhaps the most successful tool for reconciliation employed by the occupying forces was sociability—in dancing, but also hunting, theater, banquets, and freemasonry. While such sociability was most common among elite officers and the bourgeois, ordinary troops and peasants also fraternized in taverns, *guinguettes*, festivals, fields, streets, and private lodgings. Some of these contacts resulted in lasting relationships, including marriages and births (legitimate and illegitimate).

*   *   *

The various ways in which the military contributed to peacemaking during the occupation of 1815–18 are illustrated by two cases: the Austrian sector in and around Colmar, in the Haut-Rhin, under the command of General Baron Jean-Marie Philippe de Frimont, and the Russian sector around Maubeuge, in the Nord, under the leadership of Count Mikhail Semenovich Vorontsov and his officers, particularly Baron V. I. Löwenstern. During the occupation, these officers all earned a reputation for discipline, fairness, and generosity. While their leadership did not eliminate all "excesses" by Allied troops, to use the euphemism employed at the time, it did go a long way toward ensuring "good intelligence" between occupiers and occupied and ensuring peace in France.

In the first case, the Austrian sector around Colmar, the tone was set at the top, by the commanding general Baron de Frimont as well as his French civilian counterpart, the prefect of the Haut-Rhin, André de Biaudos, Comte de Castéja. Fortuitously for the inhabitants of this region, Frimont and Castéja came from similar backgrounds, noble families in northeastern France who had joined the Emigration after 1791. Born in Lorraine in 1759, Frimont had left France in 1791 to join the counterrevolutionary army of Condé (named after its leader, Louis-Joseph de Bourbon, Prince of Condé). Eventually enlisting in the Austrian army, he served as an officer under Field Marshal Karl Philipp von Schwarzenberg in the campaigns in Russia in 1812 and in France in 1814 and again in 1815. During the occupation of guarantee, he was placed in charge of the Austrian contingent of 30,000, at its headquarters in Colmar. There, he socialized regularly with the prefect, Comte de Castéja, over twenty years his junior, whose family originated in the Landes in southwestern France but had connections in the Nord. Like Frimont, Castéja's father had joined the Emigration after 1791, dying outside of France in Maastricht. After serving in a variety of administrative positions under the Empire in the Pas-de-Calais, Castéja was transferred by the Restoration monarchy to the prefecture of the Haut-Rhin in August 1815.[14]

These two men, who seemed to share mutual respect and admiration, worked together to minimize violence and promote "harmony" between occupiers and occupied in the Haut-Rhin. In addition to cooperating to lodge as many occupying troops as possible in barracks in repurposed public buildings, to minimize opportunities for conflicts, both insisted upon tight discipline. The Austrian commander was lauded (for instance, by the local newspaper) for his "moderation and wisdom." For his part, the French prefect followed the mantra "to engender neither division nor affection" between his subjects and the occupying troops. Under the leadership of Frimont, Austrian officers regularly gave alms to local mayors and priests to distribute to impoverished inhabitants of the region where they were stationed. In February 1817, for instance, the subprefect of Belfort reported to the prefect that the officers of the regiment stationed nearby,

> distinguished every day, in this season [of winter and Lent], by acts of charity toward the poor of this town, have turned to the profit of the indigent class even

their amusements: they gave, last Thursday, a Ball for which they paid all the expenses but whose entry tickets, at three francs each, yielded 433 francs, which were given entirely to the fund of the Bureau de Bienfaisance.[15]

The Austrian troops also frequented salons, parties, and festivals hosted by Castéja and other local elites and invited local inhabitants to their reviews (including visits by Wellington) and festivities, especially on the birthday of the Austrian emperor. After one such review at which Wellington was present, in the fall of 1816, the French interior minister praised the behavior of the Austrian military leadership in a letter to the prefect:

> The order that reigned, the number of spectators, the precautions that Messieurs the Generals took to cause the least damage possible to agriculture, everything that preceded and followed the review is satisfactory evidence of the good spirit of the inhabitants, of the good conduct of the troops and of the harmony that you have known how to maintain in concert with Messieurs the Generals.[16]

Of the festivities for the Austrian emperor's birthday in February 1818, which included an open-air mass and a grand ball attended by local elites as well as occupying troops, the official French newspaper the *Moniteur universel* editorialized, "It is thus that in mutually offering each other testimonies of esteem and affection, in uniting their voices for the prosperity of their respective sovereigns, these nations show themselves to be deserving of the benefit of the peace owed to them, and cooperate to assure its maintenance and endurance."[17] While officials had good reason to emphasize the "harmony" and "peace" rather than discord between occupiers and occupied, this sort of testimony nonetheless suggests that the role of Allied officers in peacemaking was appreciated by the French.

Recognizing the role these officers had played in returning peace to the region, the citizens of Colmar bestowed thanks and gifts on them at the end of the occupation. As local teacher Georges Ozaneaux wrote to his mother as the Austrian troops prepared to depart, "Colmar will be less populated, but more gay. . . . In the end, they conducted themselves like angels, and the general Frimont will carry with him our universal affection."[18] Long after his return to the Habsburg Empire where he was later assigned to lead a campaign against the Carbonari in the Kingdom of Naples, General Frimont remained in correspondence with the Comte de Castéja in Colmar.

The role of Allied officers in making peace between occupiers and occupied was even more evident in the Russian sector around Maubeuge, where not just the commander-in-chief but also his subordinate officers, were recognized by locals for their gentility, discipline, and charity. In charge of the Russian sector was Mikhail Semenovich Vorontsov, son of the Russian ambassador to London, who, after enlisting in the Life Guard Preobrazhensk Regiment at the age of four in 1786, served in various campaigns throughout the Napoleonic Wars, including at the Battle of Borodino in 1812 and in the army of the North in 1813–14.[19] As commander of the Russian occupation corps in France after 1815, Vorontsov earned a reputation for his insistence on humanity and justice. Reminding his troops that "no individual belonging to the army corps including entrepreneurs, roadmenders, etc., may take advantage of the Russian name for the least gain," he issued strict orders against arbitrary requisitioning, smuggling of contraband, and hunting or fishing outside of the conventional seasons. In a memorandum to local authorities in the arrondissement of Rocroi early in the occupation, he assured the French that he would use "police measures" to prevent "the inconveniences that at present troubled their peace." He also asked them to report any "excesses" by his troops, so that he could investigate and punish them in conformity with military law. If local authorities would ensure a bit more "exactness" in supplying provisions to his troops, he was certain that "everything will arrange itself so that the troops and the inhabitants are content with their fate and in good intelligence. I assure you that that is my primary desire, and that on my part there are no efforts I am not ready to make to contribute to it."[20] In fact, under Vorontsov, Russian officers insisted upon punishing troops for misbehavior, often by forcing them to run a gauntlet of lashes. To minimize misbehavior in the first place, the Russian officer General Count Barclay de Tolly required soldiers under his command to obtain each week a certificate of good conduct from the mayor of the place where they were stationed.[21] Such measures, particularly joint Russian and French policing, were appreciated by local authorities, such as the subprefect of the arrondissement of Avesnes, who wrote in March 1817, "The Russian Army comports itself according to the principles of its general [Vorontsov]. The officer and the soldier live in peace with the inhabitant, and the army joins with the national guard to conduct the night patrols and prevent the disorders that might be occasioned, either by the military occupation, or by the horrible misery that reigns in this country."[22]

To smooth relations with French inhabitants, however, Russian officers relied at least as much on carrots as on sticks. Vorontsov allowed and even encouraged his officers to fraternize with French bourgeois in balls, theaters, and Masonic lodges—something which made him suspect with tsarist authorities back home. Throughout the occupation, Russian troops participated enthusiastically in French festivities, such as the feast day of Saint Louis and the anniversary of the return of Louis XVIII. In July 1816, at Maubeuge, for instance, they joined in festivities to celebrate the marriage of the Duc de Berry, including a parade, church service, banquet, and ball, at which "was never seen more union," according to a local official. "The French and the Russians battled for the attentions, the actions and the regards [of the crowd]. In one word, it was a family party."[23] Across their zone, the Russians also helped regularly in harvesting grain and donated generously to charities for local inhabitants.[24]

In particular, Estonian Baron Löwenstern, who was commandant in Givet from 1816 to 1818, prided himself on treating the occupied population with kindness. Early in 1816, Löwenstern obtained permission from the Duke of Wellington to donate provisions left over from the Allied siege to the inhabitants; the next year, he arranged for regular shipments of grain from the Netherlands (payment of which was guaranteed by the department), to alleviate dearth in the region. He also donated money for the repair of the organ, iron grill, and bell of the parish church in nearby Rethel. To protect diligences and wagons on the roads from bands of thieves, he employed convoys of Cossacks. A bon vivant who was fluent in French, Löwenstern hunted and fished frequently with local lords and ladies, and he organized many a dinner and ball, to which he invited the inhabitants to fraternize with his troops. At these festivities, he later remembered, "Our soldiers, mixed with the villagers, waltzed, danced the Cossack to the great joy of the women, paid court to all, and did not seem the least astonished to find themselves participating in a French contra-dance." For his efforts in smoothing relations between occupiers and occupied, at the end of his stay in France Löwenstern was offered a sword of honor by local authorities, which touched him greatly: "I had relieved as much as possible the inhabitants: that was my heart's first desire."[25] Throughout the occupation, officers such as Löwenstern played a crucial role in ensuring peace between former enemies.

*   *   *

Ultimately, however, the success of the occupation depended not just on these exemplary officers but on the thousands of soldiers who were stationed in towns and villages throughout northeastern France for three years. To be sure, some of these occupying soldiers misbehaved, for instance, by drinking, stealing, raping, and brawling. However, most lived in relative peace with French inhabitants. While primary sources on ordinary soldiers are rare, except when they attracted the notice of the police or judiciary, anecdotal evidence suggests that they too made an effort to smooth relations with their former enemies.

To take just one example, the small Danish contingent around Bouchain was recognized by French as well as Danish authorities for their goodwill toward the occupied population. At their headquarters, Danish troops attended open-air church services led by their own pastor, K. Nyholm, who reminded them that France and Denmark were "the most loyal friends and allies." At these services, money was collected to benefit the families of Danish troops but also local French in need. In June 1816, a Danish battery under the command of Captain Gerstenberg helped to extinguish a fire in Lens, preventing a catastrophe, and then donated money to the fire's victims. On another occasion, a crew from the Queen's Battalion helped the French customs administration to capture a band of smugglers on the Belgian border and then declined the reward they were offered by the General Director of Customs, in favor of the region's poor. During their stay, the Danes repaired a number of fortifications, bridges, and sewers in Bouchain, leaving the town in a better state than when they arrived. These troops became so respected that one inhabitant of Lens supposedly exclaimed that a Danish soldier could be given the keys to one's house! The Danish troops also participated actively in local social life. On the anniversary of the return of King Louis XVIII in July 1816, for example, three Danish military bands participated in a music competition alongside French national guards. Some twenty Danish soldiers even married local women, most of whom accompanied them home to Denmark at the end of the occupation.[26] Such positive interactions between foreign troops and French inhabitants certainly helped to secure peace after 1815 (Figure 6.3).

*   *   *

In late 1818, satisfied that the French government had stabilized itself and indemnified its former enemies, Allied leaders decided to end the occupation two years ahead of schedule. Concerned to maintain peaceful relations with locals until the very end, they carefully planned the evacuation of the occupying troops from northeastern France. As they left, they were recognized by French authorities for their good conduct during the occupation. Typical of the language of these testimonials is a letter from the mayor and adjuncts of Valenciennes to the British commandant and majors who had been stationed there:

> Receive as a proof of the honorable memories that you leave to us, the expression of the sentiments of esteem that you have inspired in us [;] it is shared by our inhabitants who are pleased to render justice to your moderation toward them and your firmness in maintaining Discipline among your troops [;] it is these

Figure 6.3 Danish fourth Auxiliary Corps in France, 1816–18. Source: F. V. Nerland, "Danske fredsbevarende tropper i Frankrig, 1815–1818" ["Danish Peace-Keeping Troops in France, 1815–1818"], *Krigshistorisk Tidsskrift* 39:1 (2003): 3–27.

two qualities that distinguish you as military Chiefs, to which we have owed this good harmony that reigns between your soldiers and our Citizens.[27]

Moderation and *firmness*: these were the two qualities exemplified by many, if not all, of the Allied officers and soldiers who occupied France between 1815 and 1818. Even more than the celebrated Duke of Wellington, these military troops were instrumental in peacemaking in France and Europe in the aftermath of the Napoleonic Wars.

In conclusion, while it borrowed from earlier practices of both aristocratic sociability and revolutionary "liberation," the occupation of guarantee constituted a novel response to peacemaking in the aftermath of "total" war. In this new sort of occupation, officers and, by extension, soldiers drew on their previous experiences in the Revolutionary and Napoleonic Wars. However, they also developed fresh, positivist practices to promote good "harmony" and "intelligence"—in short, peace—between the victors and the defeated. The model of the occupation of guarantee would inform peacekeeping operations in other contexts, including against domestic unrest in the UK, with indigenous populations in the British empire, and (via American General Winfield Scott, who observed the approach of the Duke of Wellington while on a trip to Europe in 1815) in the American occupation of Mexico and the post–Civil War South. Although it was forgotten, at great expense, during the Versailles Conference after the Great War, it was the forebear of the "good" occupations after the Second World War, in which US soldiers were employed to reconstruct West Germany and Japan after even more devastating total war.[28]

Notes

1   For an example of the regulation of dancing, see letter from Prussian commander von Zieten to mayor of Sedan, regarding a Carnival ball which many of his officers planned to attend: "I beg you, Monsieur the Mayor, to be my voice to the ladies of Sedan to assure them that the regards due to their sex will be observed toward them, under the masks [worn at such balls], as they have always and everywhere been by the Prussian officers. I will be charmed to see there a frank and decent gaity mixing with the good tone and spirit that are the soul of society," February 21, 1816, H/70, Archives Municipales de Sedan, Charleville-Mézières, France. Unless otherwise noted, all translations from the French are my own.

2   François-Simon Cazin, *Les Russes en France: Souvenirs des années 1815, 1816 et 1817* (Avranches: J. Durand, 1880), 2.

3   To take just two examples, see John Dower, *Embracing Defeat: Japan in the Wake of World War II* (New York: W. W. Norton/The New Press, 1999), and Susan Caruthers, *The Good Occupation: American Soldiers and the Hazards of Peace* (Cambridge, MA: Harvard University Press, 2016).

4 Beatrice de Graaf, Ido de Haan, and Brian E. Vick, eds., *Securing Europe after Napoleon: 1815 and the New European Security Culture* (Cambridge: Cambridge University Press, 2019).

5 Henry Kissinger, *A World Restored: Metternich, Castlereagh and the Problem of Peace, 1812–1822* (Boston: Houghton Mifflin, 1957); Adam Zamoyski, *Rites of Peace: The Fall of Napoleon and the Congress of Vienna* (New York: Harper Perennial, 2007); Mark Jarrett, *The Congress of Vienna and Its Legacy: War and Great Power Diplomacy after Napoleon* (London: I. B. Tauris, 2013); Brian E. Vick, *The Congress of Vienna: Power and Politics after Napoleon* (Cambridge, MA: Harvard University Press, 2014).

6 For example, see Thomas Dwight Veve, *The Duke of Wellington and the British Army of Occupation in France, 1815-1818* (Westport: Greenwood Press, 1992); Marc Blancpain, *La vie quotidienne dans la France du Nord sous les occupations, 1814–1944* (Paris: Hachette, 1983); Jacques Hantraye, *Les Cosaques aux Champs-Élysées: L'occupation de la France après la chute de Napoléon* (Paris: Belin, 2005); Volker Wacker, *Die allierte Besetzung Frankreichs in den Jahren 1814 bis 1818* (Hamburg: Dr. Kovac, 2001); and Yann Guérin, *La France après Napoléon: Invasions et occupations, 1814–1818* (Paris: L'Harmattan, 2014).

7 See, for instance, Beatrice de Graaf, *Fighting Terror after Napoleon: How Europe Became Secure after 1815* (Cambridge: Cambridge University Press, 2020), esp. ch. 4, "A Moderate Occupation"; Glenda Sluga, *The Invention of International Order: Remaking Europe after Napoleon* (Princeton: Princeton University Press, 2021); and Erik de Lange, "Menacing Tides: Security, Piracy and Empire in the Nineteenth-Century Mediterranean" (forthcoming book).

8 Christine Haynes, *Our Friends the Enemies: The Occupation of France after Napoleon* (Cambridge, MA: Harvard University Press, 2018).

9 On the role of sociability in the Congress of Vienna, see Vick, *The Congress of Vienna*

10 Wellington to Viscount Castlereagh, K. G., Paris, August 11, 1815, *The Dispatches of Field Marshal the Duke of Wellington*, ed. Lt. Col. Gurwood, 12 vols. (London: John Murray, 1836–39), 12: 596–600.

11 The Council of Allied Ambassadors has been studied more extensively by Beatrice de Graaf, for instance, in *Fighting Terror after Napoleon*.

12 The dissolution of the Chamber was endorsed by the Austrian commander, Baron de Frimont, and, while on a visit to the Bas-Rhin in September 1816, Wellington himself reportedly told local functionaries that it was a "useful and salutary measure" that they needed to support. See reports on Wellington's visits to localities in Bas-Rhin, September 1816, F7/9904 Archives Nationales [hereafter, A.N.], Pierrefitte-sur-Seine, France.

13 See, for example, letter from Major General Heuckel de Donnersmarck, commandant of the Prussian brigade in arrondissements of Bar and Commercy, to prefect of the Meuse, June 26, 1817, regarding donation of 800 francs his troops

collected for inhabitants of commune of Brillon who lost dwellings and furnishings to fire, 8R/29, Archives Départementales de la Meuse, Bar-le-Duc, France.

14 Paul Leuilliot, *L'Alsace au début du XIXe siècle: Essais d'histoire politique, économique et religieuse (1815–1830)*, vol. 1, *La vie politique* (Paris: S.E.V.P.E.N., 1959), 95–6.

15 Letter from subprefect of Belfort to prefect of Haut-Rhin, February 10, 1817, 8R/1174, Archives Départementales du Haut-Rhin, Colmar, France.

16 Letter from minister of interior to prefect of Haut-Rhin, Paris, October 7, 1816, 8R/1172-1173, Archives Départementales du Haut-Rhin.

17 *Moniteur universel*, February 25, 1818.

18 Georges Ozaneaux, *La vie à Colmar sous la Restauration*, letter of August 24, 1818, Bibliothèque de la Revue d'Alsace (Paris: Paul Hartmann Éditeur, 1929), 129.

19 On Vorontsov, see Alexander Mikaberidze, *The Russian Officer Corps in the Revolutionary and Napoleonic Wars, 1792–1815* (El Dorado Hills: Savas Beatie, 2005), 438–9, and Anthony L. H. Rhinelander, *Prince Michael Vorontsov: Viceroy to the Tsar* (Montreal: McGill-Queen's University Press, 1990), esp. ch. 3, "Commanding the Occupation Army."

20 Vorontsov circular to deputies of arrondissement of Rocroy [*sic*], January 17, 1816, 3D/19, Service Historique de la Défense, Vincennes, France.

21 Regulation of "military economy" of Russian troops issued by Barclay de Tolly [n.d., prob. late 1815], 8R/29, Archives Départementales de la Meuse.

22 Subprefect of Avesnes to minister of police, March 1, 1817, F7/9901, A.N.

23 Archives Départementales du Nord, M/135, file 38, cited in Bruchet, "L'invasion et l'occupation du département du Nord par les allies, 1814-1818 (suite)," *Revue du Nord* 7, no. 25 (1921): 44–5; also reported in *Journal de Paris*, July 13, 1816.

24 On the Russian sector, see Blancpain, *La vie quotidienne dans la France du Nord sous les occupations, 1814-1944*, esp. 68–83; Jean Breuillard, "L'occupation russe en France (1816–1818)," typescript ms. for *Revue des Études slaves*, Archives Départmentales des Ardennes, 1J/486; André Sacrez, "Les Russes en 'Ardenne wallonne,'" *Ardenne wallonne* 97: 2–11, and 98: 10–17; R. Wauthier, "Les Russes à Givet, 1816-1818," *Revue historique ardennaise* 19 (1912): 155–61.

25 "L'occupation russe de 1816 à 1818: les Mémoires du général-baron V. I. Löwenstern," typescript ms., 1J/486, Archives Départementales des Ardennes, esp. 84 and 136; Wauthier, "Les Russes a Givet," 155–61; Breuillard, "L'occupation russe en France," Part I, 15; and Jean Breuillard, "L'occupation russe à Givet de 1816 à 1818, d'après les mémoires du Gén.-Baron V. I. Loewenstern," *Revue historique ardennaise* 12 (1977): 57–77.

26 Finn V. Nerland, "Danske fresbevardende tropper I Frankrig, 1815–1818," *Krigshistorisk Tidsskrift* 39, no. 1 (2003): 3–27, and Finn V. Nerland, Danish: "Danske tropper i Frankrig efter Napoleons fald," in *Danmark og Napoleon*, ed. Eric Lerdrup Bourgois and Niels Høffding (Gjern: Forlaget Hovedland, 2007), 233–47, both translated for me by Willem Osuch; Jules Duvivier, "La ville de Bouchain

et l'Ostrevant de 1814 à 1818: L'occupation danoise," *Bulletin de la Commission historique du Nord* 34 (1933): 322–38; and "Lecture par M. Duvivier d'un mémoire sur l'occupation étrangère de la région du Nord de 1816 à 1818: Journal du lt. danois Muller," October 24, 1938, *Bulletin de la Commission historique du Département du Nord* 36 (1948): 47–79.

27 Mayor of Valenciennes to Col. Arbuthnot, L. Col. Blair, and Capt. Hay, Valenciennes, November 9, 1818, H7/38, Départ des troupes d'occupation, Bibliothèque Multimédia de Valenciennes.

28 On Winfield Scott's adoption of this model in the American context, see John Berdusis, "Crossing the Pond: How General Winfield Scott Adopted the British Model of Military Occupation for Use in the United States Army in the Early Nineteenth Century" (MA thesis, University of North Carolina at Charlotte, 2021). On the later occupations, see, for example, Gregory P. Downs, *After Appomattox: Military Occupation and the Ends of War* (Cambridge, MA: Harvard University Press, 2015); Dower, *Embracing Defeat*; Caruthers, *The Good Occupation*; David Edelstein, *Occupational Hazards: Success and Failure in Military Occupation* (Ithaca: Cornell University Press, 2008); and Peter Stirk, *The Politics of Military Occupation* (Edinburgh: Edinburgh University Press, 2009).

7

"War against War"

The Anti-militarist Activities of Greek War Veterans (1922–5)

Alexandros Makris

The First World War was undoubtedly a colossal event that influenced the belligerent nations in various ways. One of the social consequences of the conflict was the emergence of diverse kinds of pacifism: the absolute rejection of the use of military force (e.g., conscientious refusal to be conscripted), the belief that political reforms could ultimately abolish war (e.g., liberal initiatives like the League of Nations or socialist calls for the overthrow of capitalism), and the aversion to war motivated mainly by material factors and expressed through strikes or mutinies. As Martin Ceadel remarked, "the various varieties of pacifism had little impact on the war itself, though rather more on the politics of the two decades that followed."[1] In this context, in the interwar period, there was "an upsurge of militant pacifism."[2] In Greece, also one of the belligerents, the veterans' movement that arose between the end of the Greek-Turkish War (September 1922) and the dictatorship of General Theodoros Pagkalos (June 1925) expressed a radical pacifism with a Communist orientation.

The roots of the transnational Communist current among ex-servicemen during the interwar period can be traced to the impact of the Bolshevik Revolution, in the aftermath of which many radicals considered veterans and war victims as a new dynamic and revolutionary part of the proletariat.[3] The French *Association Republicaine des Anciens Combattants* (Republican Veterans' Association; ARAC) declared a pacifist standpoint from its formation in November 1917. It gradually expressed increasingly revolutionary views and in 1923 was affiliated to the Communist Party of France. The leading figure in the ARAC was the well-known novelist Henry Barbusse, author of the anti-war novel *Le Feu*, published in 1916.[4] A characteristic illustration of Barbusse's antimilitarism was his appeal to French occupation troops during the 1923 Ruhr crisis to disobey military orders. He later faced prosecution in a Parisian court because of these provocative statements.[5] The ARAC's political attitude was not unique; similar political and anti-war rhetoric was expressed by the *Lega Proletaria fra Mutilati, Invalidi, Reduci, Vedove et Genitori di Caduti in Guerra* in Italy (est. 1918), and the *Internationaler Bund der Opfer des Krieges und der Arbeit* in Germany (1919).[6] The international embodiment of the ex-soldiers' Communist element was *Internationale des Anciens Combattants* (the Veterans' International), established in Geneva in May 1920 on the initiative of the ARAC and Barbusse personally. The Veterans' International considered war a consequence of the capitalist system; a struggle against war was thus essentially a fight to overthrow capitalism. Despite being the first international organization of veterans to emerge during the interwar period, the Veterans' International soon declined and, after the mid-1920s, existed on paper only.[7]

In Greece, the warfare did not begin in 1914 or end in 1918. The country's "National Wars" started with the Balkan wars (1912–13), continued with the participation in the Macedonian front during the Great War (1917–18) and ended with the Greek-Turkish War (1919–22). In the course of this decade, a total of some 450,000 men were mobilized[8] and processes that shaped interwar politics were set in motion. The question of entering the Great War led to the "National Schism," the division of Greek society into two opposing "worlds." On one side were the Venizelists, named after their leading figure, Prime Minister Eleutherios Venizelos, who wanted to enter the war on the side of Entente, and on the other side were the Antivenizelists under King Constantine I, who proposed neutrality. At the same time, socialists appeared in the political spectrum with the establishment of the Socialist Labor Party of Greece in November 1918 (later to become the Communist Party of Greece). After the defeat by Kemalist Turkey in 1922, the "Revolution of 1922," a pro-Venizelist military dictatorship seized power until January 1924. The prolonged instability that followed, with five different governments, abolition of the monarchy, and failed military coups, eventually led to the dictatorship of General Pagkalos in June 1925.[9]

In Greece, the Communist-oriented veterans' movement originated from two roots: the radicalization of injured veterans from 1921 onwards and the activities of anti-war cells in the army in the final phase of the Asia Minor Campaign. During the war, the only association of injured servicemen was the Panhellenic Union of Injured Soldiers (PETP). From 1918 to 1921, the PETP was loyal to Greek governments regardless of their political beliefs (Venizelists or anti-Venizelists) and collaborated with the Ministry of Relief on the distribution of kiosks to disabled veterans.[10] Until 1921, the majority of PETP members were veterans of the Balkan wars and the First World War, who were already military pensioners or kiosk owners, making them moderately militant in demanding additional welfare provisions. The continuation of the Greek-Turkish War and especially the operations of the summer of 1921 resulted in a large number of newly injured men (28,134 during the operations of 1921 alone).[11] That caused new problems and delays in their welfare provisions, which made them feel neglected and susceptible to Communist propaganda. In the meantime, from 1918 onward, some nuclei of injured soldiers were radicalized especially in the *Stegi Patridos* (Homeland's House) Rehabilitation School in Athens and in other military hospitals, primarily through propaganda in the form of books and pamphlets orchestrated from a leftist faction of the Socialists ("Communist Union").[12] Gradually, radicalized injured men collaborated with the Socialists, whose official newspaper *Rizospastis* (Radical) from May 1921 onwards increasingly focused on their issues.[13] This leftist trend gained power inside PETP, which had a Communist president from mid-1921 to October 1921, when the finance minister dismissed him and appointed a new administration council composed of members loyal to the government.[14] The close relationship between the political left and disabled veterans lasted not only until the end of the war (1922) but continued until the mid-1930s.[15]

After the military operations of August 1921 in Anatolia, the front was stabilized for almost a year. The lingering inactivity in combination with the postponed demobilization, multiple supply problems, and political "conflicts" between (Venizelist and anti-Venizelist) officers led to a crisis of morale and some minor incidents of insubordination. The Socialists disapproved of the Asia Minor Campaign and in the 1920 elections, their primary demand became demobilization. Simultaneously, while not openly encouraging desertion, they were the only political force which did not condemn it. Within this framework, anti-war cells appeared in many units. Their main activity was the publication and distribution of newspapers and pamphlets questioning the necessity of war. These anti-war nuclei had a limited effect on the Greek defeat, though their main significance was that many of those who participated in them played a prominent role both in the veterans' and the Socialists' movements after the war.[16]

In the aftermath of the Greek-Turkish War, from as early as October 1922, veterans' organizations were established all over Greece. Most of them, and especially their leaderships, developed progressively intimate relationships with the Socialists. The Archive of the Political Office of the Greek Prime Minister contains hundreds of police and gendarmerie reports from all over Greece, which confirm this development.[17] The bond between veterans' unions and Communism became so strong that, in December 1924, the British ambassador in Athens wrote to the Foreign Office that "Unions of Old Soldiers [. . .] now form the chief executive of the [Communist] Party: it may almost be said that Old Soldier means Communist."[18]

Veterans' associations were unified in the First Conference of Ex-Soldiers and Military Victims, held in May 1924 in Athens. The anti-war atmosphere of the conference is clear from the description of one delegate: "We gathered in a hall with 300–400 representatives, and there was an indescribable anti-militarist spirit. Men who had served for ten years as soldiers. Nobody wanted to hear about armies and weapons. They were fed up with them."[19] During the conference, the Federation of Ex-Soldiers and Military Victims was established, declaring as its aims: (a) the struggle against war and militarism, (b) the defense of material and moral interests of veterans, and (c) the protection of war victims. Besides the usual welfare requests of a typical veteran organization (higher pensions, protection from unemployment, etc.), the anti-militarist demands were ubiquitous. Originally, the Federation embraced not only veterans and war victims but also the "victims of militarism," a rather wide term which included military convicts and active privates. Demands included suffrage during military service and improvement of nutrition in the army. In addition, the Federation adopted a resolution aimed at "a real and effective struggle against war" and stating that military conflicts "derive from the imperialist conflicts of oligarchs." The Federation also deprecated the League of Nations as a "coalition of imperialist victors of the Great War, which had as its real goal their interests." There were also broad anti-militarist demands like a decrease in military spending and the sabotage of the manufacture and transport of military armaments.[20]

In addition, the Federation announced its affiliation to the Veterans' International, which addressed a greeting to the conference welcoming the newly founded Federation as a member.[21] The instant admission of the Greek Federation to the Veterans' International was thanks to Leon Trotsky's mediation with Barbusse, as the Soviet Minister of Defense informed the Central Committee of the Greek Communist Party in February 1924.[22] In the early 1920s, there were frequent references to the "fighter of peace" Barbusse, ARAC, and the Veterans' International in Greek Communist publications.[23] The influence of Communist veterans among organized Greek ex-servicemen was clear. Besides its political views, the Federation's newspaper had the same name as that of the ARAC (*Palaios Polemistis, L' Ancien Combattant*) and the two organizations shared the same motto ("Polemos kata tou Polemou," "Guerre à la guerre"). The vigorous link between the veterans' movement and the Communists was highlighted with the election of Pantelis Pouliopoulos as president of the Federation. He and other leading figures of the Federation played a pivotal role in the bolshevization of the Socialists in December 1924, when the party joined the Third International, was renamed as Communist, and Pouliopoulos was elected as its first General Secretary.[24]

The anti-war rhetoric attracted widespread new members to the Communist Party. As the British chargé d' affaires pointed out in August 1924, "there is little doubt that the pacifist side of Communism has been the most potent factor in the success gained."[25] There are numerous examples of pacifist proclamations by veterans during this period. A leaflet distributed by a veterans' union from the Pelion region in central Greece reads: "Join our Union to effectively fight a new war [. . .] to fight the roots of wars [. . .] our slogan is one: War against War!"[26] In another case, at a veterans' demonstration in Valtetsi, a village in the Peloponnesus, agitators called on future soldiers to turn their arms "against their officers."[27] Declarations like these were common from local veterans' clubs and motivated more and more ex-conscripts with pacifist beliefs to subscribe to their local (often Communist-oriented) associations.

Weaving a web of Communist privates inside the army using the propaganda of veterans also helped the Communist Party in its aspirations to seize government. Despite the fact that it was a minor party at that time (with approximately 2,000 members in 1924),[28] the influence of Communist veterans in society was much stronger, especially because of the remarkable membership of the Federation of Ex-Soldiers, which ranged between 40,000 and 60,000 members.[29] As early as August 1923, the British chargé d' affaires had warned about a potential reaction in the event of a new mobilization. As he wrote,

> "Communism has at its disposal just that section of the people who [have] the military strength and which is now being inoculated with anti-militarist ideas and may cause much trouble in the event of a mobilization."

Also, he considered that the impact of Communist veterans in a situation like that would be critical since they were men who "have much influence on local feeling."[30] As many officers of the Gendarmerie noted, Communists believed that a revolution could be supported mainly by ex-servicemen, tobacco workers, and the army and, regarding the latter, their "hopes" derived from veterans.[31]

The Federation of Ex-Soldiers would play an essential role regarding the ambitions of the Communists. The veterans' associations attempted in various ways to recruit the soldiers of the first postwar training series ("Class of 1923"), which remained in service for nearly thirty months (from September 1922 to February 1925). The associations frequently organized demonstrations for their earlier discharge.[32] Moreover, the Federation distributed pamphlets and brochures with instructions so that soldiers could create Communist-oriented cells inside the army. As one leaflet mentioned, these nuclei would in the future "relieve soldiers from officers and would lead them to the struggle against war-friendly governments and the establishment of a workers' and peasants' government."[33] The radical anti-militarist rhetoric urged even Trotsky to warn Communists, suggesting that the party should be more moderate and only against bourgeois militarism, not in general against the army, because "a revolution could not be done without a red army."[34]

In early 1925, there was significant tension between Greece and Turkey, caused by the deportation of Ecumenical Patriarch Constantine VI from Constantinople (Istanbul).[35] The crisis peaked during the final days of January, when a mobilization and a new war seemed imminent. The diplomatic crisis also led to a delay of almost a month in the discharge of the soldiers' class of 1923.[36] At this crucial moment in Greek-Turkish relations, the Federation of Ex-Soldiers activated its mechanisms to prevent a new war or a mobilization. Meanwhile, from mid-1924, veterans' anti-war propaganda had already increased both in the army and in wider society.[37] During the crisis, the Federation released a statement, in which it accused the "plutocracy" of attempting to create a "war-friendly atmosphere because of the Patriarch crisis" and it protested about the delay in the soldiers' discharge. The announcement closed with the mottos "War against War! War against racial passions! War against plutocracy, which prepares new wars!"[38] In the same vein, the Federation published a joint announcement with the Communist Party and the General Confederation of Greek Workers (also controlled by Communists) against a potential mobilization.[39]

The theoretical concept underlying the policy of the Communists, which was implemented by the Federation of Ex-Soldiers, was Leninist revolutionary defeatism, which derived from the "Zimmerwald Left." Whereas the majority at the Zimmerwald Conference (September 1915), a congress of socialist parties opposed to the Great War, adopted the resolution of a "peace without annexations or indemnities, on the basis of the self-determination of peoples," a minority under Vladimir Lenin expressed a more radical proposal. Lenin strongly supported the view that the primary duty of a socialist was to work for the defeat of his own country in order to convert the "imperialist" war into a civil "class" war.[40] As Lenin wrote in *Socialism and War* (1915) that war "inevitably creates revolutionary moods among the masses. It is our duty to help the masses become conscious of these moods, deepen them and give them shape. This task finds correct expression only in one slogan: convert the imperialist war into a civil war."[41]

In the Greek case, while 1925 was not a wartime period, the prospect of a war was realistic. At that key moment, veterans' unions literally instructed revolutionary defeatism inside the army. For this reason, in early 1925, the Federation of Ex-Soldiers published the *Book of the Soldier*, an anti-war pamphlet "written by veterans." The conclusion of the brochure was:

> If there is a destination to a man who becomes soldier, this is to be a Red Soldier. A soldier who in cooperation with veterans will crush the plutocratic government, and he will create a workers', peasants', and soldiers' government. Then, unified with the rest armies of the world, he will crush international capitalism in order to consolidate the internal peace.[42]

An additional act of revolutionary defeatism was committed in late January 1925, when "Communist pamphlets" were distributed in barracks in Athens, calling on the soldiers, in case of war, to "assassinate their officers and not their brother Turkish and Bulgarians workers and peasants."[43] In the aftermath of the discharge of the class of 1923, this rhetoric inspired numerous former privates to join veterans' associations.[44] The anti-militarist campaign of the Federation of Ex-Soldiers put revolutionary defeatism into practice. With this agitating attitude, the organized veterans threatened a vital pillar of the state—the army— especially during a period when a new military mobilization was considered likely.

At the same time, the veterans were in the spotlight for another reason. In January and February 1925, forceful peasant protests, which were also expressed through land occupations, were held in many regions of Greece, with their epicenter in Thessaly and Boeotia. The protests reached a climax in Trikala on February 2, 1925, where an angry rally of almost 1,000 demonstrators occupied the Prefecture Building and riots took place. The Fifth Infantry Regiment was called in to quell the disturbance, resulting in six deaths and numerous injuries. During these agrarian rallies, the veterans' associations, and in some cases the local Communist clubs, guided the struggle of the peasants, who were not necessarily veterans or Communists.[45] In some rural areas, the veterans' movement represented the landless peasants, who saw agrarian reform being implemented in the rest of the country but not in their region, due to local causes.[46] The agrarian demonstrations, which manifested the dynamic of the veterans' movement, and the anti-war campaign were the highlights of the

Federation of Ex-Soldiers' activities but were subsequently also the main reasons for its decline.

The activities of the Federation of Ex-Soldiers revealed the limits of anti-war propaganda in Greek society. When veterans' expressed not only pacifist but anti-militarist and anti-patriotic views and openly promoted revolutionary defeatism, they crossed a red line. This challenge against an essential institution like the army was understandably unacceptable for the state. The government had already issued public warnings to the veterans in 1924. In November of that year, Prime Minister Andreas Michalakopoulos had warned the Federation of Ex-Soldiers about its behavior, saying that veterans should "stop the propaganda against the state, otherwise the state will crush them."[47] Gradually, an increasing number of military and political officials openly proposed the suppression of the veterans' movement. In March 1925, the commander of I Army Corps, General Z. Papathanasiou, demanded that the Army Ministry dissolve the veterans' associations "because they had been converted into Communists, and they had become pioneers of any insubordination and disturbance of order."[48] Numerous similar reports, sent to the prime minister, ministers, and army units, make clear why the state eventually decided to suppress the veterans' movement.[49] Between 1924 and 1925, anti-Communism was progressively strengthened both in society and in the state, which legislated many measures against dissidents.[50] In this context, from the beginning of 1924 veteran unions' activities like rallies and even assemblies were prohibited. In the aftermath of the agrarian demonstrations of early 1925, the police carried out raids in veterans' associations across the country, arrested their members, and confiscated their archives. Furthermore, leaders of the veterans' movement, like Pouliopoulos himself, were arrested as Communists.[51] In February 1925, Prime Minister Michalakopoulos said to the British ambassador about this policy that "as they [Communists] declared war on the state, the challenge would be taken up."[52] The Federation of Ex-Soldiers responded with confidence that the prosecutions would not disintegrate the veterans' movement.[53] The circle of leftist veterans' associations was, however, practically closed.

During the first half of 1925, most of the Communist-oriented veterans' associations became weaker, and by mid-1925 they had almost disappeared.[54] Besides suppression by the government, other causes contributed to their decline. First, many landless veterans received land due to the agrarian reform.[55] Furthermore, most of the disabled veterans and war victims received pensions. Care for ex-soldiers was limited during the initial postwar years and the most significant law on war pensions was adopted as late as mid-1924.[56] Gradually the process of awarding pensions was accelerated.[57] There were also announcements in 1924 about additional welfare measures, such as the creation of a Fund for War Victims, the monopolizing of tobacco in small cities by disabled veterans, and the drafting of a general protective law for ex-servicemen.[58] These measures were, however, not adopted until October 1925 by the Pagkalos administration.[59] However, we should keep in mind that, at the time, the Greek state had to care for approximately 1.5 million refugees from Asia Minor and Eastern Thrace.[60] Moreover, the direct bond between the Veterans' Federation and the Communist Party, which adopted a resolution in December of 1924 for an "independent Macedonia and Thrace," alienated many non-Communist veterans.[61] However, the primary factor of the decline of the veterans' associations was the state repression in response to the veterans' close relationship with the Communists. After the establishment of General Pagkalos' dictatorial regime on June 25, 1925, the Federation of Ex-Soldiers and Communist veterans' associations still existed but after new persecutions against Communists in August 1925, it finally dissolved.

To conclude, the pacifist dimension of the Greek veterans' movement provides us with a solid example of ex-soldiers' anti-war sentiment in the aftermath of the First World War. Furthermore, the Greek case is one of the most powerful expressions of the extreme leftist current among Great War veterans. The veterans' movement not only promoted peace but also supported a hard anti-militarist line and finally expressed clearly revolutionary defeatism. The extreme anti-war activities of the Federation of Ex-Soldiers, in the event of a potential new mobilization, in combination with other factors, led to a harsh response from the state. During the remaining interwar period, the veterans' movement was never again so vehement or had such close ties to the Communist Left. However, ardent pacifist beliefs, though not anti-militarist, did not fade and were always a cornerstone of the Greek veterans' movement.[62]

Notes

1   Martin Ceadel, "Pacifism," in *The Cambridge History of the First World War*, vol. II, ed. Jay Winter (Cambridge: Cambridge University Press, 2014), 576, 605.

2   Annette Becker, "Faith, Ideologies, and the 'Cultures of War,'" in *A Companion to World War I*, ed. John Horne (Chichester: Wiley-Blackwell, 2010), 243.

3   Ángel Alcalde, "War Veterans as Transnational Actors: Politics, Alliances and Networks in the Interwar Period," *European Review of History* 25, no. 3–4 (2018): 494.

4 Chris Millington, "Communist Veterans and Paramilitarism in 1920s France: The Association Républicaine des Anciens Combattants," *Journal of War & Culture Studies* 8, no. 4 (2015): 303–5.

5 Alcalde, "War Veterans," 498.

6 Gianni Isola, "Socialismo e Combattentismo: La Lega proletaria. 1918–1922," *Italia Contemporanea* 141 (1980): 5–29; Gregg Eghigian, "Injury, Fate, Resentment and Sacrifice in German Political Culture, 1914–1939," in *Sacrifice and National Belonging in Twentieth-Century Germany*, ed. Gregg Eghigian and Matthew P. Berg (Arlington: Texas University Press, 2002), 97–9.

7 Adrian Tixier, "The Evolution of International Relations between the Disabled and Ex-service Men's Organizations," *FIDAC. Bulletin of Allied Legions* 2, no. 6–7 (1926): 6; Henry C. Wolfe, "War Veterans Who Work for Peace," *World Affairs* 98, no. 3 (1935): 175; Alcalde, "War Veterans," 496–7.

8 For statistics on the Greek veterans, see Alexandros Makris, "Oi kirikes tis ideas tou ethnous. Palaioi polemistes, anapiroi kai thimata polemou stin Ellada (1912–1940)" ["The preachers of the idea of the nation." Veterans and War Victims in Greece (1912–1940)] (PhD Thesis, National and Kapodistrian University of Athens, Athens, 2021) 312–21.

9 Richard Clogg, *A Concise History of Greece* (Cambridge: Cambridge University Press, 1997), 81–108; John S. Koliopoulos and Thanos M. Veremis, *Modern Greece: A History since 1821* (Chichester: Wiley-Blackwell, 2010), 68–102.

10 Makris, "Oi kirikes," 293–5.

11 Hellenic Army General Staff, *Epitomos Istoria Ekstratias Mikras Asias 1919–1922* (History of Asia Minor Campaign 1919–1922) (Athens: Army History Directorate, 1967), 486.

12 Kostas Paloukis, "I organosi Archeion Marxismou (1919–1934)" [The Organization "Archeion Marxism" (1919–1934)] (PhD Thesis, University of Crete, Rethymno, 2017), 108–10.

13 For example "Yper ton anapiron" (For the injured and disabled), *Rizospastis*, May 7, 1921, 3; "I organosis ton anapiron polemou" (The organization of disabled veterans), *Rizospastis*, August 24, 1921, 1.

14 "Praxikopima kata ton anapiron" (A coup against the disabled), *Rizospastis*, October 17, 1921, 4.

15 Makris, "Oi kirikes," 295–310, 407–10, 598–610, 728–32.

16 "Bolshevik propaganda," 1922, f. 20.7, Central Service, Diplomatic and Historical Archives of the Greek Ministry of Foreign Affairs, Thrace Army; Philip Carabott, "The Greek 'Communists' and the Asia Minor Campaign," *Bulletin of the Centre for Asia Minor Studies* 9 (1992): 99–118.

17 General State Archives of Greece (GAK), Central Service, Archive of the Political Office of the Prime Minister (APM), f. 738, 739, 877, 878, 879.

18 The National Archives/Foreign Office (TNA/FO) 371–9891, Milne Cheetham to
    Austin Chamberlain, Athens, December 18, 1924.

19 Ilias Lefousis, *To ergatiko kinima tou Volou 1881–1936* [The labour movement of
    Volos 1881–1936] (Volos, 1986), 241–2.

20 Minutes of the Conference at *Rizospastis*, from May 6 to 12, 1924. The resolutions
    and the constitution of the Federation at Philippos Orfanos [Pantelis Pouliopoulos],
    *Polemos kata tou polemou. Apofaseis tou Protou Panelliniou Synedriou Palaion
    Polemiston kai Thimaton Stratou* [War against War. Resolutions of the First
    Panhellenic Conference of Ex-Soldiers and Military Victims], 3rd edn. (1924; repr.,
    Athens: Diethnis Vivliothiki, 2008).

21 "Diaggelma tis Diethnous" [Greeting of Veterans' International], *Rizospastis*, May 7,
    1924, 1.

22 GAK, APM, f. 738, Special Security Review, February 16, 1924.

23 For example "O agon tou gallikou laou enantion tou neou polemou" [The struggle
    of French people against a new war], *Rizospastis*, April 29, 1921, 1; "Diethnis
    traumation kai anapiron polemou [Injured and disabled veterans' International],"
    Rizospastis, January 23, 1922, 3; "Henri Barbusse," *Rizospastis*, December 25, 1924,
    1. Moreover, chapters from Barbusse's *Le Feu* published in *Rizospastis* from May
    23 to July 25, 1921.

24 Gunnar Hering, *Ta politika kommata stin Ellada, 1821–1936* [The Political Parties
    in Greece, 1821–1936], vol. II (Athens: MIET, 2004), 1132–5.

25 TNA/FO 371–9896, Charles H. Bentinck to Ramsey MacDonald, Athens, August
    30, 1924, Annual Report 1923, 26.

26 Educational Centre Charilaos Florakis, Archive of the Communist Party of Greece,
    Interwar Period, Union of Ex-Servicemen of Pinakates, "Pros tous efedrous
    polemistas" [To reservist warriors].

27 GAK, APM, f. 739, Gendarmerie Directorate of Arcadia to the Political Office of the
    Prime Minister, Tripolis, November 5, 1924.

28 Hering, *Ta politika kommata*, 1123.

29 TNA/FO 371–8827, Charles H. Bentinck to Lord Curzon, Athens, August 6, 1923;
    GAK, APM, f. 878, P. Katsotas [Police Director of Athens] to Gendarmerie Chief,
    Athens, April 9, 1925.

30 TNA/FO 371–8827, Charles H. Bentinck to Lord Curzon, Athens, August 6, 1923.

31 GAK, APM, f. 739, Gendarmerie Directorate of Magnesia to the Political Office
    of the Prime Minister, Volos, August 1, 1924 and Police Directorate of Piraeus
    to the Political Office of the Prime Minister, Piraeus, October 21, 1924, f. 877,
    Gendarmerie Directorate of Kavalla to the Interior Ministry, Kavala, December 24,
    1924.

32 "Polemos kata tou polemou" [War against war], *Foni tou Efedrou* [Reservist's Voice],
    September 23, 1924, 1.

33 GAK, APM, f. 878, Gendarmerie Directorate of Patras to the Political Office of the
    Prime Minister, Patras, March 16, 1925. A cell like that disorganized in May 1925 at
    III Army Corps in Thessaloniki. GAK, APM, f. 879, III Army Corps "Review of 28
    May 1925. Communism in the Army."

34 GAK, APM, f. 738, Special Security Review, February 16, 1924.

35 Dimitris Kamouzis, *Greeks in Turkey. Elite Nationalism and Minority Politics in
    Late Ottoman and Early Republican Istanbul* (London, New York: Routledge, 2021),
    198–202.

36 "I apolisis tis klaseos tou 1923 [The dismissal of 1923 class], *Empros*, January 10,
    1925, 5; "I eygnomosini tis patridas pros tous apolimenous" [Homeland's gratitude
    to the discharged soldiers], *Empros*, February 18, 1925, 2.

37 For example GAK, APM, f. 739, Police Directorate of Piraeus to the Police
    Headquarters, Piraeus, July 20, 1924, f. 877, Gendarmerie Directorate of Ioannina
    to the Political Office of the Prime Minister, Ioannina, December 17, 1924.

38 GAK, APM, f. 877, Police Directorate of Athens to the I Army Corps, Athens,
    February 3, 1925.

39 Communist Party of Greece, *Episima Keimena* [Official Texts], vol. II (Athens:
    Sichroni Epoxi, 1974), 35–8.

40 Craig Nation, *War on War. Lenin, Zimmerwald Left and the Origins of Communist
    International* (Durham, London: Duke University Press, 1989), 81–2, 85–91,
    136–43; Sean McMeekin, *The Russian Revolution: A New History* (London: Profile
    Books, 2017), 128, 281.

41 Vladimir I. Lenin, *Collected Works*, vol. 21 (Moscow: Progress Publishers, 1964),
    313.

42 P. Nikas, *To vivlio tou fantarou* [The Book of the Soldier], (Alexandria, 1925), 3–5.

43 TNA/FO 371–10769, Milne Cheetnam to Austin Chamberlain, Athens, February 4,
    1925.

44 GAK, APM, f. 877, Piraeus Police Department to Police Headquarters, Piraeus,
    March 6, 1925.

45 GAK, APM, f. 877, Skandilas [Prefect of Trikala] to the Interior Ministry, February
    4, 1925, N. Tzikas [Chief of Gendarmerie] to the Interior Ministry, February 14,
    1925.

46 In some places of Thessaly, there were delays and exceptions in expropriation
    of some large estates. In Boeotia, the uncertain ownership of dried lake Copais
    between the English Lake Copais Ltd and Greek state prevented the agrarian
    reform. *Efimiris tis Kiverniseos* (Government Gazette), A/215/1924; Apostolos
    K. Papadopoulos, "The Drainage and Exploitation of Lake Copais (1908–1938)"
    (PhD Thesis, University of Bradford, Bradford 1993), 320–45. For veterans and the
    agrarian reform see Makris, "Oi kirikes," 446–73.

47 "Mia dilosi tou prothipourgou" (A statement of Prime Minister), *Eleutheron Vima*,
    October 15, 1924, 3.

48 GAK, APM, f. 878, Zafirios Papathanasiou to the Army Ministry, Athens, March 16, 1925.

49 For example, GAK, APM, f. 739, Prefect of Heraklion (Crete) to the Political Office of the Prime Minister, Heraklion, October 1, 1924, P. Katsotas [Police Director of Athens] to the Interior Ministry, Athens, October 28, 1924, f. 877, P. Klados [Chief of Gendarmerie] to the Interior Ministry, Athens, January 23, 1925.

50 Nikos Alivizatos, *Oi politikoi thesmoi se krisi 1922–1974* [The Political Institutions in crisis 1922–1974] (Athens: Themelio, 1983), 38–9, 44–5, 56, 71; Dimitris Bacharas, "La Grèce Après la Guerre: Dictature et République Dans un Monde en Mutation (1922–1925)" (PhD Thesis, Ecole des Hautes Etudes en Sciences Sociales, Paris, 2010), 467–82.

51 For example "Syllipseis kommouniston" (Arrests of Communists), *Rizospastis*, February 9, 1925, "Neo kima dioxeon" (New wave of prosecutions), *Rizospastis*, May 8, 1925.

52 TNA/FO 371–10769, Milne Cheetnam to Austin Chamberlain, Athens, February 4, 1925.

53 "I Opospondia apanta" [The Federation answers], *Rizospastis*, March 11, 1925, 2.

54 For example GAK, APM, f. 877, Prefect of Heraklion (Crete) to the Political Office of the Prime Minister, Heraklion, February 3, 1925, Gendarmerie Directorate of Patras to the Interior Ministry, Patras, February 16, 1925.

55 Benaki Museum's Historical Archives, Archive of Eleutherios Venizelos, f. 145, "Report for Protective Measures for Veterans" [1931].

56 Law 3122/1924, *Efimiris tis Kiverniseos* (Government Gazette), A/175/1924.

57 GAK, Central Service, Archive of the Health Ministry, box 232, "Confidential" (1927), f. 12, D. Fragkopoulos [Director of the Ministry] to Minister of Hygiene and Relief, Athens, February 17, 1927.

58 Dimitris Pazis [former Minister of Relief], "I drasis tou ypoyrgiou Pronoias" (The activities of Ministry of Relief), *Dimokratia*, August 4, 1924, 2; Hellenic Literature and Historical Archive (ELIA), Archive of Andreas Michalakopoulos, f. 2, Introductory reports (no. 17): "Introductory Report and Law Plan for Protective Measures for Veterans."

59 *Efimiris tis Kiverniseos* [Government Gazette], A/301/1925.

60 Elisabeth Kontogiorgi, *Population Exchange in Greek Macedonia: The Rural Settlement of Refugees 1922–1930* (Oxford, New York: Oxford University Press, 2006), 41–70.

61 GAK, APM, f. 877, Gendarmerie Directorate of Drama to the Political Office of the Prime Minister, Drama, February 10, 1925.

62 Makris, "Oi kirikes," 651–2. For example, "Oi efedroi polemistai" (The reservist warriors), *Proia*, January 26, 1931, 2; "Ta efedrika synedria" (Veterans' Conferences), *Akropolis*, June 18, 1936, 5.

8

Building Insecurity?

Military and Paramilitary Forces in Postwar Czechoslovak Borderlands (1945–8)

Paul Lenormand

Introduction

This chapter explores the emergence from war in Czechoslovakia, focusing on the role played by uniformed personnel in "peacemaking." It argues that the use of military and paramilitary forces in the borderlands as "peacekeepers" was a way to wage war after the conflict was officially over because the Czechs and Slovaks had not yet achieved all their war aims.

Officially one of the victorious Allied nations, Czechoslovakia suffered less from the war than most Central and East European countries. Poland or Yugoslavia, for instance, though nominally victors, were materially broken and politically unstable. Former enemies, Germany and Hungary, had been occupied, or even dismantled, and posed no immediate threat to Czechoslovak security, at least for many years. Soviet and Western Allies proved relatively supportive and agreed to restore Czechoslovakia's territorial integrity (except Ruthenia). However, because of their unique experience of the Second World War, Czechoslovaks—and notably Czechs—feared that difficult times were ahead. As a result, they took steps to prevent a disaster of the amplitude of the 1938–45 national disintegration from ever happening again.

As a reminder, after the Munich Agreement of October 1938 and the German invasion in March 1939, Central Europe's last democracy was dismantled. Czech lands were occupied by Nazi Germany for more than six years, while Hungary seized border territories in Slovakia and the whole of Subcarpathian Ruthenia. Smaller Slovakia, under priest-president Jozef Tiso, fell under German domination.[1] The occupation or satellization of former Czechoslovak territories had deep consequences for the demographics and power balance of the country. Many Czechs were expelled from the so-called Sudetenland (annexed by the Reich), prompting triumphalism among German speakers. Other Slavic groups (Slovaks and Rusyns) also suffered from German-Hungarian domination. Even worse, almost the entire Jewish population was murdered. As a result, Czechoslovak society went through a quasi-civil war (and an actual one on several counts), mostly along ethnic lines, but also opposing pro-Axis and pro-Ally groups. Military clashes and killings occurred until the very last days of the war.[2]

With the Allied victory—under Soviet leadership in most of Central Europe—and the fall of the German nemesis in May 1945, other problems appeared. In reoccupied Sudetenland, Nazified Germans seemed to pose a permanent threat to national security. In the eastern half of the Republic, Slovaks had developed a taste for independence and resented the idea of being subordinated to Prague again. Additionally, Subcarpathian Ruthenia was occupied by the Soviet army and incorporated in the Ukrainian SSR (a territorial change which officially came into force in late June 1945)—creating uncertainty about the exact location of the future border.[3] In short, Czechoslovak leaders feared for the security of the state during most of the postwar period.

As a rule, most borderlands were home to national minorities, by order of importance Germans (Czech lands and some pockets in Slovakia), Hungarians (southern Slovakia), Ruthenians (eastern Slovakia), and Poles (Czech Silesia). Some Slovaks also perceived their people as an oppressed minority. Long before the war ended, the Czechoslovak government-in-exile had started to think about a "final solution" to the multinational problem, increasingly resorting to radical and violent plans. Substantial changes were indeed to take place, mirroring the ethnic reorganization conducted in most of Central and Eastern Europe: Poland, successfully "purifying" its national body through population displacement in 1945–7, was a perfect example of this pattern.[4]

Paradoxically, Soviet domination contributed to regional stability in Central Europe: Moscow did not want interstate conflicts to erupt in its sphere of influence. Consequently, the customary clashes between small and sometimes irredentist states seemed doomed to disappear and the militarization of the zone would then lose its traditional rationale. As a result, national military and paramilitary forces would no longer focus on protecting East European countries from an invasion. Under the "protection" of the Soviet Union, East Europeans could finally stop fighting each other. However, some countries seemed to do the opposite. Yugoslavia, clashing with Western powers over Trieste, never really demobilized.[5] Czechoslovakia, for reasons we will explain, also appeared reluctant. Far from turning the page on the war, the state recreated and mobilized military and paramilitary forces. But did this remilitarization after the official end of the war really serve the consolidation of peace? Or did it contribute to widespread insecurity and violence, legitimizing illiberal behavior and postponing the return to peace?

This chapter shows that due to specific wartime and postwar conditions in Czechoslovakia, the peacemaking process was impelled: relying on a reorganized military-security apparatus, the Czechoslovak leadership pushed for a violent form of "pacification," notably in the borderlands. This transition led to the rise of a new society, more willing to subscribe to the nationalistic and statist discourse of the Soviet-backed Communists.

Peacemaking versus Pacification

First, it is important to stress the violent nature of the emergence from the war in many territories, notably in western Ukraine, Lithuania, and Transylvania, and in various European colonies (French Algeria, or British Palestine).[6] The Second World War mutated into civil wars or decolonization conflicts, which lasted years or even decades. Many factors played against peace: ethnic rifts, mass migrations, and social and economic insecurity, as well as more traditional unsolved military and diplomatic disputes.

The wartime response of the state to these kinds of challenges—or mortal threats—is general mobilization, the distribution of weapons, legalizing and easing lethal violence, and military combat. As a rule, the legal rights of the population are reduced or suspended. By contrast, "peacemaking" involves ending combats, preventing extreme violence, demobilizing, and disarming. Though gradual, the emergence from war implies the implementation of new norms and practices, a process often called "cultural demobilization."[7] In particular, and even more in liberal democracies (what Czechoslovakia claimed to be), the civilian population is not supposed to be treated as an enemy or an expandable resource, at least not without a minimal level of consent. Indeed, peacemaking is a complex process of co-making, with both state actors and the populations willing to compromise. Pacification, by contrast, does not require the participation of all: the state assumes that some citizens or even large groups of them are still fighting a war and preventing the return to peace. State leaders will mobilize security or military means to suppress opposition, preferring counter-insurgency over the political settlement.[8]

To a large extent, Czechoslovak leaders did not stop fighting the war once the country was free of German occupation troops. The postwar challenges were met with aggressive policies, in which the military and security forces played a significant role.

Profiling the Peacemakers: Military and Paramilitary Forces in Postwar Czechoslovakia

Before exploring the peacetime missions of the Czechoslovak postwar military, it is important to look back at the creation and evolution of the armed forces in the country. As in much of Europe, uninformed personnel were increasingly associated with the nation-state: before 1918, most soldiers and policemen were—justifiably—perceived as supporters of the Habsburg imperial order. After the First World War, the newborn Czechoslovak state pensioned off the majority of the German- and Hungarian-speaking military/security cadres, to the benefit of the Slavic nationalities and especially the Czechs. Among them, many came from the anti-Habsburg nationalist "Legions" fighting on the Entente side. In other words, the military apparatus embodied the nation, while the state remained ambiguously multinational, fueling a growing discontent among minorities (and above all among Germans). The old tradition of national militias did not disappear: nevertheless, compared to most of Central Europe, little paramilitary violence occurred in post-imperial Czechoslovakia.[9] By and large, the Czech leaders, in cooperation with some of the minority leaders, successfully obtained the support of the majority of the people. Democracy worked fairly well, at least until the late 1930s. In spite of the sometimes petty-minded behavior of Czechs, national minorities were granted rights (locally) and even in the army under monopolistic Czech command, young draftees were not particularly harassed.[10]

During the First Republic (1918–38), the military focused on classical defense tasks: protecting the borders behind a Maginot Line-style network of bunkers and cooperating with its French sponsor and regional allies to face any hostile resurgence from Germany or Hungary. As Hitler's expansionism and Horthy's irredentism grew, the Czechoslovak army was further modernized and praised for its readiness.

Enforcing law inside the country was mainly the task of the police, the gendarmerie, and the customs service, often uniformed and lightly armed. As a rule, the army was not mobilized for internal troubles, though notable exceptions occurred, for instance, in the early 1920s against leftist strikers. Only later, when local German nationalists started to threaten stability in the borderlands did the military intervene more directly: army officers took command of combined military and security battalions in charge of deterring potential Nazi insurgents.[11] In this era of tension, militarism infused public life, and even the Communists supported the perspective of fighting against their now-fascist German ex-comrades.

Military operations never materialized because of the Munich Agreement, a capitulation without combat which also impacted the prestige of the army. After the invasion of the Czech lands in March 1939, the Germans attempted to symbolically "castrate" their new subjects: indeed, they stripped young Czech men of the right to wear uniforms and bear arms, even on the Axis side.[12] The Czechoslovak army was dissolved soon after the establishment of the Protectorate, while most police officers de facto obeyed the Germans, contributing to law enforcement and easing the job of the occupation forces. Most professional soldiers refrained from active collaboration but, as little military action took place in Bohemia and Moravia until late April 1945, few former career soldiers took part in armed action against the Germans. Liberation came from abroad, almost completely unexpectedly. Most Czechs remained "passive," causing much frustration and depriving a majority of young Czechs of any serious training—usually provided by the army—and valuable combat experience. Paradoxically, in the midst of a total war, Czechoslovak society (and significantly its Czech segment) was demilitarized.

The postwar state was soon confronted with a double challenge: cleansing the military and security apparatus and mobilizing and remilitarizing society to make sure that the peace would be a "good peace." Altogether, this process changed the sociological profile of the armed and security forces, their respective importance, and their missions. Inevitably, these changes also altered the way the army and security would enforce peace.

From 1945 onward, a broad process of regeneration of the state apparatus through cleansing and incorporation of new personnel started. The pro-Communist general Ludvík Svoboda took command of the Ministry of National Defense (MNO). Under his leadership, the army lost at least 10 percent of its officers and a majority of its top generals, leading to a major identity crisis. Thousands of new junior officers entered the army permanently, notably in the Communist-led intelligence and education departments. This process was even more evident in the security forces, under the Communist Minister of the Interior Václav Nosek: the police and gendarmerie were merged into a new

Corps of National Security (*Sbor národní bezpečnosti* or SNB), incorporating former Czech insurgents and partisans, many of them fresh members of the Communist Party.[13] Additionally, former insurgents (mostly in Prague and in big cities) and partisans (mostly in the countryside and in Slovakia) continued to perform security duties for many weeks or months, mutating into militias (notably the factory militias securing industrial sites against potential sabotage). Overall, veterans' organizations played a key role in the local power balance.[14] As all these forces were placed under the authority of Nosek's ministry, the security apparatus was centralized and strengthened.[15] The new balance of power between the military and the security forces reflected the weakening of the army: the Ministry of the Interior received proportionally more budget than the military as compared to the prewar period, while some of the SNB and partisans' units were equipped with heavy infantry weapons (machine guns and mortars) usually associated with wartime combat. Moreover, the military was often used as a reserve force providing troops for SNB operations and for other non-military tasks. Escaping army supervision and authority, some uniformed personnel even clashed with members of the military: for instance, the Prague insurgent Václav Kotál, who took up arms in the last days of the war and later participated in the reoccupation of the borderlands, felt confident enough to confront an army general during a street defile. Wearing his hair long, Kotál publicly claimed to be a real commander despite his official rank of private in the army reserve.[16] Such behavior would have been unthinkable before the war, when the army embodied national strength and shielded the country against its hostile neighbors. More importantly, all Germans and Hungarians were banned from the army and security forces, even the very few who were recognized as "anti-fascists." Non-Slavic civilians were now alone in facing Slavic troops full of resentment about years of occupation and vexation. In short, tens of thousands of "new men" joined the army and security apparatus, sometimes temporarily, contributing to its ethnicization and politicization. It strongly impacted the way these actors would deal with the minorities and borderland issues.

The other major phenomenon of this postwar era was the mobilization and remilitarization of society, at least its Slavic component: many Czechs (and to a lesser extent, Slovaks) had to serve for short or longer periods in the militias, the SNB or the army. While many European countries demobilized partisan units and disarmed irregular fighters as soon as possible in the name of security and peacemaking, Czechoslovakia did quite the opposite.[17] The military and paramilitary components of the state apparatus grew stronger and appeared to be the ultima ratio of governance. This transformation was not simply the result of a topdown reordering. The identity of the military also changed because of its new missions: managing the transition from war to peace.

Peace Enforcement in Uniform

As Central and Eastern Europe was left in ruins by the war, all governments relied on a fair amount of authoritarian leadership and violence to restore and reinvent the state.[18] Czechoslovakia was no exception. The aforementioned military and security apparatus was tasked with a number of vital missions. For Czechoslovak leaders, militarizing the transition was the way to face both external threats and internal instability.

The first mission of the defense and interior ministries' troops was to fight armed "bands" entering Czechoslovakia. These postwar enemies were irregular fighters clashing with the Czechoslovak authorities for different reasons. Some groups came from national minorities and opposed the centralist conception of the state, supporting either separatism or autonomism. The Werwolf organization, made up of former Nazis in the German-speaking borderlands, was a fairly modest network of sabotage and intelligence cells, supposedly waiting for the resurrection of the Reich to shake off the hated Slavic domination. Some Hungarian troops of uncertain origin were also crossing the border in southern Slovakia, helping Hungarian-speaking families to escape Czechoslovakia or maintaining some presence in these disputed territories, formerly part of Great Hungary. Similar incursions of lesser magnitude also took place near the Polish border. Even in Slovakia, where radical nationalists rejected what they called Czech dictatorship, some "white partisans" (by contrast with "red" partisans of the Second World War, often leftist or Communist-oriented) were causing concern to the Prague authorities. Until 1947, when peace was signed with Poland and Hungary, the possession of some border territories remained uncertain, even if in the end Czechoslovak leaders successfully retained all disputed areas. These internal troublemakers—Germans, Hungarians, and Slovaks—never threatened the survival of the state but justified more surveillance and a more radical response from the Czechoslovak government.

The other set of "bands" was not looking to destroy the Czechoslovak state: they were merely collateral damage of regional insecurity. Of least concern was the Polish Home Army (AK), whose members sometimes used Czechoslovak territory as a rear base in their war against the Polish Communist state. Much more impressive was the Ukrainian Insurgent Army (UPA), made up of nationalists opposing the Soviet takeover of their country. Increasingly pressured by the Soviet security forces, more and more veterans of this neighboring civil war tried to reach Western Europe. Czechoslovakia was on their way, and free of Soviet troops, unlike Poland, occupied Eastern Germany and Hungary. Well-equipped and experienced, they needed supplies and sometimes plundered villages. Staunchly anti-Communist, they also represented an ideological threat to the left-wing Czechoslovak government.

The anti-UPA (whose members were called by the derogatory term *banderovci*, i.e., "Bandera's followers") campaign lasted from early 1946 to early 1948. A blockade was imposed in the northeast corner of Slovakia, with several lines of defense, fortified hubs of communication, and mobile pursuit units, totaling more than 10,000 men by August 1947 (c. 22 percent of available servicemen), not counting the policemen and partisans also mobilized in the area. If the incursions progressively stopped, it was more a consequence of Polish and Soviet operations against the Ukrainian nationalists than a reflection of the military efficiency of the Czechoslovaks. Overall, the press coverage given to the anti-UPA fighting gave this threat much more importance than it really had and contributed to raising insecurity in the public space, favoring a more nationalistic and authoritarian vision of the state.[19]

Moreover, contributing to the transition from war to peace, the armed forces helped to clear the land of mines (mostly in Slovakia) and to secure the numerous ammunition depots (in Bohemia), suffering 116 casualties (including 69 dead).[20] The state also tried to recover the thousands of individual weapons in the possession of civilians, mostly trophy rifles, submachine guns, and pistols taken from the enemy during the war. Despite calls to restitute these weapons, many citizens kept them. Furthermore, the army provided manpower for the national economy. Though not unusual for armed forces, this decision roused opposition among servicemen, who felt exploited.

Fighting armed groups, clearing mines and collecting weapons, and even helping the economy seemed sound goals for the military in this postwar period. Other tasks, however, had less to do with the primary vocation of the army and more with an ethnic rearrangement of the country.

Politically, postwar Czechoslovakia was a binational compromise between a Czech majority and a Slovak minority. Admittedly, the Slovaks had loyally served Hitler, until an anti-Axis uprising broke out in late August 1944. From that moment, Slovakia was considered friendly again by the Allied and Czechoslovak officials. However, bilateral conflicts never ceased and were even reactivated by the postwar transition and purges. The Czechs suspected their partners of seeking independence, and the Communists in particular feared that the religious inclinations of the majority of the Slovak population (conservative Catholicism) might prevent them from acquiring their support and vote. In late May 1946, the first postwar elections took place. To prevent any "disturbance," Czech troops from Moravia were sent to Slovakia: precisely where, under the postwar compromise between Czech and Slovak leaders, only Slovak soldiers were to be garrisoned in peacetime. For instance, one battalion of the Forty-Third Infantry Regiment left south Moravia in early May, traveling by truck for several days before reaching Hažín, a relatively remote village in eastern Slovakia, home of Ján Ferjak, a Democratic Party leader favoring autonomy. There, the Czech soldiers were assigned propaganda duties, playing music and promoting Czechoslovakia. On the Slovak side, the reception was not enthusiastic: locals accused the Czechs of supporting "a Communist putsch" or trying "to influence the social and political environment of Slovakia." As a rule, the Czech soldiers felt unwelcome and resented what they called "Slovak chauvinism," also suspecting the Slovaks of being anti-Semitic (as demonstrated by a riot in Topoľčany in September 1945).[21] By 1946–7, the army had become a potential law enforcer in Slovakia in the event that the population might resist political orders from Prague.

Slovaks, at least, were granted a future in the Czechoslovak state project. Non-Slavic minorities, by contrast, were subjected to more radical measures. To a large extent, the army was in charge of rounding up and expelling "hostile" members of national minorities, notably Germans and Hungarians. The latter were suspected of irredentism and some 50,000 of them were deported from southern Slovakia to the Czech borderlands, where they were subjected to forced labor until most of them were allowed to return home. The former, the German archenemies, did not benefit from such—relative—leniency. Hundreds of thousands of German-speaking civilians had already fled Bohemia and Moravia during the final days and weeks of the war. But more than two million Germans still lived in the Czech and Moravian borderlands, in fairly compact strips along the Silesian (now Polish), Saxon, Bavarian, and Austrian borders. Some German pockets also existed in Slovakia. Following plans prepared during the war and validated by the Allies in Potsdam in June 1945, the Czechoslovak authorities started to round up Germans in 1946. Soldiers had to separate the "Germans" from the "Slavs." The former were designated as "the mortal enemy of Slavic nations" and the "Ten Commandments of the Czechoslovak soldier in the borderlands" included "to behave as a victor, [. . .] to be tough with Germans [. . .]" and "hard with [the German women and the Hitler Youth who] also bear the guilt of the Germans' crimes."[22] Such a distinction between "us" and "them" could be equated with a brutal ethnicization of the population. For instance, an artillery detachment was sent to Silesia, in a territory called Hlučínsko, known for the widespread pro-German feelings of its inhabitants, independently of their native language.[23] In any case, only people of German nationality were expelled, as if the wartime standpoint of individuals did not matter: ethnicity, not loyalty, was a valuable criterion for Czechoslovak leaders.[24] By the end of 1946, most of the three million Czechoslovak Germans had been deported (mainly by train) to occupied Germany, under military supervision.

In some cases, the Czechoslovak soldiers went further: recent research counted around 30,000 Germans killed during massacres after the war, mainly in 1945. In several cases, the Czechoslovak authorities tolerated or encouraged violence. On at least one occasion, military men decided to kill unarmed civilians because of their ethnicity. On June 18, 1945, a rail convoy repatriating hundreds of Slovak Germans (and a few Hungarians) back to their homes stopped in the Moravian town of Přerov. The passengers had been evacuated by the German authorities during the last phase of the war. As the convoy came to a halt, Czechoslovak lieutenant Karol Pazúr decided that the travelers were Nazis and ordered his men to shoot them near the railway station. Altogether, 265 people were executed, including 120 women and 74 children. The inquiry showed that no active Nazi activists were among the victims, while some had supported the resistance in wartime Slovakia. Pazúr, the main perpetrator, later faced trial but served only one year in prison. He never expressed regrets.[25] That members of the military perceived Germans as mortal enemies was not only the consequence of the occupation. Strengthening hate and dehumanization, the army itself depicted the Germans as foreigners—their legal status after they were deprived of their citizenship by the Beneš decrees—and dangerous, even contagious, people. Even the Allies who had liberated Czechoslovakia sometimes felt uncomfortable with the Czechoslovak warfare against civilians from national minorities.[26] Once the Americans and Soviets had left Czechoslovakia in December 1945, there was no counter-power to protect them from the vengeful spirit of the Czech and Slovak masters.

During the postwar period, the Czechoslovak military was thus mobilized rather than demobilized to confront politically or ethnically defined threats: it gave birth to a new kind of state, more authoritarian and hostile to ethnic diversity. Focusing on the borderlands as the main space for "peace enforcement," the final section discusses the meaning of the voluntarism that Czechoslovak armed forces displayed after the war.

A Pyrrhic Victory in the Borderlands?
Peacemaking as the Last Stage of the War

European borderlands have been studied as places of both cooperation and conflict. Some cities and regions were home to multiethnic coexistence and the birthplace of unique cultural identities.[27] At the same time, nineteenth-century nation-building helped grant a special significance to borderlands, often associated with the quintessence of the nation, where healthy competition with hostile neighbors shaped a better-quality population.[28] This was, with local specificities, true of Transylvania, Alsace, Tyrol, Istria, Galicia, and many other multinational regions. In Czechoslovakia, the struggle for national supremacy was particularly strong in Bohemia and Moravia.[29] Germans and Czechs steadily reached a power balance, as the Czech national movement grew stronger in the late nineteenth century. The fall of the Habsburg Empire in 1918 further weakened the German nationalists: their leaders mobilized the so-called "Sudeten Germans" against the new state in the borderlands, aiming for secession and an *Anschluss* to Germany, but to no avail. However, throughout the interwar period, a mix of *völkisch* and more radical politics contributed to a pernicious revival of German nationalism. Until 1938, the Czechoslovak state had proven viable and Czech society quite vibrant and tolerant, but Nazi expansionism put an end to this multinational (though not fully satisfying for minorities) experiment. Again, the Czech-German contest was replayed, reducing most borderland Czechs to subjects of the Reich, if they did not flee their occupied land to seek refuge in central Bohemia and Moravia.

Consequently, as the war was being lost by Germany, the Czechoslovak leaders started to think about a way to win the historical contest between Slavs and non-Slavs. This project permeated internal army debates about the border. As it was clear that liberation and victory would be obtained and guaranteed by the great powers, it was the task of the national units to secure both this territorial recovery and new gains beyond the prewar border, if possible. As early as June 1944, a cartographic proposal was drafted, with minimum and maximum claims. Six months later, in January 1945, another proposition was made, with different maps and inflated "gradual" demands. The army leadership was pursuing at least three sets of goals: first, protecting the weaker flanks of elongated Czechoslovakia, by annexing portions of Silesia and lower Austria. Then, improving the economic position of the country, through better access to navigable rivers (notably the Oder), more agricultural flatlands, and ore deposits (for instance, bauxite in northern Hungary). And finally, making the

Slavic nation bigger, by the addition of border territories supposedly populated by Czechs (Kladsko/Glatz) or Slavs (Lusatia), a process complemented by the "remigration" of tens of thousands of people of Czech or Slavic descent living abroad.[30] This effort was largely ineffective, as the Allies—including the USSR—favored a relative territorial status quo in the region, in order to prevent further tensions: Hungary lost only a few villages on the southern bank of the Danube, to increase the size of the Bratislava bridgehead, and even Austria and Germany were left intact (setting aside the enormous losses to Poland and the Soviet Union in the East). If Czechoslovak military leaders had also envisioned occupying the German and Austrian slopes of the mountains surrounding the Czech lands, it never materialized: the American and Soviet troops retained their positions on the Bavarian and Saxon side.

Even without additional conquest, the reoccupation of the borderlands by the Czechoslovak troops was a challenge in itself, a war to be won after the official end of hostilities. Until late 1946, the overwhelming majority of the population was German. At the same time, Slavic (mostly Czech) colonists came to settle in this area, attracted by opportunities to seize abandoned properties and companies. The territorial repartition of military and security forces reflected the priorities of the Czechoslovak leadership: in addition to SNB border units (the most militarized of the police forces), local police and customs stations covered the towns and the countryside. The army itself maintained 177 territorial commands, each supervising one or several local military detachments.[31] In rural areas, a company or battalion-size unit was generally garrisoned in a small town, covering the adjacent area. Naturally, many of the units were located in the Czech and Slovak hinterland, where Habsburg and later First Republic Czechoslovak units had been accommodated for decades. Yet, a great number of units were also stationed in the borderlands, notably along the northern and western border, the new "frontier" of Czech nationalism.[32] There, Czech and Slovak soldiers were garrisoning the main "German" cities of Tepliz, Reichenberg, Mährisch Schönberg, and Freudenthal but also smaller municipalities, at the heart of the former Sudetenland.

The military played an important role in the increasingly empty border territories. For local authorities under Czech control, soldiers provided security against the German majority and, after the expulsion of most of them, against returning Germans looking for their abandoned belongings or for resettlement. Moreover, because both the manpower and the consumers had vanished, the Czech colonists being too few, the military offered cheap labor and captive clients for the local markets. That is why many municipalities, including Benešov nad Černou (southern Bohemia), Bor u Tachova (western Bohemia), Josefov (northern Bohemia), and Valašské Meziříčí (eastern Moravia), were asking for a permanent military presence.[33] In Benešov nad Černou, the municipal council explained to the Ministry of Defense that 80 percent of its inhabitants had left (i.e., had been expelled) and that the police station of five men was insufficient to control the territory. Located 10 kilometers from Austria, the municipality faced thefts from Germans crossing the border and offered its empty school and other buildings to host a full battalion, also hoping for some help with agricultural work. The demand was supported by a few MPs from the area. The other small towns gave similar justifications, also fearing the departure of the few colonists who had settled in the borderlands. In Bor, the postwar garrison was planned for departure in the fall of 1947. The soldiers had to resettle in Stříbro, a bigger town close to Plzeň, the regional capital. The military reoccupation of what had been known in German as Haid (Bor) and Mies (Stříbro) was part of the transition to peace, at least a peace for the Czechs. Once the area was secured, the security troops (SNB) and the civilian administration (the municipality councils) would fully take over the local governance from the army. It was probably a sign that the military peacemaking was over, and garrisoning in Bor was no longer necessary by the end of 1947. Rather than pursuing peace and local stability, the military and other Czechoslovak state organs had made sure that the victory over the Germans had been completed. Settling the national struggle by eliminating the Germans certainly brought unilateral "peace," but it contributed to new social and economic problems the Czechoslovak state would try to overcome for decades (Figure 8.1).[34]

Whatever the national importance of the task, the military leadership was not really happy with the "pacification" mission assigned to the army. During the

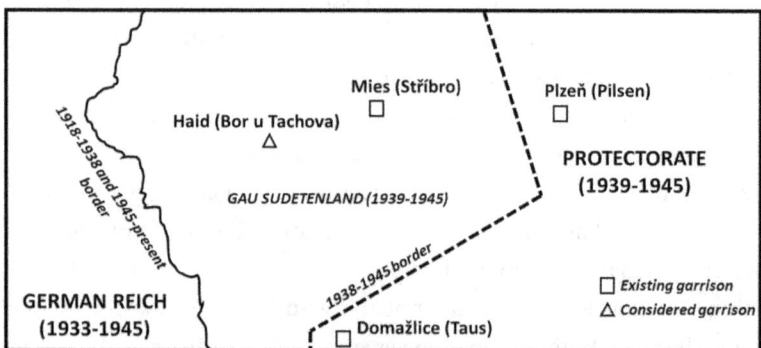

Figure 8.1 Location of a few garrisons in western Czechoslovakia (indicative wartime borders) designed by P. Lenormand, 2023.

weeks and months following the liberation, the reoccupation of the borderlands had been a legitimate military duty. But over time, it seemed that peacekeeping, which encompassed security missions and economic participation in national reconstruction, prevented the army from doing its job. Indeed, with soldiers allocated to agriculture, foresting, mining, construction work, engineering, and clearing minefields, as well as supervising the *odsun* (expulsion of Germans) and assisting security forces against "bands," military training was neglected. Many in the ministry felt that it was not the army's vocation to make the inhabitants of the borderland feel safe or to support the local economy. The army often rejected requests from municipal councils, arguing that the borderland towns lacked adequate buildings for accommodation, space for training, or even decent hygienic conditions. In most cases, small units were left temporarily in remote border districts, until the Germans were gone—in Bor, for example, it was just one company. Peacekeeping was the result of a compromise between the army and the government bodies, but the military was not enthusiastic about it. By 1947, more important Cold War challenges requiring a stronger and more "military" army had already appeared and "peacemaking" in the borderlands was no longer a priority.

Conclusion

Postwar Central Europe suffered from widespread destruction and chronic instability, justifying a militarization of society to deal with the transition from total war to uncertain peace. In Czechoslovakia, the first aim of this mobilization was to ensure a complete victory over the ethnically defined enemies, the Germans. Additionally, mobilizing the military for reconstruction and national warfare served an internal political struggle for power. By assuming security and economic duties, the army was getting closer to civilians and, as a result, was increasingly politicized. Performing non-military duties involved daily contact with municipalities, cultural committees, and, by and large, political parties. In some areas, notably in the Czech borderlands, the local administrators were mostly Communists. For the "peacekeepers," enhanced cooperation with these fairly friendly partners eased the relationship between the military and the militancy, two historically hostile spheres. In other words, the borderlands witnessed the emergence of a militarized conception of governance shared by both Communists and nationalists, who tended to develop a common position on the ethnic question. The perspective of a nationally purified, more progressive, and pro-Soviet state seduced military audiences.

The Communist takeover in February 1948 put an end to the peace process in Czechoslovakia by initiating a new confrontation between the aggressive imperialistic West and the vulnerable democratic East. The borderlands, once again, became a place of—potential—warfare, justifying decades of militarization.

Notes

1   James Mace Ward, *Priest, Politician, Collaborator: Jozef Tiso and the Making of Fascist Slovakia* (Ithaca: Cornell University Press, 2013).

2   Mark Mazower, *Dark Continent: Europe's Twentieth Century* (London: Penguin Books, 1999).

3   Sabine Dullin, "How the Soviet Empire Relied on Diversity: Territorial Expansion and National Borders at the End of World War II in Ruthenia," in *Seeking Peace in the Wake of War: Europe, 1943–1947*, ed. Stefan-Ludwig Hoffmann, Sandrine Kott, Peter Romijn, and Olivier Wieviorka (Amsterdam: Amsterdam University Press, 2015), 217–46.

4   Catherine Goussef, *Échanger les peuples: Le déplacement des minorités aux confins polono-soviétiques (1944-1947)* (Paris: Fayard, 2015).

5   Bojan B. Dimitrijević, *Jugoslovenska armija 1945–1954: nova ideologija, vojnik i oružje* (Belgrade: Institut za savremenu istoriju, 2006).

6   Timothy Snyder, *Bloodlands: Europe Between Hitler and Stalin* (New York: Basic Books, 2010); George Reklaitis, "Cold War Lithuania: National Armed Resistance and Soviet Counterinsurgency," *The Carl Beck Papers in Russian & East European Studies*, no. 1086 (2007): 1–43.

7   John Horne, "Demobilizing the Mind: France and the Legacy of the Great War, 1919-1939," *French History and Civilization: Papers from the George Rudé Seminar* 2 (2009): 101–19.

8   Elie Tenenbaum, *Partisans et centurions: Une histoire de la guerre irrégulière au XXᵉ siècle* (Paris: Perrin, 2018).

9   Miloslav Čaplovič, *Branné organizácie v Československu 1918–1939 (so zretelom na Slovensko)* (Bratislava: Ministerstvo obrany SR, 2001); Robert Gerwarth and John Horne (eds.), *War in Peace: Paramilitary Violence in Europe after the Great War* (Oxford: Oxford University Press, 2012), 16.

10 Martin Zückert, *Zwischen Nationsidee und staatlicher Realität: Die tschechoslowakische Armee und ihre Nationalitätenpolitik 1918–1938* (Munich: Oldenbourg, 2006).

11 Radan Lášek, *Velitelé praporů SOS* (Prague: Codyprint, 2009).

12 Paul Lenormand, "Vers l'armée du peuple: Autorité, pouvoir et culture militaire en Tchécoslovaquie de Munich à la fin du stalinisme" (PhD manuscript, Sciences Po Paris, Paris, France, 2019).

13 Tomáš Jakl, "Povstalci, gardisté, vojáci a příslušníci SNB—vývoj ozbrojených složek ČSR v létě 1945," in *Od svobody k nesvobodě 1945–1956,* ed. Ivo Pejčoch (Prague: MO České republiky, 2011), 50–69.

14 Lenormand, "Vers l'armée du peuple," 363–434.

15 Molly Pucci, *Security Empire: The Secret Police in Communist Eastern Europe* (New Haven: Yale University Press, 2020).

16 Report from SNB, April 5, 1950. Resistance group "Alex-Mimoň." SPB, box 109, Czech National Archives, Prague, Czech Republic.

17 On France, see Claire Miot, "Rentrer dans le rang? L'intégration des combattants issus de la Résistance intérieure dans la Première armée française (1944–1945)," in *Pratiques militaires et globalisation. XIXe-XXIe siècles,* ed. Walter Bruyère-Ostells and François Dumasy (Aix-en-Provence: Bernard Giovanangeli, 2014), 147–60.

18 Czechoslovakia, however, had better postwar conditions than Poland or Romania: no Soviet "occupation" and mass stationing of forces, less destruction, and a relatively consensual political coalition of six parties. For a general overview, see Bradley Abrams, "The Second World War and the East European Revolution," *East European Politics and Societies* 16, no. 3 (2002): 623–64.

19 Prokop Drtina, *Československo, můj osud,* vol. 1 (Prague: Melantrich, 1991), 412.

20 Report from general Kratochvíl, December 31, 1945, box 6, file 906, Vojenský ústřední archiv (VÚA).

21 43th infantry regiment (Hodonín), box 1, VÚA.

22 *Svobodné Československo,* June 16, 1945, 2.

23 Regimental diary. May 24, 1946 entry, June–July 1947 entries, 107th artillery regiment (Opava), box 1, VÚA.

24 Hlučínsko was a former Prussian territory, annexed by Czechoslovakia in 1920, reannexed by Nazi Germany in 1938, and reintegrated again to Czechoslovakia in 1945. The majority of the population spoke a Czech dialect (and was registered in the census as people of Czech nationality) but supported Germany—most of them voted for the Nazis in the 1935 elections and many served in the German military during both world wars.

25 Indictment from attorney Rašla, June 16, 1948, Vrchný Vojenský Sud Bratislava, box 3, Slovak Military History Archives. Bratislava, Slovakia.

26 Justine Faure, *L'ami américain : La Tchécoslovaquie, enjeu de la diplomatie américaine, 1943–1968* (Paris: Tallandier, 2004).

27 Delphine Bechtel and Xavier Galmiche (eds.), "Villes multiculturelles en Europe centrale," *Cultures d'Europe centrale,* no. 8 (2009).

28 Anne-Marie Thiesse, *La création des identités nationales* (Paris: Seuil, 1999).

29 Jeremy King, *Budweisers into Czechs and Germans: A Local History of Bohemian Politics, 1848–1948* (Princeton: Princeton University Press, 2002).

30 See, for instance, the postwar studies on Kladsko. Report from March 18, 1947, D 13469, AKPR.

31 List of territorial commands, August 11, 1945, MNO45, box 198, file 20019, VÚA.

32 These areas were the most densely populated of the Bohemian German-speaking districts. The south and southwest was more sparsely populated and required less "peacemakers." Population maps, Jana Jíchová (eds.), *Historický atlas obyvatelstva českých zemí* (Prague: Karolinum, 2017), 30.

33 Postwar correspondence, 1945–7, MNO47, box 2, file 834; box 8, file 4711; box 15, file 12273; VR PPV, box 1, VÚA.

34 Eagle Glassheim, *Cleansing the Czechoslovak Borderlands: Migration, Environment, and Health in the Former Sudetenland* (Pittsburgh: University of Pittsburgh Press, 2016).

Part III

The Military as a Source of Expertise

9

Alexei Orlov, General of the Russian Army and Military in the Service of Diplomacy

Elena Linkova

Annotation

This chapter is devoted to the diplomatic activity of the Russian general Count Alexei Orlov, who took a direct part not only in military operations but also in the process of drafting and signing key treaties on behalf of Russia with the countries of Western Europe and the Ottoman Empire in the period from the 1820s to the 1850s. This study shows that the military is often quite active in the peace process and has good training that helps in diplomacy. Count Orlov was one such military figure. Examining Orlov's personality makes it possible, using the methods of historical and military-historical anthropology, to study the peculiarities of the influence of the individual on the development of the country's foreign policy.

Examining the activities of Alexei Orlov is all the more interesting, since his name is associated with the solution of the Eastern question, so relevant for Russia and Western countries in the nineteenth century. Both as a general of the Russian army and as a diplomat, Orlov played an important role in establishing Russia's authority in the Middle East.

Introduction

Peace agreements have often become the fruit of the work not only of diplomats but also of the military. These are servicemen, with accurate data on the capabilities of the army, on the deployment of troops, who became the heads of diplomatic missions when concluding treaties. Russian General Alexei Orlov represented Russia at the largest international congresses in the years 1820–50. Thanks to its activities, Russia signed a number of important agreements, for example: the Treaty of Adrianopole (also called the Treaty of Edirne) in 1829, the Treaty of Unkiar-Skelessi in 1833, and the Treaty of Paris in March 1856.

The Purpose and Objectives of This Research

The purpose of this research is to analyze the characteristics of the actions and the role of the military in international congresses and conferences. To achieve this goal, the author proposes to study the diplomatic activities of Russian Army General Alexei Orlov.

The relevance of the topic lies in the need to study a statesman in the extreme conditions generated by war or international tension. The participation of the military in the peace process, in negotiations, and in the settlement of the conflict presents us with a rather rare situation for the nineteenth century, but this practice can serve as an example for our days.

It is important to note that the study of the activities of Alexei Orlov makes it possible to analyze the events of the mid-nineteenth century from the point of view of historical anthropology. Often, when describing battles and diplomatic struggles, Russian and foreign scientists lose sight of the person with his passions and thoughts, the creator of these events. In our opinion, the attempt to analyze a historical event through the personality and its active participation is a kind of prism for understanding the subject of the study.

Research Sources and Methodology

The corpus of sources gathered for this study includes a set of published documents, in particular, the correspondence of Count Alexei Orlov with Louis Napoleon[1] and official documents: manifestos for the conclusion of peace, international treaties, and so on.[2]

Degree of Development of the Subject

Turning to the historiography of the problem allows us to form an idea and draw a conclusion about the degree of study of the topic among researchers. Historians have studied the personality and activities of Alexei Orlov in the framework of studies on the history of the Crimean War and the Conclusion of the Treaty of Paris,[3] analyzing the nature of Russian-Turkish relations in the late 1820s–30s,[4] as well as in the study of Russian-French relations in the 1840s–50s.[5] However, until now, none of this work offers a study dedicated to the analysis of the role of a military in the diplomatic process of settling international disputes.

This study aims to partially fill the gap that has formed in this regard for the personality and diplomatic activities of Alexei Orlov.

Methodological Basis of the Chapter

In addition to the general principles of historiography (historicism and method of comparative history), the methodological approaches used in this study correspond to the specificity and nature of the corpus of sources. The methods of analysis of intellectual history and the history of international relations were used for this purpose. The present study thus involves the methodology of historical anthropology by reconstructing the emotional aspect of diplomacy.

Research

Referring to the diplomatic activities of Alexei Orlov, it seems necessary to analyze the events of the late 1820s.

For the first time as a diplomat, Alexei Orlov participated in the negotiations with Turkey that led to the signing of the Adrianople peace treaty in 1829. The text of this treaty was drawn up in St. Petersburg, and Orlov had to convince the gate to accept Russian terms. Orlov's perseverance and especially the military measures taken by the Russian commander-in-chief Ivan Dibich-Zabalkansky forced the Turks to sign this document. After that, in October 1829, Orlov was appointed ambassador to Constantinople, where he successfully solved the task assigned to him and managed to ensure the conditions of the Treaty. The July Revolution of 1830 in France prompted Nicholas I to send Orlov to Vienna to find opportunities for joint actions with Austria against France. However, his journey did not succeed. Before his arrival in Vienna, Austria, like England and Prussia, recognized Louis-Philippe as king of France.

In 1831, Orlov led the suppression of the "cholera revolt" in St. Petersburg and of uprisings in military settlements.[6] In 1832, he carried out a diplomatic mission to Prussia, the Netherlands, and England. In 1833, he was Ambassador Extraordinary and Plenipotentiary to the Turkish Sultan; he managed to sign the Treaty of Unkiar-Skelessi, which was very advantageous for Russia. This treaty with Turkey was a great success of Russian diplomacy in the Middle East. The Treaty of Unkiar-Skelessi was very carefully prepared by Alexei Orlov, who remained almost two months before the signing of the treaty in Constantinople. Then in diplomatic circles, it was joked that in Constantinople at the beginning of July, there remained only one person who was not bribed by Orlov and it was Sultan Mahmud II. But only this fact cannot explain Orlov's brilliant diplomatic success. This victory was all the more valuable because it was achieved without war, only through diplomacy.

This was the rare case when the military force lost diplomacy. With the level of development of international relations that took place in the nineteenth century, the best and most effective way to resolve the foreign policy conflict was to wage a war. The example of the Treaty of Unkiar-Skelessi demonstrates another possibility.

The prerequisites for the Unkiar-Skelessi treaty were worked out in St. Petersburg and delivered by Orlov to Constantinople. This treaty was signed on June 26, 1833, was defensive in nature, and was concluded for a period of eight years.[7]

Russian historians of the nineteenth century believed that the Treaty of Unkiar-Skelessi was the crowning achievement of Russian diplomacy and, at the same time, a kind of beginning of confrontation with the West because of the Eastern question. This document is "worthy of completion . . . of a number of our glorious treatises with the Sublime Porte, determining the dominant position of Russia in the Eastern question."[8] In addition, the agreement with Turkey contributed to the stabilization of the situation in the region; during this period the influence on the Sultan by the Western powers was small, so the Ottoman Empire "gave itself under the patronage of the Russian tsar, the ruler sincerely refused any intention to conquer on his own."[9] But such a state of affairs did not satisfy neither the British, nor the Austrians, nor the French, for them the Russian-Turkish treaty became literally a "thunder in a cloudless sky."[10] Russian publicist and diplomat Sergei Tatishchev stressed the legality of the agreement from the point of view of international law. According to him, "Turkey was an independent power and able to enter into alliances with those it wanted, without reporting to anyone on their terms. Moreover, the treaty did not create a new provision, but only legitimized the fact of Allied aid, in fact deposited by Russia to the Sultan."[11] But the reaction of European courts was clearly hostile. The victory of Russian diplomacy "was perceived as a threat to British and French interests, as a 'treaty by force torn from the Sultan.'"[12] Therefore, immediately after 1833, Western countries took a number of actions aimed at leveling the successes of Russia and limiting Russian influence in the Middle East.

Sergei Tatishchev emphasized that the position of Western countries at that time was consistent in its anti-Russian orientation. And although "Prince Metternich kept silent, he even claimed that he was not at all disturbed by the new manifestation of Russian influence on the Bosphorus. But in London and especially in Paris, there was a loud cry that Russia had transformed into supremacy and patronage the pre-eminence it had enjoyed for a long time in Constantinople."[13] The historian quoted the text of the official dispatch from France, which contained an accusation against Russia: "The St. Petersburg cabinet wanted, in front of the whole of Europe, to openly proclaim, to erect as a principle of popular law its exclusive and out-of-reach predominance in the affairs of the Ottoman Empire."[14] The statement of the Ministry of Foreign Affairs of France seemed quite loyal in relation to the statements made to Russia by François Guizot.

As Sergei Tatishchev noted, in his accusations, the French leader "goes even further," baselessly claiming that "by this treaty, Turkey was transformed into an official client of Russia, The Black Sea into a Russian lake, the entry of which was guarded by the designated client against the enemies of Russia, while the exit remained free for her, and she could at any time send her ships and troops to the Mediterranean."[15]

At the same time, Count Orlov's diplomatic activity was not limited to his participation in international congresses. In 1830, he was sent to Vienna to carry out an armed intervention project of the powers of Saint Alliance to restore the Bourbon dynasty in France. By the way, for Orlov, the failure of his mission was obvious, and after enjoying in Vienna, he returned to Russia.

In 1847, even before his election to the presidency of the French Republic, Louis Napoleon made several attempts through the head of the Russian secret police, Count Orlov, to enter into personal contact with Nicholas I in the hope of obtaining the tsar's help in the implementation of his plans in France.

Louis Napoleon asked Count Orlov to become his lawyer, and this was the term used by the future emperor of the French: "I therefore beg you, Monsieur le Comte, to be my lawyer, and I would be happy to owe you such a great service."[16]

Documents from the Archives of Foreign Affairs of the Russian Empire show that the history of the relations of Nicholas I and Louis Napoleon began in 1847, that is, before the latter's election to the post of President of the French Republic in December 1848. Analyzing documents from the Archives of Foreign Affairs of the Russian Empire historian Peter Cherkassov demonstrated that personal contacts with Nicholas I and the St. Petersburg cabinet "the future president and Emperor of the French tried to establish as early as the spring of 1847, when he lived in London as an emigrant."[17] In these attempts, an important role was assigned to Alexei Orlov.

In 1847, Louis Napoleon in a letter to Alexei Orlov asked the emperor permission to come to St. Petersburg on a private visit. Louis Napoleon motivated this request by his desire to get acquainted with Russia. He wrote to Orlov: "for a long time one of my greatest desires has been to have the honor of being presented to the emperor, for since my earliest childhood I feel for the memories of your great empire the feelings of gratitude that the generous conduct of Emperor Alexander towards my mother in 1814 inspired me."[18] But all these attempts turned out to be unsuccessful. Nicholas I was very concerned about the threat of the spread of the revolution in European countries. Even the promise of Louis Napoleon to restore order in France and thus contribute to the restoration of "calm" in Europe in exchange for financial assistance from Russia (1 million francs a year) did not impress the Russian emperor. Louis Napoleon asked for money, and he stressed that restoring order in France was "a difficult but not impossible undertaking. But to achieve this great goal, there is a lack of money."[19] Nicholas I refused Louis Napoleon his financial support.

Subsequently, Count Orlov, while chief of the gendarmes, continued to perform diplomatic missions to the Russian emperor. He met with general Lamorissier to express his concern about the situation in France.

I wonder how Nicholas I would behave if he knew that in three months, in December 1848, Louis Napoleon would become president of the French Republic, and then emperor of France? Obviously, this was a miscalculation of Nicholas I against Louis Napoleon. This fault, committed in 1847–8, was aggravated in the years before the Crimean War. And perhaps in September 1855, when the French flag was flown over the destroyed bastions of Sevastopol, the young Emperor Alexander II became angry with his father who so stubbornly rejected the friendship that had been offered to him by Louis Napoleon.

Another example of Orlov's successful diplomatic activities is the Paris conference in 1856, which was convened as a result of the Crimean War, lost by Russia. Due to the fact that Orlov managed to find a common language with Napoleon III, the Russian delegation obtained sufficiently advantageous solutions on a number of issues. For example, with regard to concessions on the territory of Bessarabia, where Austria was the main opponent, the Russian Commissioner—Orlov, with the effective support of Napoleon III, managed to win over the negotiating limits that he wanted to grant. As a result, the territorial concessions of Russia in Bessarabia were minimal. Orlov conducted negotiations correctly, gave in where it was inevitable, and showed firmness where it was possible to succeed.

According to Russian historians, it was thanks to Orlov, his excellent knowledge of the military potential and capabilities of Russia and the international position of Great Britain, that the confrontation with Lord Clarendon ended, and the latter was not able to implement British diplomacy projects regarding the Caucasus. These projects provided for large territorial concessions from Russia and the neutralization of not only the Black Sea but also the Sea of Azov. It is known that the peace treaty as a result of the Crimean War was signed on March 18, 1856, which recorded the defeat of Russia in the war. But it should be noted that Orlov managed to give the Treaty such a worthy appearance that the French ambassador in Vienna had every reason to say: "one can not understand, after reading this document, who is the winner here, and who is defeated."[20] He said this about the treaty signed after the defeat when it was very heavy for Russia. After signing this document, Orlov participated in the elaboration of the articles of the Paris Declaration on the law of the sea, an important international instrument aimed at regulating maritime trade and blockade in time of war as well as prohibiting corsairs.

Orlov was a supporter of the rapprochement between Russia and France. In 1847 and 1855–6, he had the opportunity to express his feelings toward France. From the first moment of the stay at the Paris conference in February to March 1856, Orlov concentrated all his activities to get closer to the emperor of the French, Napoleon III. Several secret negotiations took place between the French emperor and Orlov. Arriving in Paris, Orlov, during the first conversation with Napoleon III, took the course for a close rapprochement between Russia and France, saying that there is, indeed, no contradiction between our countries.

As a qualified serviceman, Orlov chose his original tactics for negotiations. For example, before the solemn sessions of the Paris Congress, he spoke to Napoleon III, clarifying the position of the emperor of the French on certain points of the future Treaty of Paris. Thanks to this situation, close interaction with Napoleon III, Orlov was able to face England and Austria. According to the memories of Russian diplomats, the head of the Russian mission always had figures and exact information about the possibilities of the Russian army. He was collecting information about the army from Russian opponents and all these allowed him to make the right decision and course of action in Congress.

As a result of Orlov's actions, Austria had to leave the Congress, not receiving from the allies the payment of its ultimatum to Russia on December 2, 1855.

Orlov, like several Russian servicemen—General Ivan Paskevich, General Rostislav Fadeev—was convinced that it was Austria that was the main opponent of Russia in the settlement of the Eastern question. Another opponent, which was traditionally opposed to Russia, was Britain. But according to the military, France had no deep reason to be hostile toward Russia. And it was necessary to use this circumstance to strengthen the positions of Russia, lost during the Crimean War.

Knowledge of the capabilities of his own army and the enemy army, and the use of a set of diplomatic and military arguments during negotiations helped Orlov, a career military man, to succeed in the diplomatic field. Sometimes, when diplomats do not find the right solution, the military enters the negotiation process. It is they who often succeed, not allowing to start a bloody war.

It is noteworthy that the military in the capacity of diplomats sometimes presented a strategy that was distinguished by the combination of foreign and military policy aspects, taking into account the data on the armaments and fortifications of Russia.

In general, the role of the military in the service of diplomacy is of some interest. The study of this issue allows expanding the conceptual framework of research on the history of international relations to understand the specifics of the methods of a military diplomat.

However, the signing of the Treaty of Paris in 1856 became a new stage of the war, no longer by the forces of the army and navy but by diplomacy. Even before the end of military activities in Crimea, negotiations began in Vienna, in which the allies, and more precisely the Austrians, put forward quite strict demands on Russia.

Count Orlov's methods can be evaluated based on the analysis of his position at the Paris Congress of 1856. The ideas and proposals of the count show us that Russia did not behave like a defeated country.

Alexei Orlov proved himself a skilled diplomat "yielding where it was inevitable, he showed firmness in areas where it was possible to succeed."[21] At the same time, one should not forget that Orlov had serious and solid "arguments" in discussions with his opponents. This is about the victories achieved by Russian troops in the Caucasus. Being a military man, Orlov well represented the price of these trophies and skillfully used them in the negotiation process.

So, for example, the Austrians demanded Bessarabia, but at this request Count Orlov replied: "Mr. Austrian commissioner does not know what sea of tears and blood will cost his country such a correction of borders."[22]

Orlov also mocked and roughly negotiated with the English foreign minister, Lord Clarendon. Russia agreed, for example, to "neutralize the Black Sea" and not to keep on its shores naval arsenals and not to restore the Black Sea navy.

But besides the base in Sevastopol, Russia then had another base on the Black Sea—the city of Nikolaev, in which there were shipyards and a military arsenal. British diplomats believed that Nikolaev should therefore be disarmed, and his yards should be destroyed in accordance with the peace treaty. However, Count Orlov responded to this request that Nikolaev was not on the Black Sea shore, but on the Bug River, and the Paris agreements did not apply to Russian facilities on this river.

Everyone knew perfectly well that Nikolaev stood on the Bug estuary and therefore was on the Black Sea. They also knew that the estuary was navigable even for large ships. But Orlov's opponents could not bend Russia on this issue. Moreover, Russia defended its right to keep several more ships in the Black Sea, the count telling his "Western partners" that if Russia deems it necessary, it will build these ships in Nikolaev.

During the negotiations, there were also discussions about Russian forts on the Eastern coast of the Black Sea. Some of them had been destroyed during the war, and Lord Clarendon stated in this regard that the Russian forts in this area were arsenals designated by another name. Thus, in fact, according to the British diplomat, Russia had no right to rebuild these strongholds, which Count Orlov opposed because, according to him, forts and arsenals were two separate things and that as a result, Russia should not respond positively to Britain's demands.

British diplomats attempted to address the economic issue in an attempt to force Russia to make Sevastopol a free trade area, but again their demands were not accepted. Finally, Russia, through the voice of Count Orlov, refused to pay war indemnities to the winning countries.

Conclusion

As a result, the terms of the Treaty of Paris signed by Russia and its opponents in March 1856 did not seem to suit any of the participants in the war. Despite all the efforts of the Russian mission in Paris, in Russian public opinion, the Paris Agreement was treated as humiliating. Moreover, such assessments were characteristic of conservative and liberal politicians. For example, according to the Russian liberal publicist and historian Alexander Gradovsky, "the Treaty of Paris was nothing more than an attempt to bury several million Turkish Christians and put into oblivion a huge country with a population of 80 million."[23] At the same time, in the countries of Western Europe, there was also not much enthusiasm for the results of the war. Mikhail Pogodin, a Russian historian and publicist, pointed out that "at the Paris conference there were disagreements that make it possible to foresee the future struggle in other countries of Europe and with other allies."[24] In fact, this struggle did not take long, showing that the Crimean War did not end the famous Eastern question, but, on the contrary, it ignited it with new force.

However, despite the obvious incompleteness in solving the Eastern question, Alexei Orlov, both as a general of the Russian army and as a diplomat, played an important role in minimizing the damage to Russia on the southern borders, which later made it possible to restore Russia's authority, role, and influence in the region in the near future.

Notes

1 Neizvestnaja perepiska Lui Napoleona Bonaparta s grafom A. F. Orlovym, nachal'nikom Tret'ego Otdelenija (1847–8) [Unknown correspondence between Louis Napoleon Bonaparte and Count A. F. Orlov (1847–8)], Iz fondov Gosudarstvennogo arhiva Rossijskoj Federacii, Gosudarstvennyj arhiv Rossijskoj Federacii (GARF), in *Rossija i Francija. XVIII–XX veka. Vypusk 9. Otvetstvennyj redaktor i sostavitel'*, ed. Petr P. Cherkasov (Moscow, 2009), 166–89.

2 Manifest Nikolaja I po povodu revoljucii 1848 g. vo Francii, Germanii i Avstro-Vengrii i o vystuplenii russkih vojsk na podavlenie vosstanija v Vengrii [Manifesto of Nicholas I on the revolution of 1848 in France, Germany and Austria-Hungary and on the action of Russian troops to suppress the uprising in Hungary], 14 marta 1848, 672/1/198, GARF; "Parizhskij traktat, Parizh 18/30 marta 1856" [Treaty of Paris]; "Sbornik dogovorov Rossii s drugimi gosudarstvami 1856–1917" [Collection of treaties of Russia with other states], Histrf.ru, December 15, 2015, https://histrf .ru/lenta-vremeni/event/view/parizhskii-traktat; Runivers, "Dogovory Rossii s Vostokom. Politicheskie i torgovye. Saint-Peterbourg 1869" [Treaties between Russia and the East. Political and commercial. Saint Petersburg], https://runivers.ru /bookreader/book456128/#page/1/mode/1up.

3 Mikhail P. Pogodin, *Istoriko-politicheskie pis'ma i zapiski v prodolzhenii Krymskoj vojny. 1853–1856* [Historical and political letters and notes in the continuation of the Crimean War. 1853–1856] (Moscow: V. M. Frish, 1874); Vardan J. Bagdasarjan, *Russkaja vojna: stoletnij istoriograficheskij opyt osmyslenija Krymskoj kampanii*

[The Russian War: a Century-long historiographical experience of Understanding the Crimean Campaign] (Moscow: Izd-vo Moskovskogo otkrytogo universiteta, 2002); *Bor'ba imperij,* "Kruglyj stol" zhurnala Rodina, posvjashhennyj prichinam, itogam i posledstvijam Krymskoj vojny [The struggle of empires. "Round table" of the magazine "Rodina," dedicated to the causes, results and consequences of the Crimean War], *Rodina,* 1995, 3–4; Andrei M. Zajonchkovskij, *Vostochnaja vojna, 1853–1856,* vol. 2 (Saint Petersburg: Polygon, 2002); Elena V. Linkova and Marc de Bollivier, "Francuzskaja istoriografija Krymskoj vojny (1853–1856 gg.): osnovnye napravlenija i tendencii" [French historiography of the Crimean War (1853-1856): main directions and trends], *RUDN Journal of Russian History* 19, no. 3 (2020): 240–53.

4   Nikolay Nikolayevich Muravyov-Amursky, *Russkie na Bosfore v 1833 godu. Iz zapisok N.N. Murav'eva (Karsskogo)* [Russians on the Bosphorus in 1833. From the notes of N.N. Muravyov (Karssky)] (Moscow: Tipografija A. I. Mamontova, 1869).

5   *Rossija i Chernomorskie prolivy (XVIII–XX stoletija)* [Russia and the Black Sea Straits (XVIII–XX centuries).] (Institute Ros. History of the Russian Academy of Sciences: Moscow, 1999); Sergei S. Tatishchev, *Vneshnjaja politika Imperatora Nikolaja Pervogo. Vvedenie v istoriju vneshnih snoshenij Rossii v jepohu Sevastopol'skoj vojny* [Foreign policy of Emperor Nicholas I. Introduction to the history of Russia's foreign relations in the era of the Sevastopol war] (I. N. Skorokhodova: Saint Petersburg, 1887); Sergei S. Tatishchev, *Imperator Nikolaj i inostrannye dvory. Istoricheskie ocherki. Saint-Peterbourg* [Emperor Nicholas and foreign courts. Historical essays. Saint Petersburg] (Saint Petersburg: I. N. Skorokhodova, 1889); Oleg R. Airapetov, *Vneshnjaja politika Rossijskoj imperii (1801–1914)* [Foreign policy of the Russian Empire (1801–1914)] (Moscow: Publishing House "Europe," 2006); Rafael A. Arslanov and Elena V. Linkova, *Strany Zapada i ih vneshnjaja politika v vosprijatii rossijskih konservatorov i liberalov XIX veka* [The countries of the West and their foreign policy in the perception of Russian conservatives and liberals of the XIX century] (Moscow: RUDN Publishing House, 2018).

6   Military settlements were a special organization of the Russian military forces in 1816–57 (in particular, the cavalry units stationed in the south of the country and the infantry in the northwest), which combined military service and agricultural employment.

7   Runivers, "Dogovory Rossii s Vostokom. Politicheskie i torgovye. Saint-Peterbourg 1869."

8   Tatishchev, *Vneshnjaja politika Imperatora Nikolaja Pervogo,* 381.

9   Ibid.

10 Ibid.

11 Ibid., 382.

12 Ibid., 383.

13 Ibid.

14 Ibid.

15 Ibid.

16 Neizvestnaja perepiska Lui Napoleona Bonaparta s grafom A.F. Orlovym, nachal'nikom Tret'ego Otdelenija (1847–1848), GARF; Cherkasov, *Rossija i Francija*, 172.

17 Petr P. Cherkasov, *Nikolaj I i Lui Napoleon Bonapart (1848-1852)* [Nicholas I and Louis Napoleon Bonaparte (1848-1852)], 3 (Moscow, 2012), 124–65; Cherkasov, *Rossija i Francija,* 127.

18 Napoléon Louis Bonaparte au Général Orlov. Londres, le 24 Avril 1847 [Napoleon Louis Bonaparte to General Orlov. London, April 24, 1847], Political correspondence. Archives des Affaires Etrangères, Russia; Cherkasov, *Rossija i Francija*, 171.

19 Ibid., 173.

20 "Календарь: 30 марта 1856 г." [Calendar: March 30, 1856], Runiverse, https://runivers.ru/Runivers/calendar2.php?ID=62223.

21 *Rossija i Chernomorskie prolivy (XVIII–XX stoletija)*, 163.

22 "Austrian Emperor Franz Joseph and Russia: from Nicholas I to Nicholas II," *New Vienna Journal*, January 31, 2019, https://www.russianvienna.com/istoricheskie-materialy/4451-100-letiyu-okonchaniya-pervoj-mirovoj-vojny-posvyashchaetsya.

23 Alexander D. Gradovsky, *Slavjanskij vopros i vojna 1877 goda. Pol'skij vopros* [The Slavic Question and the War of 1877. The Polish question] (Moscow: M. M. Stasyulevich, 2017), 113.

24 Mikhail P. Pogodin, *Rossija v otnoshenii k vostochnym plemenam* [Russia in relation to the Eastern tribes], 1–4 (Moskvitjanin: Moscow, 1856), 28.

10

The Naval Officer, a Peacekeeper in Europe (1815–48)?

Keeping European Peace Overseas and Consolidating French Naval Power

Hélène Vencent

Introduction

This case study will focus on the years between 1815 and 1848, the period of the Bourbon Restoration and the July Monarchy in France. Those years mark a desire on the part of European powers to regain stability after the Napoleonic era, which destabilized the continent through its dynamics of hegemony. The Vienna Congress in 1815 formalized and implemented this stability and gave rise to the Holy Alliance and a Europe constructed by congresses, to which the European powers adhered in various ways.[1]

However, it should be noted that this European stability manifested itself on the continent itself rather than overseas: Britain saw its naval ambitions reinforced and confirmed its domination over a number of strategic locations (Malta, Cape Town, Mauritius, Saint Lucia, Tobago, etc.). French expansion on the European continent may have been halted and limited, but overseas France retained domination over some of its territories in the Indian Ocean and the Caribbean. These territories justified de facto the continued existence of the French navy, which secured contacts with the mainland and soon took on the role of maintaining relays and waypoints for French ambitions overseas.

During those years, by taking part in the various congresses, the French kingdom played by the rules of European stability and was careful not to provoke Britain too blatantly, so as not to concern its island neighbor. Nevertheless, successive French governments increasingly allowed themselves to dream about territorial expansion overseas. Their aim was to carry out this expansion within the limits set by the Vienna Peace treaty and continually maintain a modicum of concord with Great Britain. Naval officers found themselves key players in this expansion while having to stay within the boundaries of peace in Europe.

This conundrum, safekeeping diplomatic relations with Britain without giving up overseas expansion, was at the heart of the navy's mission in the first half of the nineteenth century.

Many locations for this expansion can be studied, but we will focus on three that showcase French ambitions to expand in extra-European territories. We will start with an observation mission in the Caribbean at the beginning of the 1820s, a region then confronting numerous tensions. We will then move to the Indian Ocean, where France's expansionary ambitions took the shape of rather tentative conquests around the time of the 1830 revolution. Last, we will study the Pacific area during the 1840s, where the navy found itself involved in influence missions and colonial wars, while tensions with Britain were flaring up again on mainland Europe.

Introductory Remarks: The Naval Officer, a Key Player in European Overseas Geopolitics

This study is based on the reports written by the naval officers in charge of the three missions mentioned earlier. Their careers reflect the evolution of French power induced by peace: they are the young men schooled at the *Ecoles spéciales de Marine* created by Napoleon in 1811 to restore the navy after the crisis caused by the Ile d'Aix fire ships in 1809.[2] They were then at the heart of a strategy to reorganize a navy that was unable to match that of Britain. But the career of these young men started in 1815, with the instauration of peace: while they were trained to be key players in the strategy to defeat Britain, they ended up being tasked to uphold European peace.

The officers' corps examined in this study led to the replacement of the war navy in the long term. This navy had its roots in the *Ancien Régime*, evolved during the revolutionary and imperial eras, and survived the Restoration. It was always a political tool: if the political power need to go to war, the navy went to war, and if it needed peace, the navy would ensure that peace. The careers of these officers show clearly that war is just one task of the navy among many others, for example, the ability to ensure contact between the government in Paris and the extra-European margins and to conduct extremely diverse scientific or deployment missions. Officers obviously played a key part in all of these tasks that had to adapt to specific political needs. The fact that their missions allowed the government to look beyond European matters also gave them a unique perspective on France (Figure 10.1).

Spaces of intervention of the naval officer

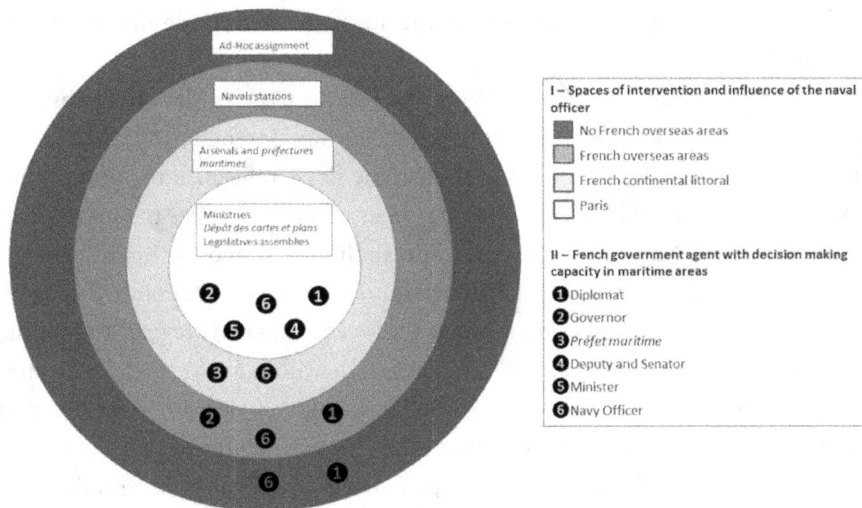

Figure 10.1 Spaces of intervention of the naval officer designed by H. Vencent, 2023.

Among agents of the French government, naval officers were the only ones who played a part in all the geographical spheres subject to French intervention: Paris, the provinces, French overseas, and non-French overseas territories. This gave them unique expertise, with two important elements:

First there was a time lag between their activities and those of the government: this time lag did not disappear entirely but started to decrease in the course of the nineteenth century with technical progress.

Secondly their missions were manifold, often with both diplomatic and military goals but also relating to scientific research and intelligence gathering.

In the years we aim to study, naval officers took part in more peacetime than wartime missions. Armed operations, like the capture of Cadiz in 1823, of Algiers in 1830, and of Vera Cruz in 1838/39 took place regularly during those years but they did not define them.

The Caribbean: showcasing France's ability to sustain civil peace overseas

Was it possible to give the navy back its ability to act without endangering the peace? The issue of abolition of the slave trade

The slave trade was not only a European matter. While legislation on the trade was passed in European capitals and European ports like Bordeaux, Nantes, and Liverpool thrived from it economically, not to mention the considerable financial interests involved, it also took place in regions far from Europe, embracing the African continent and the sugar-producing islands, mainly in the Caribbean.

In Europe, Britain had been paving the way to pass legislation against the slave trade, and it was formally abolished by law on March 25, 1807. The scope of this law was universal, aiming to abolish the slave trade all along the African coast. But it could not be abolished if there was no navy to police the seas, which made the Royal Navy a key player in the abolition. Moreover, British foreign policy made abolitionism one of its tenets, and the issue was therefore discussed in peace talks; the first additional article to the Paris treaty (May 30, 1814) thus dictates that France should abolish the slave trade within five years. Like Britain, France needed its navy to enforce this abolition, linking it de facto to the bilateral French and English peace process. From this, it can be assumed that the British did not wish to see the complete disappearance of the French navy: rather, the French navy was, in a way, subordinate to the Royal navy in its role in policing the seas. This subordinate position could, however, be seen as a potential source of tension and ultimately of instability in post-Napoleonic Europe.

Despite the return of the emperor, the Vienna Congress took place from September 1814 to June 1815 and slavery was among the matters discussed. A condemnation of "the trade of African slaves" was issued on February 8, 1815, in Vienna, but the congress did not go as far as Britain and put an end to it completely.

Once peace was back for good, the London conference on August 28, 1816, dealt with the matter once more. This conference followed the measures taken in Vienna and aligned with British foreign policy on extra-European affairs, out of the range of the Holy Alliance's concerns. The marquis d'Osmond, the French representative, officially came out in favor of abolition. In a way, the French navy's powerlessness in the face of British interventionism was thus changed into a moral endeavor that could put France back on the international stage. By making France take up the principles of British foreign policy, the marquis d'Osmond gave the initiative back to the French navy and soothed the tensions that could ultimately have threatened European peace.[3]

We can ask ourselves whether this new French standpoint was a conscious and willing effort to deprive British foreign policy of its moral impetus or merely an imitation of this British policy, in the spirit of the times in Europe; this remains an open question.

France ended up abolishing slavery through a royal ordinance on January 8, 1817, and a law of April 15, 1818. These measures did not define slave trade as a misdemeanor but simply as an infraction.[4] They did, however, provide a legal framework within which the navy could operate. In this manner, the navy regained the ability to operate independently within the authorized boundaries of European peace. It kept both its military role and its role in policing the seas. Naval officers were therefore key players in this European peace, characterized by this unlikely philanthropic alliance between France and Britain on the seas. Unlikely, because once the French navy had regained some legitimacy through this philanthropic endeavor, it gave rise to a renewed desire in France for an empire.

An ambiguous observation mission: preserving European peace and increasing French influence

In the Caribbean, the sugar-producing islands were going through economic decline, caused by revolutionary unrest, competition from sugar beet on the mainland,[5] and the rise of American power. This decline threatened to upset the civil peace, which could have aroused British interventionism and weakened peace in Europe.

In 1822–3, a young *enseigne de vaisseau* in his mid-twenties, Auguste Febvrier-Despointes, was sent to tour the area. His mission was representative of a policy that aimed to showcase France's ability to keep the peace while hinting at a desire for expansion. The decision to send Febvrier-Despointes on the mission was made after a slave uprising in le Carbet in Martinique in October of 1822,[6] which was speedily crushed by the authorities by mid-November. The young officer was to "endeavor to find out the feelings caused among the foreign colonies by the slave uprising at le Carbet."[7] A native of la Martinique, Febvrier-Despointes, was put in command of la *Légère* and sent to tour the Caribbean. He had earned some distinction during the Hundred Days after he accomplished a number of missions for the comte de Vaugiraud, governor of Martinique, who had remained faithful to Louis XVIII. The *enseigne de vaisseau* was not only a messenger tasked with announcing to the various Caribbean powers that peace had been reestablished in Martinique but also had a diplomatic role to play, reassuring these powers that France was able to maintain order in its territories without outside help; revolutionary unrest and its Caribbean counterpart was over once and for all. Foreign intervention was thus avoided.

However, this was not Febvrier-Despointes' whole mission. What follows is a perfect example of how ambiguously the French government behaved outside the European continent as early as the 1820s. Indeed, the reports he sent during his tour are not only those of a naval officer but also of an intelligence officer: his goal was also to assess the economic status of the area. According to his report, the French colonies were much better off than the British ones. Here is what he wrote about Saint Kitts:

And indeed whatever intelligence I was able to gather made clear to me that this colony is entirely ruined. Many inhabitants had just abandoned their sugar plantations, as their cost was higher than their gain. One cannot compare our colonies with this one, where poverty and discontent are apparent everywhere.[8]

There was a fear that the poverty rife in the Caribbean area, as well as the feeling of its inhabitants that they had been abandoned by the mainland, would provoke armed uprisings and loosen ties with Europe. This fear was not specific to France, as instability threatened the entire area. However, it quickly became apparent that the fear of seeing peace broken in the Caribbeans or the echoes this might have in Europe are not Febvrier-Despointes' main concern in his reports. He seems much more preoccupied with dreams of grandeur for France. In 1823, la *Légère* was wrecked off the coast of Puerto Rico (probably because there were no detailed maps of this coast). This did not stop his observation mission, however, and he noted in his report:

The harbor [of the city of Faxada][9] is very wide, and rather well protected by inlets at its mouth. The sandy seabed is very good. I believe that frigates, maybe even ships of the line could be moored here, and that it could be made into a refit port. It is very easily defended and its position is very military. The Spanish have not yet had this idea and only two twelve-pounder cannons defend its mouth. I was not able to find out why the city was not built near the beach, where there is a beautiful plateau.[10]

The Spanish expedition had not yet taken place, since this was only the beginning of 1823, but the Verona congress of the Holy Alliance regarding Spain had ended and France had been allowed to operate in the Iberic peninsula.[11] This situation opened the way to a new balance of power in the Caribbean. As Febvrier-Despointes points out:

Based on the intelligence [I was able to] gather [. . .] I am almost certain that, should the partisans of the constitution be beaten, both the government of Puerto Rico and its most prominent inhabitants would sever this island's ties with the mainland, and make it into a haven for those forced to leave Spain because of their opinions.[12]

According to the young officer's reports, General de la Torre, political and military governor of Puerto Rico from 1823 to 1827, seemed close to the Spanish constitutional faction, which explains the French surveillance. What we have here is political and strategic intelligence gathering, in order to find out which elements France could use to its advantage and where it could apply pressure. Nothing tells us, however, whether this report was written in preparation for a military intervention should the island secede from Spain; or if France, playing both sides, would play the role of protector to an island in dire need of a military alliance, weakened by a flagging economy even as the abolitionist movements were gathering momentum.

Moreover, Febvrier-Despointes' report has to be understood as a reflection on the position France should take with respect to insurgents from Spanish colonies in Central and Southern America. Indeed, as early as 1818, Richelieu's government wanted to mediate between the colonies and the Spanish government, which shows that France was already playing a role in managing European stability. At the same time, the Anglo-Saxon influence was growing in Spanish America: in 1823 the British government declared in favor of the independence of the Spanish colonies, and President of the United States James Monroe laid out the doctrine that bears his name. The balance of power in Southern America was shifting swiftly.

Finally, we must stress that Febvrier-Despointes was not only a very young man but also a native of the area, and this report also reflects his personal views. There may therefore be a gap between his point of view and the intricacies of the balance of peace on the mainland. Naval officers, through their reports, were the eyes and ears of the government in these remote regions. Nevertheless, these reports were necessarily filled with their personal viewpoints, which is interesting since, because of the nature of their positions, these views were often not focused on the European mainland. This gap could be exploited by the ministries, depending on political needs.

The officers were government agents and worked during those years toward European stability, a stability fueled by an aspiration for peace. However, peace in Europe did not mean renouncing power, be it economic power, easier to attain in peacetime, or military power, aimed at playing a bigger part on the European stage. To attain this power meant sending those young officers on observation missions fit for their rank and sometimes on influence missions to reassure the governors of other European islands in the Caribbean area.

The Indian Ocean: Accommodating European Peace with Imperial Ambitions

With the Vienna treaty, which deprived France of Mauritius, Britain endeavored to reduce France's influence in the Indian Ocean. The British needed to control the road to India through maritime routes and turn the Indian Ocean into their own private domain. France, however, still owned the Ile Bourbon (la Réunion).[13]

To compensate for the loss of Mauritius, the French government started showing interest in Madagascar, which had some previous experience with France.[14] In 1821, France took possession of the island of Sainte-Marie,[15] in the bay of Tintingue, in the northeast of Madagascar,[16] under the pretense of ending once and for all Malagasy piracy, which had already started to decline but was still active. Once more, French naval officers were playing the part of peacekeepers in Europe by preserving peace on the sea while at the same time acting on France's imperial ambitions. This location off the coast of Madagascar provided a port of call on the way to India and therefore reinforced French maritime routes to the subcontinent but also to the Pacific Ocean while opening the way for further expeditions: and indeed, in 1829, the Bourbon station navy was sent to take the Pointe-à-Larée fort, which faced Sainte-Marie island. The capture of the fort was followed by a campaign that resulted in the capture of Foulpointe and Tamatave.

This took place one year before the Algiers expedition, at a time when political upheaval was looming in France: to solve this crisis, the government looked for a way to cultivate unity and found it in the capture of Algiers. In both instances, emphasis was placed on the safety of maritime routes, be it by combating Malagasy or Barbaresque piracy. The French navy was acting ostensibly to preserve peace, with a philanthropic aspect.

However, these feats (the capture of Algiers and the Madagascar campaigns) were not enough to save Charles X's government. After the 1830 revolution, the freshly crowned Louis-Philippe ordered the evacuation of Tamatave to appease the British, who were concerned about the unrest in France. In the short term, this operation was therefore only a way to show off France's military power without any territorial gain. But in the longer term, it marked the beginning of colonization in Madagascar. France left its mark on the territory and accepted the need for patience after making its imperial ambitions clear. In this case, naval officers simply obeyed orders and had no real agency, except perhaps in their relations and the contacts they made with local populations beforehand.

These interventions on the extra-European stage were a way to preserve peace in Europe by displacing tensions: the distance appeased those tensions, but the show of power was real and effective.

The Pacific: On the Margins of European Peacekeeping

Oceania is the maritime area furthest away from Europe.[17] Because of the communication gap, naval officers could take more initiative and had greater power. This gap between the reality on the ground and the news reaching the European capitals also allowed for some flexibility in usually stiff diplomatic relations. Naval officers were essential to this flexibility: although they did obey orders, they also had to show initiative, and the distance gave them an *imperium* of sorts when they had to act. In the 1840s, the Pacific became the main area in which the thin veneer of European peace began to show cracks under the pressure of French and British expansionist ambitions over the same territory.

Before we start examining this third example, we must mention a third player besides governments and navies: the missionaries. Missionaries often provided geographical knowledge of the coveted territories but, above all, they paved the way to a form of social occupation with schools, dispensaries, catechism classes, and so on. This led Claire Laux to theorize the coexistence of a "Christian" and a "profane" geography in this part of the world,[18] which really underlines the importance of missionaries in the Oceania region. Rivalries between the Anglo-Saxon Protestant and French Catholic missionaries swiftly began to fuel maritime tensions between France and Britain, reflecting the growing French presence in the area as well as France's unwillingness to leave it solely to the British.

In Tahiti, on the recommendation of her adviser Pastor Pritchard, Queen Pomaré IV denied Catholic missionaries access to her territory after having missionaries of the order of Picpus expelled.[19] The latter then appealed to naval authorities. And at the same time in Europe, relations between France and Britain were turning sour. Palmerston's withdrawal from public affairs in the years 1841–6 allowed both countries to attempt to salvage their cordial understanding, but economic rivalries and the Spanish marriage affair cut these attempts short. In 1838, following these tensions between Protestant and Catholic missionaries, France sent Admiral Aubert Dupetit-Thouars, who was soon very busy indeed. He captured the Marquesas Islands and used political strife in Tahiti to make it into a French protectorate through a treaty signed in 1842. The troubles on Tahiti appear to have been both a cause and an effect of the deteriorating relations between France and Britain; they also allow us to see naval officers at their most ambiguous: they make good use of their distance from the mainland to be more belligerent in their reports and of their role as representatives for the French government.

The affair did not stop there: missionaries were still in Tahiti and retained a good deal of influence. Peace in Europe, if not threatened, was weakened. Using a flag as a pretense, Admiral Dupetit-Thouars annexed the kingdom in November

1843. This annexation was initially disavowed in Europe, and Tahiti returned to being a protectorate, while the French government agreed to compensate Pritchard.

On the ground, naval officers were therefore looking for French footholds that would immediately affect their missions. As such, they were more aggressive than the Paris government, which temporized once the deed was done. This being said, even if the government did temporize when it came to diplomacy, it did not withdraw the French navy. This stresses the fact that the government was playing a double game, with diplomatic discourse on the one hand and naval operations on the other.

And indeed, in January 1843, *capitaine de vaisseau* Bruat was appointed governor of the Marquesas Islands and then governor of the French Oceanian territories, which included the kingdom of Tahiti. Just before leaving the area, Bruat tackled the task of consolidating the French position in commercial exchanges, so that the British would not take up most of them. This mission involved, as usual, policing the seas: "I asked for instructions on how to crack down on smuggling, and how to mete out justice in the case of a foreign captain asking for help against mutineers." To this, he added more aggressive measures. Indeed he asked for some *"canons de 80"* and "percussion projectiles *système Billette*."[20]

On the ground, Bruat immediately introduced himself to local leaders and, in Tahiti, pursued a repressive policy, which invoked a response from the population, leading to a climate of war which led Bruat to launch a massive counterattack: he sent all the troops available to Mahaena. The war ended on December 17, 1846, when the French captured Fatahua. Queen Pomaré came back from exile in 1847 and agreed to sign a new convention, which deprived her of much of her power in favor of the commissioner, Jacques-Antoine Moerenhout. In 1863, the French put a stop to British influence by replacing the British Protestant missions with the *Société des missions évangéliques de Paris*.

This crisis did not ultimately bring peace in Europe to an end. The fact that the mainland was far away allowed naval officers to conduct a war that might threaten peace in Europe but was remote enough that the French government could both claim that they wanted peace and try to extend their hegemony by thwarting British ambitions. Nineteenth-century European imperialism was careful not to breach peace in Europe. It was an other story outside Europe. The French government gained more and more confidence as it moved away from the revolution but also as the distances lengthened. Rivalries were dealt with far away from Europe in order to keep the peace.

Conclusion

Within the boundaries of the European peace set up by the Vienna Congress, the French navy gained legitimacy by cracking down of the slave trade, allowing it to retain its independence. The navy still furthered the interests of France's territorial power and of its overseas empire: it upheld peace without renouncing France's power.

Peace in Europe was thus incorporated into naval practices in missions, be they influence or observation missions, and power strategies. These missions reflected all the ambiguity of the peace talks aiming at European stability. The fact that most tensions were now located overseas allowed those tensions to be expressed. As the years passed, imperial ambitions grew and became increasingly blatant, threatening peace with tensions, mostly between France and Britain.

Thanks to the distance, diplomatic discourse could develop; the fact that decisions could not be taken immediately left more room for attempts at hegemony. Naval officers knew they were only tools in political matters and did not generally stray from their appointed missions. Thus, in the European area, the missions of naval officers were more strictly delimited in order not to threaten the peace. General officers, however, were left with a lot of autonomy, a form of *imperium* that can be explained by the distance between them and the central government. Therefore, even if those missions were more strictly delimited the closer they were to Europe, they bore both the responsibility to uphold peace and the risk of breaking that peace. A good example is the Battle of Navarino in 1827, which greatly embarrassed both the French and British governments, which did not know how to deal with the situation. This led to baron Tupinier ironically writing about M. de Rigny in his *Mémoires*: "It is a pity that he was not killed by a Turkish cannonball, which would have excused the government from the thanks it now so fears to give him."[21] However, this battle was a joint French and British operation and therefore did not put their relations, and through them peace in Europe, at risk even though it did breach Mediterranean stability. The affair of the Spanish marriages also amply shows us that, before resorting to an armed confrontation, governments had at their disposals many tools able to weaken their adversaries' power. Those tools multiplied in an era when public opinion emerged both as a player and as a tool in political matters. Government agents must not give rise to a casus belli. As a final example, we can refer to the bombardment of Barcelona in 1842, during which, with remarkable composure, *capitaine de corvette* Gatier negotiated with the French consul Ferdinand de Lesseps the evacuation of the city before the bombardment, kept the tensions from escalating, and made sure that the conflict was limited to a national, internal stage. Meanwhile, the British were launching a campaign disparaging France,[22] to gain public support to counter the growing influence of France in the Western Mediterranean, around the triangle formed by Toulon/Marseille, Barcelona, and Algiers. But that is a different story, to be told by someone else.

Notes

1 Voir Pierre Renouvin, *Histoire des Relations internationales, t.II, De 1789 à 1871* (Paris: Hachette, 1994); Thierry Lentz, *Le Congrès de Vienne: une refondation de l'Europe (1814–1815)* (Paris: Perrin, 2015).

2 Hélène Vencent, "Les Ecoles flottantes sous l'Empire et la formation des officiers de marine, 1810–1816," *Revue de l'Institut Napoléon*, no. 197 (2008): 21–57.

3 Serge Daget, *La Répression de la Traite des Noirs au XIXe siècle. L'Action des croisières françaises sur les côtes occidentales de l'Afrique (1817-1830)* (Paris: Karthala, 1997) et Serge Daget, "L'Abolition de la traite des Noirs en France de 1814 à 1831," *Cahier d'études africaines* 11 (1971): 14–58.

4 Ibid.

5 See Nelly Schmidt, *L'Abolition de l'esclavage. Cinq siècles de combats (XVIe–XXe siècle)* (Paris: Fayard, 2005).

6 See Françoise Thésée, "La Révolte des esclaves du Carbet à la Martinique (octobre-novembre 1822)," *Revue française d'histoire d'outre-mer* 80, no. 301 (1993): 551–84.

7 Despointes (Auguste-Febvrier dit Febvrier-Despointes), "Lettre du gouverneur de la Martinique au ministre de la Marine et des Colonies," 19 mai 1823, CC7 alpha 863, Fort-Royal, Service Historique de la Défense (SHD), Vincennes, France.

8 Despointes (Auguste-Febvrier dit Febvrier-Despointes), "Rapport de M. Febvrier-Despointes, enseigne de vaisseau," 24 février 1823, CC7 alpha 863, Fort-Royal, SHD.

9 Probably Fajardo.

10 Despointes (Auguste, Febvrier dit Febvrier-Despointes), "Rapport de M. Febvrier-Despointes, enseigne de vaisseau," 24 février 1823, Fort-Royal, CC7 alpha 863, SHD.

11 Renouvin, *Histoire des relations internationales*.

12 Despointes (Auguste, Febvrier dit Febvrier-Despointes), "Rapport de M. Febvrier-Despointes, enseigne de vaisseau," 24 février 1823, Fort-Royal, CC7 alpha 863, SHD.

13 See Claude Wanquet, Jullien Benoît (dir.), *Révolution française et océan Indien. Prémices, paroxysme, héritage et déviances*. Actes du colloque de Saint-Pierre de la Réunion du 22 au 27 octobre 1990 organisé par l'Association historique internationale de l'océan Indien (Saint-Denis: l'Harmattan, 1996).

14 The *comptoir* (trading center) of Fort Dauphin, today Tolanaro, had been founded on Richelieu's orders and had been there from 1643 to 1674.

15 This location had been considered as a possible *comptoir* before the foundation of Fort Dauphin.

16 See Michel Prou, *Malagasy: Le "royaume de madagascar" au xixe siècle, 1793–1894* (Paris: l'Harmattan, 1987).

17 The word "Oceania" is a neologism created in 1812 by the French-Danish geographer Malte-Brun, based on the word "ocean," which shows the importance of the sea in the Pacific area.

18 Claire Laux, "La Construction d'une géographie de l'Océanie par les explorateurs, les missionnaires, les colonisateurs," in *L'Empire des géographes. Géographie, exploration et colonisation XIXe-XXe siècle*, ed. Singaravélou Pierre (Paris: Belin, coll. Mappemonde, 2008), 176–87.

19 Claire Laux, "Rivalités coloniales et rivalités missionnaires en Océanie (1688-1902)," *Histoire, monde et culture religieuse*, no. 6 (2008): 5–26.

20 Bruat (Armand-Joseph), 9 février 1843, CC7 alpha 347, SHD.

21 Baron Tupinier, *Mémoires du Baron Tupinier, 1779–1850* (Paris: Desjonquères, 1994), 210–11.

22 de Diesbach Ghislain, *Ferdinand de Lesseps* (Paris: Perrin, 1998); Hélène Vencent, "Les Elèves officiers de marine sous l'Empire et leur destin" (PhD Thesis, Université de Paris-Sorbonne, Paris, 2016).

11

Soldiers versus Veterans

Peacemaking in Britain after Napoleon

Evan Wilson

At first glance, the subtitle of this chapter makes little sense. Why would peace need to be made in Britain? The causal arrow usually runs in the other direction: Britain *made* the peace after 1815, heralding the onset of the *Pax Britannica*— literally the British Peace. Britain was not a victim of the Napoleonic Wars, it was the great victor. Napoleon famously never managed to land an army on British shores, sparing Britain from the destruction he wrought from Spain to Russia. In that sense, then, the story told in this chapter differs from many others in this book in that it is not one of an occupying power constructing a postwar settlement nor of a country picking up the pieces from its destruction in a brutal war. Yet, it is a story of the process of peacebuilding or more particularly of the long and nonlinear process of transitioning from war to peace. It is told by focusing on the role of ordinary soldiers in Britain in the five years following Napoleon's defeat at Waterloo.

Britain may have won the Napoleonic Wars, but it was difficult for those who experienced the victory to see what had been won in the immediate aftermath. It was a period of social and economic distress, as the disruption of demobilization intertwined with Radical agitation and threatened to overthrow the government. Even before Waterloo, in March 1815, Members of Parliament were besieged in the Houses of Parliament as protests erupted over the passage of the Corn Law. Two months after Waterloo, striking sailors shut down the port of Newcastle, and in December of that year, there were major riots in the manufacturing districts of Birmingham that had been decimated by the cancellation of wartime contracts. In the spring of 1816, East Anglia saw major disturbances, but worse came over the summer, as the eruption of Mount Tambora in Indonesia caused a global climate catastrophe, which manifested itself in Britain and Ireland as famine and a typhus epidemic. At the end of the "year without a summer," tens of thousands gathered at Spa Fields in London to call for parliamentary reform, only for the night to end in violence. The spring of 1817 witnessed two significant attempts to force change on the government, one peaceful and one violent: in March, the Blanketeers gathered petitions and aspired to walk down the spine of the country, gathering supporters as they went; and in June, Jeremiah Brandredth led the Pentrich Rising in Derbyshire. Both fizzled out, but the government became increasingly convinced that revolution was imminent and passed repressive legislation aimed at defeating Radicalism. The punctuation mark on the postwar distress was the attack on a peaceful crowd in St. Peter's Fields, Manchester, in August 1819 that left eighteen dead and hundreds injured.

That summary barely scratches the surface of the postwar years, but it gives some sense of the violence endemic to British society and the ways in which the end of the war exacerbated existing tensions. It is also a story that has been told from a range of perspectives. Labor historians have naturally gravitated to this period, and their work, building on the foundational text by E. P. Thompson, has dominated our understanding of it. Yet as others have noticed, labor historians have paid little attention to soldiers despite their potential as a well-cataloged group of working-class men.[1] Instead, the military appears vaguely and seemingly randomly: we read that Radical meetings were occasionally "invaded by the military,"[2] and that the Pentrich Rising was dispersed by a magistrate at the "head of a party of hussars." After the Spa Fields riots, "by nightfall the troops had restored order in the City."[3] In none of these cases is it explained where the soldiers came from or why they were (from the government's perspective) in the right place at the right time. Some military historians have noted the domestic presence of the army in this period, but they tend either to downplay its significance or speak only in broad terms about its deployments.[4]

This chapter takes as its premise that the government really did need to make peace with its people, and it used soldiers to do so. Today, we might expect the government to create social programs like the National Health Service or pass the G. I. Bill to ease the transition from war to peace. But British ministers in 1815 had no appetite for such initiatives. Instead, they worried about shoring up their support with the landed classes they represented and tackling the national debt by slashing government expenditure. When faced with social unrest, then, the most readily available tool was the military, and as a result, soldiers found themselves ensnared in the postwar tumult. Simultaneously, the military was in the process of discharging hundreds of thousands of men back into civilian life, and they not only participated in many of the postwar riots but also used their military experience to train protestors. Thus, this chapter focuses on filling the gap identified earlier—when and where did the soldiers come from, and what did they do when they arrived on the scene of a riot—and hints at the ways in which that analysis could be applied to the veterans they often fought. Soldiers emerge as doubly important: as both perpetrators and suppressors of riots. They were key actors in the long and tortuous process of peacemaking.

Before the establishment of the Metropolitan Police in 1829, the government left law enforcement to local officials and in particular to the landed classes. Lord Lieutenants controlled the selection of Justices of the Peace, who were often Anglican clergy. There were property and income requirements, and they had the authority to issue warrants for arrest. For all matters of enforcement, from property crimes to individual violent crimes to mass unrest, they relied on support from local amateur volunteers. Common law dictated that all citizens were required to act in the event of a riot, though of course this rarely happened in practice. Many were willing, however, to serve as informants for magistrates, warning them about approaching mobs or passing on hearsay about plots. Yet even well-organized communities with attentive magistrates had to resort to calling on military force in extreme—but not uncommon—circumstances.[5]

The larger the crowd, the more likely that this ad hoc system of self-policing would be insufficient. When confronted with a mob, a magistrate's first move was often to read the Riot Act of 1714, which gave crowds one hour to disperse peacefully before arrests would be made. Sometimes, that was enough. If it did not have the desired effect, the next escalatory step was to raise a competing but respectable mob. During the riots in East Anglia in 1816, for example, the mayor of Cambridge raised a preventive mob of 300 men, whom he swore in as special constables.[6]

Few magistrates had such foresight or sufficient time to get ahead of the mob, so they frequently had to react to rapidly changing circumstances by calling in the militia or yeomanry. The militia were dismantled at the end of the war, leaving the yeomanry as the primary amateur military force available during the postwar riots. Boasting about 20,000 members around the country, the yeomanry were locally organized and usually drawn from the middle ranks of society. A troop consisted of about fifty or sixty mounted men, and they had to pay for most of their equipment and horses. The infamous Manchester and Salford Yeomanry, who charged at Peterloo, were mainly shopkeepers and merchants. In general, the yeomanry sought to preserve the status quo. They were an anti-revolutionary organization initially designed to respond to a French invasion, but their respectability and ability to suppress popular protest made them, at least initially, an attractive rapid-response team for postwar magistrates.[7]

There are plenty of examples of the militia or yeomanry successfully suppressing riots, but there are also many examples of failures. Peterloo is the most famous of the failures, but it was exceptional in its scale and legacy. More common in the postwar years were smaller clashes between yeomanry and citizens. Most ended much less decisively than Peterloo, as well. When workers went on strike at the Merthyr Tydfil ironworks in Wales in October 1816, the Cardiff yeomanry successfully dispersed a crowd using the flats of their blades. That same year, the yeomanry in East Anglia were less successful when confronted with a crowd demanding the release of a recently captured gang of poachers. The magistrates held their nerve, but neither they nor the yeomanry could prevent the crowd from diverting to the nearest pub, which it destroyed while consuming most of its beer.[8]

When the yeomanry failed, or if the yeomanry was in danger of failing, magistrates called the army. There were plenty of soldiers available, increasingly so as the wars went on. In 1793, 17,000 troops had been quartered in Britain; by 1798, there were 40,000, and by 1808, 60,000. They slept in pubs and built camps in forests and on moors. As the postwar malaise continued, more permanent solutions were sought: barracks, which had usually only been built in coastal areas with invasion defense in mind, began appearing inland. Twenty percent of all the new barracks built from 1660 to 1847 were built after 1815, mainly in the disturbed northern areas. Eleven thousand troops were moved into the northern areas after Peterloo in 1819, double the deployment before the massacre. But there were also troops available when trouble appeared in East Anglia in 1816 and in the Home Counties in 1820. During the clashes over the funeral procession of Queen Caroline, half of all the troops in Britain—nearly 10,000—were stationed near London. As E. P. Thompson summarized, "In 1816 the English people were held down by force."[9]

The army could act in domestic affairs only on orders from the civil power. During the Gordon Riots of 1780, the perception was that soldiers had held firmly to this legal requirement, with the result that the riots had spiraled out of control. In the aftermath, there were more and more calls for the army to be turned loose.[10] Combined with the ready availability of troops in wartime and in the postwar period, the result was that magistrates began to call the army to their assistance with increasing frequency. The army, for its part, began to develop tactics for dealing with crowds. This is not to say that there was a doctrine, or that troops drilled for these eventualities—as we will see, no soldier was comfortable in front of a mob. Rather, the goal here is to trace some common techniques that soldiers deployed.[11]

Step one was simply to show up. The soldiers might parade in formation or form lines in front of the mob. Disciplined troops are intimidating and often simply being present defused the situation. Officers might feel compelled to give speeches, saying that they did not want to fight their own countrymen. When soldiers were known to the crowd, these techniques could be effective; problems arose, though, when soldiers were not from the area. The presence of Scottish soldiers attempting to suppress the Wilkes riots in London in 1768 contributed to the subsequent casualties—they were, in some sense, foreign occupiers.

If simply being present did not disperse the crowd, the soldiers were usually then deployed to guard key civic buildings. This tactic was the most challenging for the soldiers because standing guard made them tempting targets for both insults and stones. From the crowd's perspective, nothing had changed: the soldiers were still simply present rather than taking active measures to suppress the crowd. This tactic rarely lasted a long time and almost never proved sufficient to quell a riot.

The most common tactic came next: limited offensive measures. In the Boston Massacre of 1770, the soldiers who had been guarding the Custom House fired a ragged volley into the crowd that had been pressing around them for hours. But direct fire was rare. Instead, soldiers could fire blank cartridges or fire balls over the crowd's heads. That was the most effective tactic in dispersing a crowd, but it also often resulted in casualties. A more disciplined approach was for the infantry to advance against the mob, using the stocks of their muskets as weapons. If cavalry were available, they would wade into the crowd, theoretically using the flats of their blades. It is remarkable that wounds from blades were relatively rare, with the notable exception of Peterloo.

These tactics developed over time, as the examples from the middle of the previous century show. They were not fixed nor were they always followed, but they do give a general sense of how troops might approach their constabulary tasks. We can see how they played out in practice in the postwar years.

Sometimes step one—showing up—was more difficult than we might think. Despite the construction of inland barracks in the north after 1815, detachments of soldiers often had to travel long distances. Technically, magistrates could only call out local troops, but that could still mean troops a day's march away or more. While the Cardiff yeomanry were dealing with the striking ironworkers, for example, a troop of dragoons was making its way over the mountains by forced march. Upon arriving in an area disturbed by rioting, troops could be concentrated or dispersed. Opinion was divided about the best practice. During the Luddite riots, Lieutenant-General Sir Thomas Maitland kept his troops concentrated, despite pleas from magistrates to make them more available to civil authorities. Eventually, he agreed, with the result that in Huddersfield, a thousand troops were quartered in thirty-three pubs.[12]

As the magistrates argued, dispersing troops made it more likely that they would be on hand when trouble erupted and that clearly had some value. "There is nothing to fear from the rioters," wrote one officer to *Bell's Weekly Register* in 1816. "They have no plan, no arms, and flee at the sight of a soldier."[13] Well, sometimes. During the hustings for the 1818 Westminster election, supporters of Royal Navy Captain Sir Murray Maxwell built a boat on wheels and dressed in patriotic clothing. Their opponents, supporters of the Radical Sir Francis Burdett, ambushed them, captured the boat, and broke it into pieces for use as weapons in their assault on Maxwell's headquarters near Covent Garden. They used the cart that had held the boat as a battering ram. Eventually, the magistrate read the Riot Act and called out some nearby dragoons. When the soldiers arrived, the crowd pelted them with whatever was at hand, mainly cabbages from Covent Garden vegetable carts.[14]

Thomas Morris also ran into the problem of how to deal with a crowd that was not intimidated by the arrival of soldiers. His regiment, the seventy-third, returned to England from the Army of Occupation in late 1815 and was almost immediately deployed to Birmingham to deal with riots in the manufacturing districts.[15] As in Westminster, troops showing up did nothing and in fact further enraged the crowd. The high constable read the Riot Act, to which the crowd responded by throwing bricks and stones at the soldiers. Morris claims his captain proceeded to skip a few steps. Impatient under the assault from the crowd, he never attempted the limited offensive measures that might have been effective. Instead, he ordered the company to load and fire into the mob. The constable acted quickly to intervene, scolding the captain: "Sir, you are called on to aid and assist the civil power, and if you fire on the people, without my permission, and death ensues, you will be guilty of murder." Morris claimed that his captain "seemed nettled at the circumstance, but consoled himself with the thought, that we should even yet have the privilege of killing a few people." In the end, the captain never got his bloodthirsty wish, but it was a narrow escape.[16]

During the East Anglian riots in 1816, there were a number of examples of more effective management of riotous crowds. After a crowd in Norwich threw "fireballs" during a riot in May, the First Royal Dragoons arrived in the market square. Even though the crowd reacted much as it had in Birmingham, in this case, the dragoons were able to chase the crowd away. They "galloped up stone steps, rode over posts and rails, and followed wherever the ill-disposed thought themselves most secure." Later, at Littleport, two privates from the same regiment of dragoons were so enthusiastic about chasing rioters that they forded a river holding their pistols over their heads. But this was not some lark—the rioters during that summer in East Anglia were deadly serious. A man named John Hassett assaulted a soldier by grabbing his sword and yelling, "Damn your Eyes I have got your sword and will fight any of you, you Bugger."[17]

Among the more extreme cases of soldiers clashing with protestors came in March 1815 during the passage of the unpopular Corn Law. The Home Secretary ordered more than a thousand troops to London to deal with the crisis, and for three days, the capital was governed by the military and the yeomanry. The Life Guards were called in to defend the Houses of Parliament, and at the height of the protests, they charged the crowd with drawn sabers. A bystander who happened to be a midshipman was killed by gunshot in the ensuing fracas, and it could have been worse. At one point, an officer drew his cutlass in the hopes of slowing the advance of a mob of about a hundred; he later claimed that if he had been able to find a magistrate, he would have ordered his men to fire into the crowd.[18]

The Corn Law rioting was not random: protestors targeted those known to be supporters of the bill, such as the Hon. Frederick John Robinson (a future prime minister). But since Robinson and his fellow MPs were busy in Parliament, it was his servants that bore the brunt of the assault. A mob besieged his house, launching multiple assaults that his servants tried desperately to repel. One servant was a carpenter and was able to board up some of the windows and doors, but nevertheless, the mob broke in, smashed furniture, and threatened to kill every servant if they did not tell them where Robinson was. (Presumably they were more comfortable attacking a private residence than taking on the Life Guards in front of Parliament.) The next morning, the servants managed to get six privates and a corporal from one of the Guards' regiments into the house to help with the defense. Someone in the crowd drew a picture of Robinson hanging from the gallows, and the fighting intensified, particularly once the crowd realized that the soldiers were firing only blank cartridges. The soldiers naturally reloaded with shot. Jane Watson, a widow, was mortally wounded, and eventually the arrival of more troops on the street outside dispersed the crowd.

The next month, four of the soldiers who had been in the house stood trial for Watson's murder. One, James Ripley, pleaded his case by noting that he "had nothing to do with the Corn Law. We were ordered to defend a house." He argued that his life had been in danger, and he was acting in self-defense. It was corroborated by the servants who had been present, as well as Mr. Robinson himself: they all felt that they had been in mortal danger for multiple days. As Ripley's lawyers put it, the violent defense of property by soldiers was necessary to protect "the peaceable and well-disposed men of society," who otherwise would be "at all times at the mercy of a furious and enraged populace." Unsurprisingly, given the political context and the personal testimony of an MP, the soldiers were found not guilty.[19] Soldiers in such situations were certainly in difficult positions, but the casualties resulting from the Corn Law riots nevertheless reinforced the reputation of the Life Guards as poor constables: they had also killed a man during a riot in 1810, for which they earned the moniker "Piccadilly Butchers."[20]

Calling troops to a riot sometimes made matters worse rather than better. In recognition of the uncertainty inherent in dealing with a maddening crowd, some magistrates adopted a policy of keeping regular troops nearby but out of sight. At an open-air meeting calling for parliamentary reform in Staffordshire, for example, the Lord Lieutenant made a point of personally attending and keeping the troops in reserve. The same happened at Peterloo, where the Fifteenth Hussars were not initially present in St. Peter's Fields but were a reserve to be used in case of emergency.[21]

It is an understatement to call what happened at Peterloo an emergency, and unsurprisingly, the Fifteenth Hussars saw plenty of action that day—not only during the massacre itself but in the chaotic aftermath. Lieutenant William Jolliffe recalled that in the afternoon, they spent a few hours patrolling the streets, which were by that point mostly empty. That evening, two troops of horses and some infantry (from the Eighty-Eighth Regiment) were ordered to set up a picket. Immediately after they had done so, a crowd gathered around them. The crowd grew increasingly agitated as darkness fell, throwing stones at the soldiers. Jolliffe described the soldiers' attempts to use nonlethal force: "[T]he Hussars many times cleared the ground by driving the mob up the streets leading from the New Cross." Here we can see the usual pattern of escalation: show up, guard something, suffer stones from the crowd, and then advance against them without firing. It did not work. Locals used their knowledge of the narrow passages between streets to re-form and launch another attack. For nearly an hour and a half, the soldiers endured the assault, "being more and more pressed upon," as the lieutenant put it. A magistrate showed up to read the Riot Act, to no avail. Having exhausted the nonlethal options, the officer in charge, with the approval of the magistrate, "ordered the 88th to fire (which they did by platoon firing) down three of the streets. The firing lasted only a few minutes; perhaps not more than thirty shots were fired; but these had a magical effect; the mob ran away and dispersed forthwith, leaving three or four persons on the ground with gunshot wounds."[22]

That, then, is how peace was made in Britain in the turbulent aftermath of the Napoleonic Wars: with violence carried out by veterans of those wars. The Fifteenth Hussars had been with Wellington on the Peninsula and at Waterloo; many were wearing their Waterloo medals at Peterloo. They had no formal training in crowd control, they possessed no nonlethal weapons, and they were under the orders of panicked magistrates. They were in a tough spot. If they obeyed orders and fired into or above crowds, they might be accused of murder; if they disobeyed orders, they might be accused of mutiny.[23] Usually, they followed orders, with the result that British civilians were killed with remarkable regularity by British troops in the postwar years. To be fair, as a number of historians have pointed out, fewer civilians were killed than we might expect, given how frequently the army clashed with rioters. Nevertheless, the government was forced to admit that soldiers made poor policemen, and what was needed was a trained regular police force.

It is difficult to uncover how soldiers felt about all this, but some memoirs provide a few hints. Jolliffe quoted earlier began his account of Peterloo by noting that he had no experience with a large manufacturing population. He did not know whether "a great degree of distress was then prevalent," and he wondered whether the agitation was caused by outside political agitators like Henry Hunt. Perhaps "the bad feeling which appeared to exist between employers and employed, was wholly or in part caused by the agitation of political questions."[24]

Many soldiers had been gone from Britain for years, and they were unfamiliar with the communities they were policing. Some, like Captain Harry Smith, had married Spanish wives and then served in the Army of Occupation in France. When they finally returned in 1818, Smith recalled, "[W]e heard of nothing but 'the French are coming over.'" They had been gone for so long that British soldiers were now, as Smith put it, a "them." As they traversed the countryside, they looked around nervously, expecting the enemy to take advantage of their scattered deployments: "Although I repeated to myself a hundred times daily, 'You are in England,' the thought would arise, 'You are in the power of your enemy.'"

Smith and his soldiers were still fully militarized when they deployed to Glasgow to deal with riots in the manufacturing districts. They saw the country through the eyes of veteran campaigners. It was, they thought, a difficult country to make war in, and Smith recalled conversations among his men: "I say, Bill, look at that wood on the hill there and those hedgerows before it. I think we could keep that ourselves against half Soult's Army. Ah, I had rather keep it than attack it! But Lord, the war's all over now." When they arrived in Glasgow, Smith's wife had to live in the barracks "as during the war," but it soon became too dangerous for her, so he sent her to Edinburgh.

These were men used to following orders, used to preparing for combat, and used to viewing the world as perpetually in a state of war—as it had been for most of their lives. One of Smith's superiors said he was "proud . . . to see one of his old Battalions in peace the same ready soldiers they were in war." We should perhaps not be surprised, then, that, when confronted with an unruly crowd, they were ready to put their training and experience to use. When stones started flying, it did not matter if they were flying from the hands of fellow countrymen.

Suppressing rioting was "very laborious and irksome," Smith recalled decades later, and he "never had more arduous duties than on this occasion"—this from a veteran of campaigns on four continents. "We had neither enemy nor friends: a sort of *Belllum in Pace*, which we old campaigners did not understand." Smith did claim to understand the importance of deferring to the civil authority, though. When he and his men were sent to arrest some Radicals, they were confronted by a mob. He ordered his men to use the flats of their swords to "make the heads of some ache, while brickbrats, stones, etc. were flying among us half as bad as grapeshot." The magistrates were worried he would order his men to fire, but as he later explained to his commanding officer, "I did not desire to bring upon my head either the blood of my foolish and misguided countrymen, or the odium of the Manchester magistrates."[25]

The construction of barracks lengthened the distance between soldiers and civilians. In Huddersfield during the Luddite riots, every pub was overflowing with soldiers, but as more inland barracks were built, soldiers became increasingly separated from the population they were supposedly protecting. Of course, being quartered in pubs created as many problems as it solved. During celebrations of the king's birthday in Oldham in April 1820, some soldiers drank his health and began singing a song called "Waterloo." The locals in the pub responded with "Peterloo." This incident was no preview of "La Marseillaise" in *Casablanca*: the valiant locals did not outsing the soldiers. Instead, they fought, and the ensuing riot caused a number of serious injuries.[26]

The sense of dislocation was compounded, for common soldiers, by the different ways that veterans were commemorated. From 1750 to 1850, perceptions of soldiers remained fluid and contradictory. A common strain in the late eighteenth century saw soldiers as helpless victims of war, unfit for peaceful occupations. At the same time, soldiers were defenders of the nation against the chaos of revolution and the tyranny of Napoleon. Wellington naturally received the highest honors his country could bestow as well as hundreds of thousands of pounds to build his grand estate, and his officers boasted knighthoods and peerages. But his men did not share in the glory. While the Waterloo medal was given to all participants, Peninsula veterans did not receive a medal until 1847. It was politically dangerous to celebrate the achievements of ordinary soldiers in times of mass unrest. Soldiers were, according to one historian, "by turns admired, feared, despised, and pitied."[27]

In Percy Shelley's "The Masque of Anarchy," written after Peterloo, he vividly depicts common soldiers as tools of an oppressive regime.* The cabinet—represented as the four horsemen of the apocalypse—are greeted "with pomp" by soldiers:

Clothed in arms like blood and flame,
The hired murderers, who did sing
"Thou art God, and Law, and King.

We have waited, weak and lone
For thy coming, Mighty One!
Our purses are empty, our swords are cold,
Give us glory, and blood, and gold."[28]

Hired murderers thirsty for blood, soldiers are "the Tyrant's crew." Later in the poem, he calls on citizens to resist passively the coming assault:

Let the tyrants pour around
With a quick and startling sound,
Like the loosening of a sea,
Troops of armed emblazonry.

Let the charged artillery drive
Till the dead air seems alive
With the clash of clanging wheels,
And the tramp of horses' heels.

---

* A disclaimer applies: Shelley is not known for his word choice precision, and he was in exile throughout this period.

Let the fixèd bayonet
Gleam with sharp desire to wet
Its bright point in English blood
Looking keen as one for food.

Let the horsemen's scimitars
Wheel and flash, like sphereless stars
Thirsting to eclipse their burning
In a sea of death and mourning.[29]

This is the army as a tool of the state, whose exclusive purpose is to kill British citizens. Shelley is not subtle. Yet there are also hints that Shelley recognizes that the army might not be the most effective police force. He writes in "England in 1819": "An army, whom liberticide and prey / Makes as a two-edged sword to all who wield."[30] In other words, though the army kills liberty, it may also be the undoing of the tyrants. How this might happen is not clear, but to return to "The Masque of Anarchy," we can see the slimmest possibility. In listing the occupations of those who should stand against the tyrants, he includes those who use the "Loom, and plough, and sword, and spade."[31] Perhaps ordinary soldiers, men of the sword, may be allies in the fight for revolutionary change.

The "four horsemen," that is, the cabinet, were aware that soldiers might not always be the most reliable tools of suppression. Four different acts passed in 1817 included measures to punish attempts to tamper with the loyalty of the armed forces. With no regular police, yeomanry of uncertain quality and memories of the storming of the Bastille still very much alive (Lord Liverpool, the prime minister, had seen it firsthand), the government could not afford any distance between it and its armed forces.[32]

Some Radicals seem to have sensed the opportunity this dilemma presented. At the Spa Fields meetings, soldiers were greeted with a banner reading, "The Brave Soldiers are our Friends." As London braced itself for the arrival of Queen Caroline's carriage in 1820, rumors spread about mutiny among the Life Guards—the same regiment that had earned a bloody reputation in previous riots. Prostitutes apparently bargained with soldiers, telling them that they could only enjoy their services if they agreed not to fight the protestors. During the ensuing rioting, a crowd urged soldiers at the barracks at Charing Cross to join the mob. The risk of defection was such that Lord Sidmouth left a dinner party near Piccadilly and personally oversaw the dispersal of the crowd by a troop of the Second Life Guards.[33] While stationed in Glasgow, Harry Smith noticed the similarities between the soldiers under his command and the protestors they were sent to arrest. In fact, many of the "half-starved weavers" were old soldiers, some of whom Smith recognized. He spoke to one former Rifleman, "an old comrade" who had lost his arm at the Battle of New Orleans. Smith claimed that a combination of the good conduct of his soldiers and the bonds that still existed between the soldiers and the veterans in the crowd helped defuse tensions.[34]

More often, though, soldiers were perceived as tools of oppression. Rumors about mutinous regiments remained baseless, and separating the army from the government proved too difficult for Radicals to undertake a serious effort. Most soldiers had been gone from Britain too long to feel a sense of solidarity with the communities they were policing. It was difficult for veterans of a long war to resist falling back on their recent combat experience when they were confronted with an angry mob. Even if, from a socioeconomic perspective, soldiers on active duty shared much in common with protestors, there does not seem to be much evidence that soldiers showed any inclination to act in solidarity.

The same cannot be said of discharged veterans. While there is no space in this chapter to examine the role that veteran soldiers played in organizing the riots, it is a promising area for further research.[35] They used their skills learned in the army to increase the effectiveness of rioters; they organized protests into military-style regiments and companies; and they trained protestors on the moors to march and turn, using sticks and pitchforks in place of muskets and bayonets. When Harry Smith spoke with the Rifleman he had served with, he learned that the protestors in Glasgow had appointed a general and a central committee of delegates ("a House of Lords," according to the Rifleman), and the city was organized into sixteen regiments. Each sent a representative to the committee, and each also coordinated a street-by-street rapid-response plan, "so that in case of a turn-out they could parade—'Ah, just as we did in the towns of Spain and France,'" said the Rifleman.[36]

Britain may have won the wars in part by marching an army through Spain and France, but the fighting was not over. The army was deployed throughout the British Isles to create the peace after Waterloo. It was a violent and turbulent process, and while it did prevent the British equivalent of the storming of the Bastille, it was not wholly successful. Calls for parliamentary reform grew louder, especially after the yeomanry and hussars killed innocent protestors at Peterloo. Of course, Britain was not alone in experiencing postwar distress: all of the delegates at Vienna returned home to suppress Radicalism in the hopes of preventing a repeat of the worst wars that Europe had ever seen. The British case is a useful reminder that even the victorious powers struggled to transition from war to peace.

Notes

1 Nick Mansfield, "Military Radicals and the Making of Class, 1790–1860," in
   Soldiering in Britain and Ireland, 1750–1850: Men of Arms, ed. Catriona Kennedy
   and Matthew McCormack (Basingstoke: Palgrave Macmillan, 2013), 57–75.

2 Edward P. Thompson, *The Making of the English Working Class* (London: V.
   Gollancz, 1963), 610.

3 Reginald J. White, *Waterloo to Peterloo* (New York: Russell and Russell, 1973/1957),
   144–5, 172.

4 Ian F. W. Beckett, *The Amateur Military Tradition, 1558–1945* (Manchester:
   Manchester University Press, 1991), 126–7; Frederick Myatt, *The British Infantry,
   1660–1945: The Evolution of a Fighting Force* (Poole: Blandford Press, 1983), 110.
   There are two exceptions—works which take the role of the army in suppressing
   domestic unrest seriously. Tony Hayter's *The Army and the Crowd in Mid-Georgian
   England* (London: Rowman and Littlefield, 1978) provides an excellent survey of an
   earlier period. Historians of the development of the police have also discussed the role
   of the army in riot suppression. See especially Stanley H. Palmer, *Police and Protest in
   England and Ireland, 1780–1850* (New York: Cambridge University Press, 1988).

5 White, *Waterloo to Peterloo*, 110.

6 Charles M. Clode, *Confidential Memorandum for the Secretary of State for the War
   Department*, February 2, 1867, WO 33/18, The National Archives, Kew; Palmer,
   Police and Protest, 57–65; White, *Waterloo to Peterloo*, 105–9; A. J. Peacock, *Bread
   or Blood: A Study of the Agrarian Riots in East Anglia in 1816* (London: V. Gollancz,
   1965), 118–19.

7 George Hay, *The Yeomanry Cavalry and Military Identities in Rural Britain, 1815–
   1914* (Basingstoke: Palgrave Macmillan, 2017), 2–4, 84–5, 245–7; Beckett, *Amateur
   Military Tradition*, 132–7; Palmer, *Police and Protest*, 189.

8 Peacock, *Bread or Blood*, 87–9; James Hobson, *Dark Days of Georgian Britain:
   Rethinking the Regency* (Barnsley: Pen and Sword, 2017), 28.

9 White, *Waterloo to Peterloo*, 111–12; Palmer, *Police and Protest*, 61–2, 159–62, 172,
   180–90; Thompson, *Making of the English Working Class*, 605.

10 Clode, *Confidential Memorandum*.

11 The tactics described here are modified from Hayter, *The Army and the Crowd*,
    167–86.

12 Hobson, *Dark Days*, 28; Palmer, *Police and Protest*, 181–2.

13 Hobson, *Dark Days*, 28.

14 Ibid., 63.

15 On the Army of Occupation, see Christine Haynes, *Our Friends, The Enemies: The
    Occupation of France after Napoleon* (Cambridge, MA: Harvard University Press,
    2018).

16 Thomas Morris, *The Napoleonic Wars*, ed. John Selby (London: Longman, 1967), 109–16. Morris is not entirely reliable on these points, as he set out explicitly to counter the more traditional narratives of high-ranking officers receiving all the glory. See Gavin Daly, "British Soldiers and the Legend of Napoleon," *The Historical Journal* 61 (2018): 131–53.

17 Peacock, *Bread or Blood*, 78–84, 107–12.

18 Thompson, *Making of the English Working Class*, 603; Jenny Uglow, *In These Times: Living in Britain Through Napoleon's Wars, 1793–1815* (London: Faber & Faber, 2014), 609–15; *The Times*, March 13, 1815.

19 *Old Bailey Proceedings Online* (www.oldbaileyonline.org, version 8.0, July 18, 2019), April 1815, trial of James Ripley, Robert Herbert, Richard Burton, Richard Mathews (t18150405-13).

20 Palmer, *Police and Protest*, 166–75.

21 Thompson, *Making of the English Working Class*, 679.

22 Sir William Jolliffe, *The Charge of the 15th Hussars at Peterloo* (1845), reprinted in *Three Accounts of Peterloo*, ed. F. A. Bruton (Manchester: Manchester University Press, 1921), 56–7.

23 Palmer, *Police and Protest*, 65.

24 Jolliffe, *Charge of the 15th Hussars*, 48–9.

25 Harry Smith and George C. M. Smith, *The Autobiography of Lieutenant-General Sir Harry Smith, Baronet of Aliwal on the Sutlej* (London, 1903), 319–28.

26 Palmer, *Police and Protest*, 62; Robert Poole, "The March to Peterloo: Politics and Festivity in Late Georgian England," *Past and Present* 192 (August 2006): 109–53; *Manchester Observer*, April 29, 1820.

27 G. W. Stephen Brodsky, *Gentlemen of the Blade: A Social and Literary History of the British Army since 1660* (New York: Greenwood Press, 1988), 46–52. Or, in a slightly different framing, common soldiers remained seen as a "socially disruptive and criminal force." Catriona Kennedy, *Narratives of the Revolutionary and Napoleonic Wars: Military and Civilian Experience in Britain and Ireland* (Basingstoke: Palgrave Macmillan, 2013), 192; Daly, "British Soldiers and the Legend of Napoleon," 131–53.

28 Percy Bysshe Shelley, *The Masque of Anarchy* (London: Edward Moxon, 1832), stanzas 15–16.

29 Ibid., stanzas 41, 75–8.

30 Percy B. Shelley, *England in 1819* (London: Edward Moxon, 1839), lines 8–9.

31 Shelley, *The Masque of Anarchy*, stanza 41.

32 57 Geo. 3, cap. 3, 6, 7, 19; White, *Waterloo to Peterloo*, 149; Kennedy, *Narratives*, 193.

33 White, *Waterloo to Peterloo*, 143; Palmer, *Police and Protest*, 172.

34 Smith and Smith, *Autobiography*, 325.

35 See my latest book, *The Horrible Peace: British Veterans and the End of the Napoleonic Wars* (Amherst: University of Massachusetts Press, 2023).

36 Smith and Smith, *Autobiography*, 325.

12

The Price of Disobedience

The Eastern French Army in Albania (1918–25)

Renaud Dorlhiac

On October 23, 1916, the first *Régiment de chasseurs d'Afrique* (African cavalry regiment), commanded by Colonel Joseph Bardi de Fourtou, entered Korça (Korytsas in Greek), the main city in the southeast of the newly created country of Albania.[1] The move had been decided by General Maurice Sarrail, commander of the Eastern Allied Armies redeployed in northern Greece in the autumn of 1915 after the failure of the Gallipoli campaign, in order to make a junction with the Italians established on the eastern shores of the Adriatic Sea. The need to secure the army's left flank, weakened by the Bulgarian advance in the summer of 1916, was also politically driven. First, it aimed to replace Greece's royalist regime, present in Korça since the beginning of the Balkan wars, by a Greek administration supportive of the Entente;[2] the second aim was to cut off communications between the said regime and the central powers occupying Albanian territory.

If the officers on the ground stuck with the second objective, they rapidly bypassed the first, believing that it would weaken their strategic position by arousing a strong armed opposition. This shift stemmed from a situational awareness drastically different to that of the Ministry of Foreign Affairs and of the Greek government, eager to foster the Hellenization of a region outside the remit of the Ottoman Empire and without defined borders, so as to promote its allotment to Greece at the end of the war. For three and a half years, the Eastern French army's policy, implemented without the approval of the French authorities, had far-reaching consequences by binding this region to Albania, cementing its border with Greece and helping train elites that, from the interwar period to the Communist one, would make it a modern and francophone country.

The rich archives of the French Ministries of Foreign Affairs and of Defense provide us with ample information, in the form of officers' profiles visible through their memoirs and employers' records, to allow us to understand the reasons for their political choices in Albania. Broadening the scope, with the aim of nurturing a general reflection on the military's contribution to peace, it seems equally relevant to examine the competences and know-how mobilized by these officers in a war context, before considering how they reinvested them in the immediate postwar period.

Soldiers as Political Actors

In Service to the Nation

For strategic reasons, the French gradually extended the territory that they occupied in southern Albania between the autumn of 1916 and the summer of 1918. One year after their arrival in this region, the borders of the occupied zone matched those of the former Ottoman kaza of Korça and Pogradec, the first constituting the eastern starting point for the forthcoming Greek-Albanian border (according to the Conference of London on August 11, 1913),[3] while the second marked the boundary between Serbia and Albania. For the newly occupied territories, to avoid administrative and political interference with Greece and Serbia, the French resorted to mechanisms differing from the one in force in Korça. First, they set up a buffer zone along the border with Greece on the model of the one established in Thessaly in November 1916 to prevent clashes between Greek liberal and royalist regimes. Second, they maintained the northern territories on the shores of Ohrid's lake (the Territory of Pogradec), seized in September 1917, under a military administration. At no time did they attribute a political dimension to these confines or try to preempt future political decisions.[4] However, the need for strategic stability underlying these measures practically led to the fixing of a border contested and still not delineated at that time even—if it could rely on local realities. A clear demonstration of this lies in the fact that the Treaty of Kapshticë, signed on May 28, 1920, by local Albanian and Greek authorities, without any governmental approval on both sides, fully respected the demarcation line, even if Greece only returned the villages of the buffer zone occupied since May 1920 to Albania in October 1924. But, if the French dismissed the political dimension of their actions in southeast Albania, the setting-up of an area preserved from external meddling constitutes a turning point for the local identities at a moment when the region was leaving the Ottoman Empire and being embedded in a nation-state.

Less than one month after their arrival in Korça, the French officers radically changed their approach to pacifying the region. Now convinced that the majority of the population did not favor a Greek regime, they put aside their former beliefs and guidelines by driving away the liberal authorities and by taking on all the executive duties. The robust armed resistance presented by Albanian bands operating under the Austro-Hungarian or Bulgarian flags led the French to seek agreement with them. Once achieved, a memorandum signed on December 10, 1916, enshrined this goal by recognizing a *Région autonome de Korytza* (Autonomous Region of Korytza). The French and the Albanians, however, interpreted this document differently, the former giving it a local dimension, while the latter strove to give it a national one. It is noteworthy that the French refused to establish an Albanian government in Korça to allow the coming of high-level Albanian politicians or the opening of a consulate of the autonomous region in New York. However, the Albanians seized all the opportunities to amend the designation, first in *Albanie autonome* (Autonomous Albania) in January 1917 and then in *République de Korytza* (Republic of Korytza) in March. Furthermore, they also succeeded in raising the national flag on public buildings and did not give up their idea of setting up customs posts.

Despite such different views on the ground, the French took a set of measures that helped promote the spread of an Albanian national ideal that was both multiconfessional and centered on the mother tongue. To that end, they allowed the free use of the Albanian language in the public space by permitting Albanian newspapers to be published and by introducing, for the first time, public teaching in Albanian. They also tried to reduce the confessional element by placing laics at the head of the monasteries, nationalizing the resources of religious foundations and diminishing religious rivalries in the public space by establishing equal representation between Muslims and Christians in all public bodies. In addition, for more than one year, these measures were supported by rigorous steps against Hellenism, such as the closing of Greek schools and banning of the Greek press. The return to a more balanced politics between Albanian and Greek interests in February 1918 did not call into question the recent achievements of the former.

The fact that such measures espoused the goals at the core of the Third Republic certainly made them acceptable for the French officers acting under the command of General Sarrail, fiercely republican and in close contact with socialist circles. Colonel Andre Ordioni's memoirs substantiate this:

Il me semblait en outre qu'il y avait quelque chose à faire dans cette république naissante et embryonnaire de Korça. . . . En ma qualité de républicain, d'admirateur sincère de la république athénienne et de notre république de 1848, je ne pouvais que m'intéresser à cette fille de nos principes de justice et de liberté! [It seemed to me, moreover, that there was something to do in this nascent and embryonic republic of Korytza. . . . As a republican, as a sincere admirer of the Athenian republic and of our republic of 1848, I could not but be interested in this daughter of our principles of justice and freedom!][5]

In order to improve the level of knowledge and spread the spirit of enlightenment, the officers brought in and developed French courses. In their mind, and most certainly because at that time schooling in Albania did not go beyond the secondary level, it would give the pupils access to a more Europeanized literature. In the long term, this measure had a deep impact to the extent that all the Albanian political regimes through the twentieth century, royalists as well as Communists, relied on French teaching to train elites free from neighbors' influences. Moreover, they did not limit their involvement to educational or religious matters. They also endorsed the setting up of a republican regime, whereas the Conference of London provided the new Albanian state with a royalist one.[6] Albanians and French converged on the necessity to set up a more egalitarian regime representing all the categories of the population. This intended to reduce the privileges of the powerful Muslim landowners as well as those of the great Orthodox merchants. In parallel, they centralized and streamlined public services by establishing some central services (education, finance, forests, the police, etc.).

From Obedience to Defiance

The political consequences of the measures taken under French protection are not accidental. If the decisions mainly met strategic and military requirements, they were sometimes the result of brave personal considerations in that they deviated from the instructions received.

Such behavior is clear in the decision, approved by General Sarrail without the endorsement of the Ministry of Foreign Affairs, to replace the Greek administration by an indigenous regime. According to the orders given by General Sarrail, this led to the arrest of the more radical Greek leaders and their subsequent deportation to Thessalonica: "Tous les fonctionnaires grecs (royalistes et vénizélistes) doivent être supprimés à Korytza et dépendances.

L'autorité militaire française désignera les fonctionnaires autochtones." ("All Greek officials (royalists and venizelists) must be removed from Korytza and its dependencies. The French military authority will appoint the native officials.")[7] General Sarrail did not give way in the face of the outcry provoked by the decision in Rome and Athens, both capitals strongly interested in the fate of this region. For nearly one year, he resisted the French diplomats, mocking their dissatisfaction for not having been consulted on diplomatic matters[8] and dismissing the policies he endorsed in southern Albania. To oust the Greek authorities in Korça, General Sarrail entrusted Colonel Descoins, a close friend of Perikles Argyropoulos,[9] who was assigned by Prime Minister Vénizélos the task of setting up the Greek administration in the town.

But on the ground, the French officers went far beyond than what was agreed. Despite the term "Autonomous Region" retained in the memorandum, Colonel Descoins undoubtedly endorsed its nationalization, as reflected in his memories:

> Sous peine de compromettre notre situation militaire à Korytza, nous devions faire pour les gens du pays plus que nous n'avions fait déjà, nous devions faire quelque chose qui liât à nous le peuple albanais d'une manière irrévocable et définitive. Si l'indépendance du Kaza de Korytza était proclamée, le nouvel Etat serait un belligérant qui prendrait place à nos côtés, il nous fournirait des troupes, ce qui permettrait de tenir ne vaste étendue de pays avec un minimum d'effectifs français. [On pain of jeopardizing our military situation in Korytza, we had to do more for the people of the country than we had already done, we had to do something that would bind the Albanian people to us in an irrevocable and definitive way. If the independence of Korytza Kaza was proclaimed, the new state would be a belligerent that would take its place on our side, it would provide us with troops, which would make it possible to hold a vast area of the country with minimal French troops.][10]

Moreover, numerous officers did not accept Sarrail's decision to revert to a more balanced politics when French political pressure became too strong. Colonel Descoins openly refused to amass evidence against his assistant, Themistokli Gërmenji, the main protagonist of the autonomy, for the purpose of bringing him before a court-martial. This disobedience led to his transfer to the island of Mytilene in May 1917, and a harsh assessment from General Sarrail, in August of the same year:

> Je connais depuis longtemps cet officier supérieur et c'est par suite dans son propre intérêt que je l'avais retiré de Korça. Postérieurement à cette mesure, j'ai d'ailleurs reçu l'ordre de le relever de son commandement pour raisons

diplomatiques. . . . J'estime que le colonel Descoins a de belles qualités, qu'il a rendu des services en Orient, mais il est un peu mégalomane et le mors arabe me semble devoir être bon pour les chevaux de Spahis comme pour lui. [I have known this senior officer for a long time and it is therefore in his own interest that I had removed him from Korça. After this measure, I received the order to relieve him of his command for diplomatic reasons. . . . I believe that Colonel Descoins has good qualities, that he has rendered services in the East, but he is a bit megalomaniac and the Arab bit seems to me to be good for the horses of Spahis as for him.][11]

On the contrary, some other high-level officers, like General Henri Mesplé, commander of the Algerian cavalry, deemed it necessary to promote Descoins to a higher rank on the grounds that "Le colonel Descoins tranche nettement au milieu de la banalité des bons serviteurs ordinaires. Il doit être nommé au plus vite au grade de général de Brigade." ("Colonel Descoins stands out from the banality of ordinary good servants. He must be appointed as soon as possible to the rank of Brigadier General").[12] But Descoins was far from an isolated case. In 1919 and 1920, when French diplomacy planned to return the region to Greece without waiting for the Peace Conference's decisions, some local officers covertly informed Albanian nationalist circles of these imminent plans in order to mobilize foreign governments opposed to such decisions and to foster armed resistance.[13] According to Italian sources, a significant number of Senegalese riflemen also disfavored such a project from sympathy for the Albanian Muslim element.[14]

However, if some soldiers disobeyed orders and political instructions, they did so rarely for religious or sentimental reasons or for material interests. The explanation lies rather in their lofty conception of the military's function, as appears from Colonel Descoins' writings:

Cette révolution, notre intérêt militaire à nous Français, qui occupions Korytza, nous commandait impérieusement de la "laisser faire." Dans le même ordre d'idées, nous devions plus tard laisser l'idée nationaliste albanaise se développer, nous devions même pousser à son développement sous peine de compromettre notre situation militaire. [This revolution, our military interest to us French, who occupied Korytza, commanded us imperiously to "let it go." In the same way, we had to allow the Albanian nationalist idea to develop later, we even had to push for its development at the risk of compromising our military situation.][15]

As testified by Colonel Ordioni, we can also find an explanation in the high regard in which they held their independence and their achievements:

De gros changements se produisaient à ce même moment dans le commandement de Salonique. . . . Si le général Sarrail partait en emmenant ses créatures fidèles, le général Guillaumat arrivait avec les siennes; de sorte que pour les indépendants, au nombre desquels je me trouvais pour avoir le droit de dire ce que je pensais, il n'y avait rien de changé! [Big changes were taking place at that very moment in the command of Salonika. . . . If General Sarrail was leaving with his faithful followers, General Guillaumat was arriving with his own; so that for the independents, among whom I was to have the right to say what I thought, nothing had changed!][16]

Skills in the Service of Peace

Beyond the political choices and the decisions taken on the ground, the soldier's contribution to peace or conflict resolution relied on a set of skills and know-how, not specifically military, acquired in various contexts and experienced in many ways. All of those came from empirical knowledge previously acquired in the Balkans and from colonial administration, to which a lot of them were accustomed. They mobilized their competences both during the conflict and in the immediate postwar period, either in a military or civil context, nationally as well as internationally.

An Arsenal of Mobilizable Skills

Even if the officers deployed in southern Albania mainly gained previous experience in the Balkans within the French Eastern Army or the Eastern Expeditionary Force (sent to Gallipoli and the Dardanelles straights from February to October 1915 along with other allies, mainly British, Australians, and New Zealanders), a handful of them acquainted themselves with the region during the Balkan wars or even, in exceptional cases, from the beginning of the twentieth century, in the international gendarmerie, which operated in Macedonia from 1904 to 1914. The competences acquired in these contexts yielded them grassroots cultural, linguistic, and geographical knowledge, as well as a subtle understanding of the local issues and balances of power. If such competences provide guarantees of impartiality, they may also interfere with political guidelines more inclined to enforce macroequilibria than taking into account local realities.

Before arriving in southern Albania, most of the officers had previous experiences in Greek (and sometimes Serb) Macedonia. This was the case of

Colonel Bardi de Fourtou who participated in the attempt to rescue the Serbian army from Thessalonica in northern Macedonia in the autumn of 1915, before leading the French detachment, which entered Korça on October 1916. Later, in September 1917, he took part in the conquest of Pogradec and then commanded the territory of Korça from August to October 1918. For his part, General Salle, who commanded the same territory for one year from May 1917, took part in the victorious onslaughts on Florina and Bitola in Macedonia in the autumn of 1916.

Some of these first-rank officers had longer experience, as they had taken part in the Eastern Expeditionary Force. In the autumn of 1915, that gave birth to the French Eastern Army after its failure and a shift of its mission toward the rescuing of the Serbian army in Macedonia. Colonel Descoins served in it as chief of staff, before joining the second as commander of the Struma detachment (in Greek Macedonia). General Gaston Foulon followed exactly the same path. Within the intelligence services, reserve officers like Réginald Kann covered the Balkan wars as a war correspondent (he also did so in Morocco and Manchuria), whereas the famous archaeologist Charles Picard had been a member and secretary general of the French School of Athens (before becoming its director from 1919 to 1925).

Such experiences in an allied environment are crucial as they help with understanding the functioning of a coalition and gaining the confidence of other partners, both guarantees of efficiency. If we consider Colonel Descoins, besides the aforementioned Greek trust, he earned the confidence of the Serbs by reorganizing their cavalry in Chalcidice, after his transfer from Corfu in spring 1916. This was also the case with General Léon-Paul Genin who, before commanding the Pogradec Territory in mid-1918 and then the *Troupes Françaises de Macédoine* (French Troops in Macedonia) in 1919, helped the Greek army to consolidate the Greek-Ottoman border in Thessaly in 1912 and headed its military schools. In the meantime, in November 1916, he took the command of the French military mission alongside the National Defense Government's army, a function in which he succeeded in setting up three Greek divisions.

Furthermore, some of these officers could rely on long-term experience, sometimes acquired in the Ottoman context. This was notably the case with General Foulon, who commanded the territory of Korça during the victorious onslaughts in Albania in the summer of 1918, which led to the breakthrough on the Macedonian front two months later. For ten years (1904–14), he helped reorganize the gendarmerie in Ottoman Macedonia and, during the Balkan wars, as a Lieutenant-Colonel of the Ottoman army, participated in the repatriation in

Anatolia of gendarmes and civil servants, as well as refugees. As appears from the following observation by General Albert d'Amade, General Foulon, the former commander of the Eastern Expeditionary Force, developed invaluable skills (all the more so if we consider that, apart from Turkish, Bulgarian, and Serb, he also spoke English, German, Italian, and Russian):

> Le Lieutenant-Colonel Foulon a rendu les plus utiles services par ses connaissances étendues de l'administration ottomane, de la langue du pays et des personnages influents de ces régions. Ses indications sont toujours précises, ses informations toujours très exactes. Esprit scientifique très développé. Expérience très complète obtenue par ses travaux, ses voyages, ses relations pendant qu'il était employé à l'organisation de la gendarmerie turque. [Lieutenant-Colonel Foulon rendered the most useful services through his extensive knowledge of the Ottoman administration, of the language of the country and of the influential people of these regions. His indications are always precise, his information always very exact. Very developed scientific spirit. Very complete experience obtained by his works, his travels, his relations while he was employed in the organization of the Turkish gendarmerie.][17]

In specific cases, understanding of or even empathy with local populations may also originate in a particular family's history. For instance, Colonel Ordioni explained his sympathy for the Greeks by the fact that four of his ancestors fought on their side during the War of Independence and fell in Missolonghi and inside the Acropolis.[18] In the same vein, he truly thought that his Corsican origin was key in understanding Albanians:

> les épiques légendes de nos bandits corses qui me sont familières depuis l'enfance m'ont préparé à comprendre les mœurs rudes ou étranges de ces populations rebelles à tout frein de l'autorité . . . ce qui m'a permis d'écrire sur leur compte des rapports officiels sur la réorganisation des forces albanaises. [the epic legends of our Corsican bandits which have been familiar to me since childhood have prepared me to understand the rough and strange customs of these populations, rebellious to any restraint of authority . . .which allowed me to write official reports on their account on the reorganization of the Albanian forces.][19]

In any event, most of the high-ranking officers serving in Albania had previous long-term experience in the colonies. General Paul Henrys, who commanded the victorious onslaughts in Albania during the summer of 1918 at the head of the French Eastern Army, served in Algeria, Morocco, the Sahara, and Sudan from 1887 to 1916. General Adolphe Guillaumat, the successor to General Sarrail at the head of the Eastern allied armies, believed that Sarrail could not have achieved such success in a command combining political and military issues equally without the experience acquired during his long stay in Africa.[20] General Genin served ten years in Algeria and three more in Indochina. General Salle served for six years in Algeria, while Colonel Ordioni spent most of his career in Tunisia, and Colonel Bardi de Fourtou arrived in Macedonia as the commander of the first African cavalry regiment. Some of them, like Colonel Descoins or Lieutenant Veauté (who performed the duties of director of the local police in Korça), relied on the *Spahis* regiment. Other central actors in southern Albania, like General Auguste Mortier (commander of the Pogradec Territory), Lieutenant-Colonel Alfred Noël, and Louis Reynard-Lespinasse, were all in the indigenous service of North Africa executives. More broadly, this also seemed to have been the case at lower level, as asserted by Colonel Ordioni: "J'oubliais de mentionner des sous-administrateurs pris parmi les lieutenants de l'Armée d'Afrique, l'Armée-école, qui remplirent remarquablement bien leurs missions." ("I forgot to mention the sub-administrators taken from among the lieutenants of the Army of Africa, the training army, who fulfilled their missions remarkably well.")[21]

If an in-depth work on the transfer of colonial competencies in the Balkans still needs to be completed, some elements seem to underpin it. First, the officers in charge of the local irregulars *Tabor albanais* (Albanian Tabor) and *Gendarmerie mobile albanaise* (Albanian Mobile Gendarmerie) used to serve in the *goums*. In the words of General Salle, they were thus "habitués au maniement des indigènes" ("used to handling natives").[22] Second, within the French Eastern Army, the cavalry detachments under the command of Colonel Bardi de Fourtou mingled frequently with colonial troops (Moroccan Spahis and Senegalese riflemen) and indigenous forces (Albanian Tabor, Greek companies, and bands of irregulars), while in spring 1916, the troops commanded by General Auguste Frotiée comprised the African cavalry regiment, *Zouaves* battalion, Czechoslovakian volunteers, and Serb bands.

But this know-how was not limited to military skills. Colonel Ordioni spearheaded archaeological excavations in Albania by identifying potential sites. His interest in archaeology started in Tunisia, where he had become acquainted with it through Alfred-Louis Delattre, a *Père Blanc*, well known for his excavations in Carthage. Several years later, in 1923, this was to have great consequences on French-Albanian relations as the Albanian state chose to entrust the famous archaeologist Léon Rey with all the excavations on its territory. It is noteworthy that the latter also worked on Macedonian burial mounds as a conscript in the French Eastern Army.

Reinvested Skills in the Postwar Period

If the signing of the armistices with the central powers between September and November 1918 halted the fighting between belligerents in the Balkans, it did not put an end to the military presence. As regards Albania, the French maintained their military occupation of the southeast until June 1920, in order to prevent its occupation by Greece, Italy, or even Serbia, without the Peace Conference's approval. During this period, Colonel Ordioni commanded successively the Territory of Pogradec and the entire southeastern region (known as *Confins albanais*), while sporadically performing strictly military duties as commander of the military camp in Skopje (Macedonia) from November 1918 to January 1919, and Galatsi (Romania) from April to August 1919. For his part, Colonel Bardi de Fourtou was appointed commander of the allied occupation of Shkodra, the main northern Albanian town, close to the borders with Montenegro, and coveted by that country as well as by Serbia and Italy. His acquaintance with the Albanian question (together with his strong pro-Yugoslav feelings) explained his selection as commander of a military occupation combining French, British, and Italian contingents and that lasted from November 1918 to the spring of 1920. When it ended, he went to Bulgaria to chair the Survey Allied Military Commission.

Once demobilized (and all the more when retired), some officers chose to reinvest their skills in a civil context for the benefit of the Balkans states or, more broadly, the region's stabilization. In particular, several decided not to go back to France but to put their know-how at the service of various local states. In that respect, General Foulon was appointed technical adviser of the French High Commissioner in Istanbul for general police matters and restructuring of the indigenous gendarmerie. As of February 1919, while holding this office, he accepted the position of inspector general of the Ottoman gendarmerie. In some ways, after the war, he reverted to his former activity in Ottoman Macedonia, but this time in a national context.[23] Nevertheless, his trajectory is not unique. In the early 1920s, Lieutenant Edouard Veauté engaged with the Albanian government to help it establish a gendarmerie. More surprisingly, he assisted the Albanian delegate, Mehdi bey Frashëri, in the Boundary Commission reactivated in 1921 to delineate and demarcate Albania's northern and southern borders, a work that could not be completed before the war broke out. In this position, he frequently met Colonel Ordioni who, from April 1923 to August 1926, led the French mission within this Commission. Ordioni, although officially retired in November 1919, was also active as Chairman of the Allied Commission for the delimitation of the Bulgarian-"Yugoslav" borders. Indeed, the presence of soldiers in such a Commission was by no means coincidental. The military conditions were a prerequisite,[24] which had some consequences on the way to envisage the peace process. As Colonel Ordioni himself explained, with a certain disdain for the political circles, he conceived his mission as highly impartial:

> Depuis que j'étais parti en Orient, c'est à dire depuis plus de quatre mois, je n'avais pas reçu la moindre directive, la moindre instruction de la part de mon gouvernement. Plus d'une fois je me demandais si nous avions une politique nationale ou une politique personnelle; d'autant que j'avais un chiffre avec lequel je pouvais correspondre personnellement avec le Président du Conseil. . . . J'en déduisais que mon gouvernement désirait tout simplement que je dise la vérité, en ne m'inspirant que des sentiments de justice et d'humanité. . . . Jusque-là c'est parfait; mais alors, après qu'on ne vienne pas me dire de changer ce que j'ai vu, paraphé et signé, parce que cela ferait du bien à notre politique. Ma signature a une valeur déterminée, je suis Commissaire français, représentant de mon pays, ce qui me donne un certain prestige et une grande fierté. Mais il me fait tenir mon rang, ma dignité: un colonel français représentant la France dans des négociations internationales et délicates ne peut renier sa signature. Il se le doit à lui-même, au nom qu'il porte, à la France qu'il représente. Il doit tenir bon et faire prévaloir son point de vue, à moins que des faits nouveaux ne soient venus se greffer sur les précédents et dont il n'était pas fait état jusqu'alors . . . j'aurais voulu, comme par le passé, que l'on m'indiquât le but à atteindre, tout en me laissant le choix des moyens d'exécution. C'est là la vraie méthode. . . . Les militaires, devenus diplomates, ne connaissent que la ligne de conduite droite, comme le glaive de leur épée; alors que les diplomates de carrière sont habitués à émettre souvent des avis diamétralement opposés; l'âme des soldats s'y oppose. [Since I had left for the Orient, that is for more than four months, I had not received the slightest directive, the slightest instruction from my government. More than once I wondered if we had a national policy or a personal policy; especially since I had a number with which I could correspond personally with the President of the Council. . . . I deduced that my government simply wanted me to tell the truth, inspiring me only with feelings of justice and humanity. . . . So far so good; but then, after that, don't come and tell me to change what I have seen, initialed and signed, because it would do our policy good. My signature has a certain value, I am a French Commissioner, a representative of my country, which gives me a certain prestige and a great pride. But it also makes me keep my rank, my dignity: a French colonel representing France in international and delicate negotiations cannot deny his signature. He owes it to himself, to the name he bears, to the France he represents. He must stand firm and make his point of view prevail, unless new facts have been grafted onto the previous ones

and of which no mention was made until then. . . . I would have liked, as in the past, that the goal be indicated to me, while leaving me the choice of the means of execution. This is the true method. . . . The military, who have become diplomats, know only the straight line, like the blade of their sword; whereas career diplomats are accustomed to expressing often diametrically opposed opinions; the soul of the soldiers opposes it.][25]

On the contrary, he interpreted his task as an expert contribution that should help the Conference of Ambassadors to shape long-term solutions in order to help the populations work safely together:

Nous autres délimitateurs, sommes-nous suffisamment armés et éclairés pour prononcer des sentences équitables? Oui, je crois que nous ne pouvons nous tromper de beaucoup et voici pourquoi: tout d'abord, les principes généraux qui nous guident sont les sentiments de justice et d'humanité. Nous apportons avec nous des idées conciliantes, d'apaisement et de concorde pour que les peuples puissent commencer à travailler en toute sécurité. Et ensuite, nos enquêtes menées sur place, très sévèrement, sont frappées au coin du bon sens et de l'examen minutieux des personnes et des choses. Nous avons enfin beaucoup de facteurs qui viennent à notre secours pour nous éclairer et nous mettre sur le bon chemin. [Are we delimiters sufficiently armed and enlightened to pronounce equitable sentences? Yes, I believe that we cannot be far wrong, and here is why: first of all, the general principles that guide us are the sentiments of justice and humanity. We bring with us conciliatory ideas, appeasement and harmony so that people can begin to work in safety. And then our investigations on the spot, very severely, are struck with common sense and scrutiny of people and things. And then we have many factors that come to our aid to enlighten us and put us on the right path.][26]

Looking for a sustainable solution, by avoiding creating situations that would fuel irredentism in the future, he could not have achieved his goal without an in-depth knowledge of the local situation. Among the qualities required, Ordioni of course mentioned a thorough and critical reading of the documents, a detailed knowledge of the context, and a sound base in history and geography. But most importantly, his long stays in the country provided him with information missing from the books. Thanks to his experience, he was deeply convinced that ethnicity could not be a decisive criterion considering the widespread multilingualism (an idea not that popular at that time). He had rather taken into consideration the economic units constituted by markets, outlets, traffic lanes . . . because people "need to live."[27]

By protecting Albanian nation- and state-building in a region leaving the Ottoman Empire, the French officers deployed in southeast Albania during the First World

War had a significant and long-lasting impact on the ongoing identity developments. Regardless of the strategic reasons that led them to follow these policies, neither the populations' peacemaking efforts nor economic and social development could have been as sustainable without the expertise and know-how acquired through their various assignments outside the mainland. Imperial (and republican) competences seem to have been largely mobilized when addressing Balkan issues, as the Italians did in their own occupied zone in Albania.[28] It is in itself reassuring to note the way in which these officers put their attention to local equilibria to use in the service of peace. It is equally reassuring to see that, during and in the immediate postwar period, the military and civil authorities were eager to make maximum use of their skills by multiplying their assignments in the same regions.

However, having the skills required is not a sufficient guarantee of success, or even that they will be mobilized in the best possible way. Apart from the issues of compliance with instructions or disobedience, other personal parameters are likely to interfere with involvement and the decision-making process. As we have seen with Generals Sarrail and Bardi de Fourtou, political convictions may play an essential role. If the latter so strongly supported Albanian national interests in Shkodra during the allied occupation of the city at the end of the war, it was only to weaken Italian influence in order to promote the Yugoslav cause. In addition, acculturation could entail risks, as revealed by General Sarrail in an assessment of Lieutenant-Colonel Foulon in 1915:

> Le Lieutenant-Colonel Foulon est un officier qui a de la valeur, mais n'a malheureusement pas toute celle qu'il croit avoir. Il a en outre gardé de son séjour en Orient tous les défauts du Levantin, y compris une attitude toute spéciale pour rechercher les recommandations et les intrigues. . . . Je l'ai envoyé en Serbie espérant que nous allions avancer et que sa connaissance de l'Orient pourrait nous être utile. Il m'a écrit officiellement—et je crois aussi officieusement—pour me vanter ses capacités et me demander à être reçu chef d'état-major de l'Armée. . . . Il a la folie des grandeurs [Lieutenant-Colonel Foulon is an officer who has value, but unfortunately does not have all the value he thinks he has. Moreover, he has kept from his stay in the East all the defects of the Levantine, including a very special attitude to look for recommendations and intrigues. . . . I sent him to Serbia hoping that we would advance and that his knowledge of the East could be useful to us. He wrote to me officially—and I think also unofficially—to boast of his abilities and to ask me to be received as Chief of Staff of the Army. . . . He has the folie de grandeur.][29]

In the most extreme cases, this "acculturation" could go as far as corruption and embezzlement; take, for example, the criminal offenses committed by

General Bardi de Fourtou during the time of his mission in Bulgaria and for which he was condemned by the Seine Tribunal in 1930. Such shortcomings underline both the advantage of deploying military men in diplomatic settings: they favored ground realities over international political issues and applied their practical skills pragmatically. Yet, this also oftentimes meant that they disobeyed their superiors, risked sanctions, and achieved a sometimes uneasy balance between obedience and disobedience in times of transitioning toward peace.

Glossary

Goum	Tribal contingents employed in Algeria and Morocco for military purposes
Kaza	Ottoman intermediate size territorial administrative unit
Père blanc	Catholic priest belonging to the *Société des missions africaines* (African missions Society)
Spahis	Indigenous traditional cavalry corps, designed on an Ottoman-inspired model, incorporated within the French Army after the conquest of Algeria
Tabor	Group of goums
Zouave	Soldier of light infantry units pertaining to the French African Army

Notes

1 The Albanian State was created by the Conference of London on July 29, 1913, on the ruins of the Ottoman Empire.
2 In September 1916, the Greek Prime Minister, Elefthérios Vénizélos, set up a dissenting government in Thessalonica, the National Defense Government, closely collaborating with the Entente, contrary to the royalist government in Athens, which—though officially neutral—remained faithful to the central powers.
3 Arben Puto, *La question albanaise dans les actes internationaux de l'époque impérialiste: 1867–1912* (Tirana: Editions "8 Nëntori," 1988).
4 They always refused, by example, to put customs posts in place at the "border."
5 Jean-André Ordioni, ed., *Un officier français dans les Balkans (1917–1925)* (Vannes: Dominique Danguy des Déserts, 2016).
6 Bavarian prince Wilhelm von Wied's reign lasted only six months, from March to September 1914.
7 Général Descoins, "Six mois d'histoire de l'Albanie (novembre 1916–mai 1917)," *Revue d'Histoire de la guerre mondiale* (1929): 335.
8 Maurice Sarrail, ed., *Mon commandement en Orient (1916–1918)* (London: Wentworth Press, 1920), 221.

9   They forged mutual bonds in the wake of the Balkan wars, as Colonel Descoins commanded Thessalonica's cavalry brigade, a city in which M. Argyropoulos was prefect.

10 Descoins, "Six mois d'histoire de l'Albanie (novembre 1916–mai 1917)," 332.

11 Ministère des Armées, Service Historique de la Défense, Dossier GR 5 YE 83367, Vincennes, France.

12 Ibid.

13 Regio Consolato generale d'Italia in Janina, no. 2059/182, Serie affari politici 1919–1930, Archivio storico diplomatico del Ministero degli Affari Esteri, Rome, Italy.

14 Regia Agenzia consolare italiana Koritza, September 18, 1919, no. 749, Serie affari politici 1919–1930, Archivio storico diplomatico del Ministero degli Affari Esteri.

15 Général Descoins, "Six mois d'histoire de l'Albanie (novembre 1916–mai 1917)," *Revue d'Histoire de la guerre mondiale* (1930): 43.

16 Ordioni, ed., *Un officier français dans les Balkans (1917-1925)*, T1, 220.

17 Ministère des Armées, Service Historique de la Défense, Dossier AC 21 P 451258, Vincennes, France.

18 Ordioni, ed., *Un officier français dans les Balkans (1917–1925)*, T2, 373, 220.

19 Ibid., T1, 53, 220.

20 Ministère des Armées, Service Historique de la Défense, Vincennes, France.

21 Ordioni, ed., *Un officier français dans les Balkans (1917–1925)*, T1, 395, 220.

22 H. Salle, "L'occupation française en Albanie," *Revue politique et parlementaire* (septembre 10, 1920): 409.

23 As if time had no effect on him, his local foothold still continues as he is buried in the Ferikoy cemetery, in Istanbul.

24 Arben Puto, ed., *Çështja shqiptare në aktet ndërkombëtare pas Luftës së Parë botërore,* T. 3, (Tiranë: Albin, 2001).

25 Ordioni, ed., *Un officier français dans les Balkans (1917–1925)*, T1: 460-1, 220.

26 Ibid., T2: 299, 220.

27 Ibid.

28 Renaud Dorlhiac, and Fabrice Jesné, "Une alliance de circonstance: l'Italie et les Musulmans d'Albanie (1912–1920)," *Revue des Mondes Musulmans et de l"a Méditerranée* 141, no. 61 (2017): 53–68.

29 Ministère des Armées, Service Historique de la Défense, Dossier AC 21 P 451258, Vincennes, France.

Bibliography

1 Introduction

Argyris, Chris and Donald Schön. *Organizational Learning: A Theory of Action Perspective*. Reading: Addison-Wesley, 1978.

Autesserre, Séverine. "Insiders and Outsiders." In *The Frontlines of Peace: An Insider's Guide to Changing the World*. Oxford: Oxford University Press, 2021: 69–92.

Cabanes, Bruno. "Aftermath, 1919." In *The Cambridge History of the First World War: Global War*, edited by Jay Winter, vol. 1. Cambridge: Cambridge University Press, 2014: 172–90.

Conze, Eckart. "Die große Illusion. Versailles 1919 und die Neuordnung der Welt." In *Jahrbuch zur Liberalismus-Forschung*. Nomos: Verlagsgesellschaft mbH & Co. KG, 2019.

Coulon, Jocelyn. *Soldiers of Diplomacy: The United Nations, Peacekeeping, and the New World Order*. Toronto: University of Toronto Press, 1998.

Davion, Isabelle. "Les sorties de guerre en Europe centre-orientale (1918–1921): comment les peuples ont eux aussi tracé les frontières." *Materiaux pour lhistoire de notre temps* 3–4, no. 129–30 (2018): 35–41.

Dessberg, Frédéric. "The Versailles Peace Settlement and the Collective Security System." In *A Companion to World War II*, edited by Thomas W. Zeiler and Daniel M. Dubois, vol. 1. Chichester: Wiley-Blackwell, 2013: 29–46.

Erlichman, Camilo and Christopher Knowles. "Introduction: Reframing Occupation as a System of Rule." In *Transforming Occupation in the Western Zones of Germany: Politics, Everyday Life and Social Interactions, 1945–55*, edited by Camilo Erlichman and Christopher Knowles. London: Bloomsbury Academic, 2018, 3–24.

Flateau, Cosima. "Les sorties de guerre. Une introduction." *Les Cahiers Sirice* 3, no. 17 (2016): 5–14.

Gerwarth, Robert. *The Vanquished: Why the First World War Failed to End, 1917–1923*. London: Allen Lane, 2016.

de Graaf, Beatrice. *Fighting Terror after Napoleon: How Europe Became Secure after 1815*. Cambridge: Cambridge University Press, 2020.

de Graaf, Beatrice, Ido de Haan, and Brian Vick, eds. *Securing Europe after Napoleon: 1815 and the New European Security Culture*. Cambridge: Cambridge University Press, 2019.

Hall, Peter A. "Policy Paradigms, Social Learning and the State: The Case of Economic Policy-Making in Britain." *Comparative Politics* 25, no. 3 (1993): 275–96.

Haynes, Christine. *Our Friends the Enemies: The Occupation of France after Napoleon.* Cambridge, MA: Harvard University Press, 2018.

Heideking, Jürgen. *Areopag der Diplomaten. Die Pariser Botschafterkonferenz der alliierten Hauptmächte und die Probleme der europäischen Politik 1920–1931 (Historische Studien; Bd. 436).* Husum: Verlag Matthiesen, 1979.

Jeannesson, Stanislas. "Les diplomates français et la paix au lendemain de la Grande Guerre." *Matériaux pour l'histoire de notre temps,* no. 4 (2012): 18–22.

Jeannesson, Stanislas, Fabrice Jesné, and Éric Schnakenbourg, eds. *Experts et expertises en diplomatie. La mobilisation des compétences dans les relations internationales du congrès de Westphalie à la naissance de l'ONU.* Rennes: Presses universitaires de Rennes, 2018.

Jones, Marcus. "Vae Victoribus: Bismarck's Quest for Peace in the Franco-Prussian War, 1870–1871." In *The Making of Peace: Rulers, States and the Aftermath of War,* edited by Williamson Murray and Jim Lacey, 177–208. Cambridge: Cambridge University Press, 2009: 177–208.

de Préneuf, Jean, Thomas Vaisset, and Philippe Vial, eds. "La Marine nationale et la Première Guerre mondiale: une histoire à redécouvrir." *Revue d'histoire maritime,* no. 20 (2014).

Prost, Antoine. *Les anciens combattants et la société française, 1914–1939: Mentalités et idéologies,* vol. 3. Paris: Les Presses de Sciences Po, 1977.

Sharp, Alan. *Versailles 1919: A Centennial Perspective.* London: Haus, 2018.

Showalter, Dennis E. "Diplomacy and the Military in France and Prussia, 1870." *Central European History* 4, no. 4 (1971): 346–53.

Smouts, Marie-Claude. *L'ONU et la guerre: la diplomatie en kaki.* Brussels: Éditions Complexe, 1994.

2 Peacemaking and Civil-Military Relations, 1918–23

von Baden, Max, *Erinnerungen und Dokumente.* Edited by Golo Mann and Andreas Bruckhardt. Stuttgart: Severus, 1968.

Bucholz, Arden. *Moltke, Schlieffen and Prussian War Planning.* New York: Berg, 1991.

Butler, William. "'The British Soldier is no Bolshevik': The British Army, Discipline, and the Demobilization Strikes of 1919." *Twentieth-Century British History* 30, no. 3 (2019): 321–46.

Cabannes, Bruno. *La victoire endeuillée: la sortie de guerre des soldats français (1018–1920).* Paris: Seuil, 2004.

Calwell, Charles E. *Field-Marshal Sir Henry Wilson, Bart., GCB, DSO: His Life and Diaries,* 2 vols. London: Cassell and Company Ltd., 1927.

Charteris, John. *At G.H.Q.* London: Cassell & Co. Ltd, 1931.

von Clausewitz, Carl. *On War.* Edited and translated by Michael Howard and Peter Paret. Princeton: Princeton University Press, 1976.

Daudet, Léon. *La guerre totale*. Paris: Kessinger Publishing, 1918.

Draper, Mario. "Mutiny under the sun: The Connaught Rangers, India, 1920." *War in History* 27, no. 2 (2020): 202–23.

Duroselle, Jean-Baptiste. *Clemenceau*. Paris: Fayard, 1988.

Foch, Ferdinand. *The Principles of War*. Translated by H. Belloc. London: H. K. Fly Co., 1918.

Fromkin, David A. *Peace to End All Peace: The Fall of the Ottoman Empire and the Creation of the Modern Middle East*. Translated by H. Belloc. New York: Avon Books, 1990.

Gerwarth, Robert. *The Vanquished: Why the First World War Failed to End 1917–1923*. London: Macmillan, 2016.

Gooch, John. *The Italian Army and the First World War*. Cambridge: Cambridge University Press, 2014.

Greenhalgh, Elizabeth. *Foch in Command; The Forging of a First War General*. Cambridge: Cambridge University Press, 2011.

Harris, J. Paul. *Douglas Haig and the First World War*. Cambridge: Cambridge University Press, 2008.

Irvine, Dallas D. "The Origins of Capital Staffs." *Journal of Modern History* 10 (1938): 161–79.

Jeffery, Keith. *Field Marshal Sir Henry Wilson: A Political Soldier*. Oxford: Oxford University Press, 2008.

Jeffery, Keith. *The Military Correspondence of Field Marshal Sir Henry Wilson 1918–1922*. London: The Bodley Head, 1985.

Masson, Philippe. *La marine française et la mer noire (1918–1919)*. Paris: Publications de la Sorbonne, 1982.

McCrae, Meighen. "'Ambushed by victory': Britain, France and American Plans to Defeat France in 1919." *War in History* 38, no. 4 (2019): 320–33.

McCrae, Meighen. *Coalition Strategy and the End of the First World War: The Supreme War Council and War Planning, 1917–1918*. Cambridge: Cambridge University Press, 2019.

Mordacq, Henri. *Le ministère Clemenceau: le journal d'un témoin*, 4 vols. Paris: Plon, 1930–31.

Mordacq, Henri. *Politique et stratégie dans une démocratie*. Paris: Plon-Nourrit, 1912.

Mordacq, Henri. *La stratégie: historique, évolution*. Paris: Fournier, 1912.

Notin, Jean-Christophe. *Foch*. Paris: Perrin, 2008.

Perry, Matt. *Mutinous Memories: A Subjective History of French Military Protest in 1919*. Manchester: Manchester University Press, 2019.

Phillipson, Coleman. *Termination of War and Treaties of Peace*. London: The Lawbook Exchange, Ltd., 1916.

Robertson, William. *Soldiers and Statesmen 1814–1918*, 2 vols. London: Charles Scribner's Sons, 1926.

Rowe, Laura. *Morale and Discipline in the Royal Navy During the First World War*. Cambridge: Cambridge University Press, 2018.

Rudin, Harry D. *Armistice 1918*. New Haven: Yale University Press, 1944.

Schneider, Isonzo. *The Forgotten Sacrifice of the Great War*. Westport: Praeger, 2001.

Stern, Eliane and Viviane Koenig. *L'étoile: le journal d'une petite fille pendant la grande guerre*. Paris: OSKAR, 2014.

von Thaer, Albrecht. *Generalstabsdienst an der Front und in der O.H.L.* Edited by Siegfried A. Kaehler. Göttingen: Vandenhoeck & Ruprecht, 1958.

Whittam, John. *The Politics of the Italian Army*. London: Shoe String Pr. Inc., 1977.

Wolz, Nicolas. *From Imperial Splendour to Internment: The German Navy in the First World War*. Barnsley: Seaforth Publishing, 2015.

Woodward, David. *Lloyd George and the Generals*. East Brunswick: Routledge, 1983.

Wright, Peter E. *At the Supreme War Council*. London, 1921 as adapted by Walter Lippmann; *Public Opinion*. New York: Harcourt, Brace & Co., 1922.

3 The Post–Cold War US Army and Debates over Peacekeeping Operations

Allen, William W., Antione D. Johnson, and John T. Nelsen. "Peacekeeping and Peace Enforcement Operations." *Military Review* 73, no. 10 (1993): 59.

Bolger, Daniel P. "The Ghosts of Omdurman." *Parameters* 21, no. 3 (1991): 32.

Bush, George H. W. "Address before the General Assembly of the United Nations." Transcript delivered online by Gerhard Peters and John T. Woolley, *The American Presidency Project*, 1992. https://www.presidency.ucsb.edu/node/267788.

Cherrie, Stanley F. "Task Force Eagle." *Military Review* 77, no. 4 (1997): 72.

Cowell, Alan. "G.I. Gets Support for Shunning UN Insignia." *The New York Times*, November 24, 1995. https://www.nytimes.com/1995/11/24/world/gi-gets-support -for-shunning-un-insignia.html.

Cuddy, Dennis. "The Case for Army Specialist." *New Fayetteville Observer-Times*, September 14, 1995.

Doyle, Francis M., Karen J. Lewis, and Leslie A. Williams. *Named Military Operations from January 1989 to December 1993*. Fort Monroe: US Army Training and Doctrine Command, 1994.

Dunlap, Charles J. "The Last American Warrior--Non-Traditional Missions and the Decline of the U.S. Armed Force." *Fletcher Forum of World Affairs* 18 (1994): 70.

Durch, William J. *UN Peacekeeping, American Politics, and the Uncivil Wars of the 1990s*. New York: Palgrave Macmillan, 1996.

Farr, Beatrice J. and Ruth H. Phelps. *Reserve Component Soldiers as Peacekeepers*. Alexandria: US Army Research Institute for the Behavioral and Social Sciences, 1996.

Fisher, Marc. "War and Peacekeeping." *Washington Post*, March 4, 1996. https://www .washingtonpost.com/archive/lifestyle/1996/03/04/war-and-peacekeeping/adfd68e7 -9be7-4e16-94fb-ea566ec3fd03/.

Fitzgerald, David. "Support the Troops: Gulf War Homecomings and a New Politics of Military Celebration." *Modern American History* 2, no. 1 (2019): 1–22.

Gerstle, Gary. "In the Shadow of War: Liberal Nationalism and the Problem of War." In *Americanism: New Perspectives on the History of an Ideal*, edited by Michael Kazin and Joseph A. McCartin. Chapel Hill: University of North Carolina Press, 2006.

Gordon, Michael R. "The 2000 Campaign: The Military; Bush Would Stop U.S. Peacekeeping In Balkan Fights." *The New York Times*, October 21, 2000. http://query .nytimes.com/gst/fullpage.html?res=9C07E4DE1E3EF932A15753C1A9669C8B63 &sec=&spon=&pagewanted=1.

"I Am Not a UN Soldier." *The New American*, October 2, 1995.

Joulwan, George A. "Operations Other Than War: A CINC's Perspective." *Military Review* 74, no. 2 (1994): 5.

Kagan, Robert. *Of Paradise and Power: America and Europe in the New World Order*. New York: Vintage, 2004.

Karacs, Imre. "US Medic Who Would Not Wear the Blue Beret Goes on Trial." *The Independent*, November 18, 1995. https://www.independent.co.uk/news/world/us -medic-who-would-not-wear-the-blue-beret-goes-on-trial-1582468.html.

Krauthammer, Charles. "The Short, Unhappy Life of Humanitarian War." *The National Interest* (Fall 1999): 8.

Krauthammer, Charles. "The Unipolar Moment." *Foreign Affairs* 70, no. 1 (1990): 23–33.

Krauthammer, Charles. "We Don't Peacekeep." *The Washington Post*, December 18, 2001. https://www.washingtonpost.com/archive/opinions/2001/12/18/we-dont -peacekeep/45dd2154-c2ac-474a-a9ca-03499d0a0c0e/.

Kretchik, Walter E. "Force Protection Disparities." *Military Review* 77, no. 4 (1997): 75.

Miller, Laura and Charles C. Moskos. "Humanitarians or Warriors?: Race, Gender, and Combat Status in Operation Restore Hope." *Armed Forces & Society* 21, no. 4 (1995): 615–37.

Moskos, Charles C. "Charles C. Moskos Papers." Northwestern University Archives, Northwestern University, Evanston.

Moskos, Charles C. "From College to Kosovo." *Wall Street Journal*, August 25, 2000.

O'Connor, Mike. "A Downsized Army Leans on Reserves for Duty in Bosnia." *The New York Times*, May 25, 1998. https://www.nytimes.com/1998/05/25/world/a-downsized -army-leans-on-reserves-for-duty-in-bosnia.html.

Powell, Collin L. "U.S. Forces: The Challenges Ahead." *Foreign Affairs*, Winter 1992/3. https://www.foreignaffairs.com/articles/1992-12-01/us-forces-challenges-ahead.

Powell, Colin L. and Joseph E. Persico. *My American Journey: An Autobiography*. New York: Random House, 1995.

"Presidential Decision Directive/NSC 25: Reforming Multilateral Peace Operations." Washington, DC: The White House, 1994.

Reimer, Denis J. "Denis J. Reimer Papers. 870–51 CSA." United States Army Heritage and Education Center, Carlisle, Pennsylvania.

Reuters. "The 1992 Campaign: Excerpts from Clinton's Speech on Foreign Policy Leadership." *The New York Times*, August 14, 1992. https://www.nytimes.com/1992/08/14/us/the-1992-campaign-excerpts-from-clinton-s-speech-on-foreign-policy-leadership.html.

Ryan, Maria. *Neoconservatism and the New American Century*. New York: Palgrave Macmillan, 2010.

Segal, David R. "Is a Peacekeeping Culture Emerging Among American Infantry in the Sinai MFO?." *Journal of Contemporary Ethnography* 30, no. 5 (2001): 607–36.

Segal, David R. and Dana P. Eyre. *The US Army in Peace Operations at the Dawning of the Twenty-First Century, US Army in Peace Operations at the Dawning of the Twenty-First Century*. Alexandria: US Army Research Institute for the Behavioral and Social Sciences, 1996.

Segal, David R., Theodore P. Furukawa, and Jerry C. Lindh. "Light Infantry as Peacekeepers in the Sinai." *Armed Forces & Society* 16, no. 3 (1990): 385–403.

Sullivan, Gordon and James Dubik. *Envisioning Future Warfare*. Fort Leavenworth: US Army Command and General Staff College Press, 1995.

Summers, Harry G. "Military Strategy: Conversations with Harry G. Summers." In *Conversations with History; Institute of International Studies.* Interview by Harry Kreisler and Thomas G. Barnes. Berkeley: University of California, 1996.

"United States v. Michael G. New: Legal Documents." *MikeNew.com*, accessed December 8, 2020. https://www.mikenew.com/thecase.html.

"US Convicts G.I. 'Who Refused To Serve Under UN in Balkans.'" *The New York Times*, January 25, 1996. https://www.nytimes.com/1996/01/25/world/us-convicts-gi-who-refused-to-serve-under-un-in-balkans.html.

Winner, Robert S. "Spc. Michael New v. William Perry, Secretary of Defense: The Constitutionality of US Forces Serving under UN Command." *DePaul Digest of International Law* 30, no. 3 (Spring 1997). http://www.kentlaw.edu/academics/courses/admin-perritt/winner.htm.

Yoshitani, Gail E. S. *Reagan on War: A Reappraisal of the Weinberger Doctrine, 1980–1984*. College Station: Texas A&M University Press, 2011.

4 Soldier or Diplomat? The Gray Area of UN Peacekeeping in Cambodia

Archives Diplomatiques Nantes. 10 POI/1 1309, POI/1 1310. Nantes, France.

Artus, Dominique. "Colère française au Cambodge." *Le Journal du Dimanche*, May 31, 1992.

Author's Interview with F. Motmans, Belgium, December 14, 2019.

Author's Interview with H. Dukers, the Netherlands, August 27, 2018.

Author's interview with M. Loridon, France, July 22, 2018.

Bais, Karolien. *Het mijnenveld van een vredesmacht Nederlandse blauwhelmen in Cambodja*. The Hague: SDU Uitgeverij, 1994.

de Beer, Patrice. "Le scepticisme tempéré du général Loridon." *Le Monde*, June 2, 1992. https://www.lemonde.fr/archives/article/1992/06/02/cambodge-le-scepticisme -tempere-du-general-loridon_3907315_1819218.html.

Berdal, Mats and Michael Leifer. "Cambodia." In: *The New Interventionism, 1991–1994: United Nations Experience in Cambodia, Former Yugoslavia, and Somalia*, edited by James Mayall. Cambridge: Cambridge University Press, 1996.

Berry, Ken. *Cambodia - from Red to Blue: Australia's Initiative for Peace*. St. Leonards: Allen & Unwin in association with the Dept. of International Relations, RSPAS, ANU, 1997.

Boutros-Ghali, Boutros. *An Agenda for Peace: Preventive Diplomacy, Peacemaking and Peace-keeping*. New York: United Nations, 1992.

Braeckman, Colette. "La drôle de paix de Kompong Thom." *Le Soir*, April 14, 1992.

Brown, MacAlister and Joseph F. Zasloff. *Cambodia Confounds the Peacemakers, 1979–1998*. Ithaca: Cornell University Press, 1998.

Chanda, Nyan. "UN Divisions: Signs of Growing Franco-Australian Rivalry within Peacekeeping Force." *Far Eastern Economic Review*, July 23, 1992.

Coulon, Jocelyn. *Soldiers of Diplomacy: The United Nations, Peacekeeping, and the New World Order*. Toronto: University of Toronto Press, 1998.

Evans, Gareth. *Incorrigible Optimist: A Political Memoir*. Melbourne: Melbourne University Press, 2017.

Findlay, Trevor. *Cambodia: The Legacy and Lessons of UNTAC*. Oxford University Press, 1997.

Findlay, Trevor. *The Use of Force in Peace Operations*. Oxford: Oxford University Press-SIPRI, 2002.

Gregory, Shaun. "France and missions de paix." *The RUSI Journal* 145, no. 4 (2000): 58–63, 62.

Hatto, Ronald. *Le maintien de la paix: L'ONU en action*. Paris: Armand Colin, 2015.

Heininger, Janet E. *Peacekeeping in Transition: The United Nations in Cambodia*. New York: The Twentieth Century Fund Press, 1994.

Horner, David and John Connor. *The Good International Citizen Australian Peacekeeping in Asia, Africa and Europe, 1991–1993*. New York: Cambridge University Press, 2014.

"Inquiétude au Cambodge." *L'Humanité*, June 1, 1992.

Interview by James S. Sutterlin with Sir Marrack Goulding. *Yale United Nations Oral History Project (YUNOP)*. Oxford, United Kingdom, June 30, 1998.

Jennar, Raoul M. *Croniques Cambodgiennes 1990–1994: Rapports au Forum International des ONG au Cambodge*. Paris: Éditions l'Harmattan, 1995.

"Le retour à la paix Cambodge: timide progrès sur le terrain." *Le Figaro*, April 1, 1992.

Loridon, Michel. "Cambodge, les raisons d'un échec." In *Opérations des Nations unies, leçons de terrain: Cambodge, Somalie, Rwanda, ex-Yougoslavie*, edited by Jean Pierre Cot and Franck Debié. Paris: La Documentation française, 1995.

Loridon, Michel. "La fermeté: un droit et un devoir pour l'ONU." In *Les interventions extérieures de l'armée française*, edited by Pierre Pascallon. Brussels: Bruylant Bruxelles, 1997.

Loridon, Michel. "Le rôle des casques bleus." *Le Casoar* (July 1993): 86–8, 87.

Loridon, Michel. "The U.N. intervention in Cambodia 1991/1993." Unpublished Paper given at the RUSI-Swedish War College Seminar April 23 and 24, 1996.

Luizet, Francois. "Cambodge: la paix en panne, les Khmers rouges bloquent l'ONU." *Le Figaro*, June 11, 1992.

Message from Phnom Penh. *Agence France Presse*, accessed via Dow Jones Factiva database, July 29, 1992.

Ministry of Foreign Affairs Archives. BZ-00391. Ministry of Foreign Affairs, The Hague, The Netherlands.

Nederlands Instituut voor Militaire Historie (NIMH). UNTAC-099. The Hague, The Netherlands.

"No Shooting War for us in Cambodia, Evans Says." *The Canberra Times*, August 25, 1989.

O'Meara, Sean. "Keeping the Peace a Cambodian Diary Dec. 1991 –June 1993." *An Cosantóir – The Defence Forces Magazine* 52, no. 10 (1992): 34–36.

Peou, Sorpong. *Conflict Neutralization in the Cambodian War From Battlefield to Ballot Box*. Oxford: Oxford University Press, 1997.

Peter, Mateja. "Between Doctrine and Practice: The UN Peacekeeping Dilemma." *Global Governance* 21 (2015): 351–70.

Pons, Frédéric. "Le syndrome du buffle." *Valeurs Actuelles*, June 22, 1992.

Prasso, Sheri. "Generals Refuse to Halt Fighting in Central Cambodia." *Agence France Presse*, 1992.

Ruggie, John Gerard. "The UN and the Collective Use of Force: Whither or Whether?." In *The UN, Peace and Force*, edited by Michael Pugh. London: Frank Cass, 1996.

Ruggie, John Gerard. "Wandering in the Void-Charting the UN's New Strategic Role." *Foreign Affairs* 72 (1992): 26–31.

Sanderson, John. *Command at the Operational Level*. Presentation to the Australian Command and Staff College. Unpublished paper given at Queensclif on June 26, 2000.

Sanderson, John M. "Dabbling into War: The Dilemma of the Use of Force in United Nations Intervention." In *Peacemaking and Peacekeeping for the New Century*, edited by Olara A. Atunnu and Michael W. Doyle. Oxford: Rowman & Littlefield publishers, 1998.

Sanderson, John M. "The Incalculable Dynamic of Force." In *UN Peacekeeping in Trouble: Lessons Learned from the Former Yugoslavia Peacekeeper's Views on the Limits and Possibilities of the United Nations in a Civil War-like Conflict*, edited by Wolfgang Biermann and Martin Vadset. Aldershot: Ashgate Publishing, 1998.

Sanderson, John M. "Peacekeeping or Peace Enforcement? Global Flux and the Dilemmas of UN Intervention." In *The United Nations at Fifty: Retrospect and Prospect*, edited by Ramesh Thakur. Dunedin: University of Otago Press, 1996.

Sanderson, John M. "UNTAC: The Military Component View." In *Institute of Policy Studies Singapore, The United Nations Transitional Authority in Cambodia Debriefing and Lessons*. International Conference UNTAC: Debriefing and Lessons Singapore – August 3, 1994. London: Kluwer Law International, 1995.

Schmidl, Erwin A. "Speak Softly and Carry a Big Stick: The Use of Force in Peace Operations, Past and Present." In *Peacekeeping with Muscle: The Use of Force in International Conflict Resolution*, edited by Alex Morrison, Douglas A. Fraser, and James D. Kiras. Clementsport: Canadian Peacekeeping Press, 1997.

Semi Statisch Archief Ministerie van Defensie (SSAMD). Ministerie van Defensie, The Hague, The Netherlands.

Sitkowski, Andrej. *UN Peacekeeping Myth and Reality*. Westport: Praeger Security International, 2006.

Smouts, Marie-Claude, ed. *L'ONU et la guerre: la diplomatie en kaki*. Brussels: Éditions Complexe, 1994.

Stern, Brigitte. "Conclusion." In *United Nations Peace-Keeping Operations: A guide to French Policies*, edited by Yves Daudet, Philippe Morillon, and Marie-Claude Smouts. Tokyo: UN University Press, 1998.

Tardy, Thierry. "The Reluctant Peacekeeper: France and the Use of Force in Peace Operations." *The Journal of Strategic Studies* 37, no. 5 (2014): 770–92, 776.

Thayer, Nate. "Phnom Penh Launches Offensive as Cease-fire Efforts Stall." *Associated Press*, March 29, 1992.

United Nations Archives New York. S-0794-0011-0001, S-0794-0012-0001, S-0794-0020-0001, S-0794-0043-0001, 0794-0046-0004, S-0794-0047-0003, S-0794-0047-0004, S-0794-0048-0002, S-0794-0048-0002, S-0794-0049-0001, S-0795-0043-0005, S-0795-0045-0003, S-0796-0056-0002, S-0995-0001-0004, S-0997-0006-0003, S-1829-0314-0003, S-1854-0060-0004, S-1854-0080-0006. New York, USA.

5 United Nations Military Observers in Former Yugoslavia: Strategic Influencers or Sitting Ducks?

Archive ECMM, Semi Statisch Informatie Beheer (SSIB). Rijswijk, The Netherlands.

Archive European Council (AEUR). ECMM 50.16A. Brussels, Belgium.

Bellamy, Alex J. and Paul D. Williams. *Understanding Peacekeeping*. Cambridge: Polity Press, 2010.

Berdal, Mats and David H. Ucko. "The Use of Force in UN Peacekeeping Operations: Problems and Prospects." *The RUSI Journal* 160, no. 1 (2015): 6.

Biermann, Wolfgang and Martin Vadset, eds. "UN Military Observers' Role in De-escalation of Local Conflict: Lessons Learned from a Soldiers Perspective." In *UN Peacekeeping in Trouble: Lessons Learned from the Former Yugoslavia*, edited by Søren Bo Husum. London: Routledge, 2019.

Bloed, Arie, ed. *The Conference on Security and Co-operation in Europe: Basic Documents, 1993–1995*. The Hague: Martinus Nijhoff Publishers, 1997.

Blue Helmets: A Review of United Nations Peacekeeping, third edition, v–vi, 672, 691–773. New York: UN Reproduction Section, 1996.

Buurman, L. and P. Poharnok. "Het vervolg van de ervaringen van onze UNMOs in Sarajevo." *Achterbanier* 14, no. 8 (1992): 6.

ten Cate, Arthur. *Sterven voor Bosnië?* Amsterdam: Boom uitgeverij, 2007.

ten Cate, Arthur. *Waarnemers op heilige grond: Nederlandse officieren bij UNTSO 1956–2003*. Amsterdam: Boom uitgeverij, 2003.

Dawson, Pauline. *The Peacekeepers of Kashmir*. New York: St. Martins Press, 1994.

Diehl, Paul Francis. *International Peacekeeping*. Baltimore: Johns Hopkins University Press, 1993.

van Dijk, W. A. M. "UNMO actie naar Zepa." *Carré* 7/8 (1993): 22.

Dorn, Walter. *Keeping Watch: Monitoring, Technology and Innovation in UN Peace Operations*. New York: UN University Press, 2011.

Doyle, Colm. *Witness to War Crimes: The Memoirs of a Peacekeeper in Bosnia*. Barnsley: Pen and Sword, 2018.

European External Action Service (EEAS) Archive. A030.2-030. Brussels, Belgium.

Fleitz Jr., Frederick. H. *Peacekeeping Fiascoes of the 1990s: Causes, Solutions and U.S. Interests*. Westport: Praeger Publishers, 2002.

Gelissen, Jos. *De Gijzeling en de gevolgen*. Amsterdam: Brave New Books, 2015.

Gelissen, Jos interviewed by Dion Landstra, February 10, 2018.

Goulding, Marrack. *The Evolution of United Nations and NATO in Former Yugoslavia*. 's Gravenhage: Netherlands Atlantic Commission, 1994.

Goulding, Marrack. *Peacemonger*. Houston: Johns Hopkins University Press, 2002.

Harbom, Lotta and Peter Wallensteen. "Armed Conflict, 1989–2006." *Journal of Peace Research* 44, no. 5 (2007).

Harry Konings, interviewed by Dion Landstra, October 27, 2020.

Hatto, Ronald. "From Peacekeeping to Peacebuilding: The Evolution of the Role of the United Nations in Peace Operations." *International Review of the Red Cross* 95 (2013).

Horner, David and John Connor. *The Good International Citizen: Volume 3, The Official History of Australian Peacekeeping, Humanitarian and Post-Cold War Operations: Australian Peacekeeping in Asia, Africa and Europe 1991–1993*. New York: Cambridge University Press, 2014.

van Kaathoven, L. L. G. M. "Het werk van de United Nations Military Observer in het voormalig Joegoslavië." *Komma* 14, no. 3 (1992).

Klep, Christ and Richard J. A. van Gils. *Van Korea tot Kabul: De Nederlandse militaire deelname aan vredesoperaties sinds 1945*. Netherland: Sdu Uitgevers, 2005.

Koops, Joachim. *The Oxford Handbook of United Nations Peacekeeping Operations*. Oxford: Oxford University Press, 2013.

Landstra, D. *Informatiemakelaar en Schietschijf. De inzet en effectiviteit van waarnemers in vredesoperaties op de Balkan, 1991–1995*. Amsterdam: Boom, 2022.

van der Lijn, Jaïr. *Walking the Tightrope: Do UN Peacekeeping Operations Actually Contribute to Durable Peace?* Amsterdam: Rozenberg Publishers, 2006.

Londey, Peter, Rhys Crawley, and David Horner. *The Long Search for Peace: Observer Missions and Beyond, 1947–2006.* Cambridge: Cambridge University Press, 2019.

Lutgert, Willem Hendrik and Rolf de Winter. *Check the horizon: De Koninklijke Luchtmacht en het conflict in voormalig Joegoslavië, 1991–1995.* Sectie Luchtmachthistorie, Staf Bevelhebber der Luchtstrijdkrachten: Sdu Uitgevers, 2001.

MacKenzie, Lewis. *Peacekeeper: The Road to Sarajevo.* London: Douglas & McIntyre Limited, 1993.

Maloney, Sean M. "Operation bolster: Canada and the European community monitor mission in former Yugoslavia, 1991–92." *International Peacekeeping* 4, no. 1 (1997): 26–50.

Morillon, Philippe. *Croire et oser: Chronique de Sarajevo.* Paris: B. Grasset Publisher, 1993.

Nederlands Instituut voor Militaire Historie (NIMH). Collectie Vredesoperaties. The Hague, The Netherlands.

NIOD. *Srebrenica (band I).* Amsterdam: Boom uitgeverij, 2002.

O'Shea, Brendan. *The Modern Yugoslav Conflict 1991–1995: Perception, Deception and Dishonesty.* London: Routledge, 2005.

Pellnas, B. interviewed by Dion Landstra, September 18, 2018.

"Report of Proceedings." *NZ-UNMO Gwyn Rees,* May–June 1992.

United Nations Archive New York. S-1828-0003-0005, S-1829-0182-0001, S-1829-0181-0005, S-1829-0181-0006, S-1829-0185-0006, S-1829-0332-0004, S-1830-0009-0004, S-1830-0009-0005, S-1830-0009-0006, S-1834-0009-0006, S-1835-0040-0005, S-1837-0030-0001, S-1834-0053-0006, S-1838-0076-0003, S-1838-0079-0002, S-1837-0092-0006, S-1837-0122-0001, S-1837-0127-0001, S-1837-0129-0002, S-1837-0129-0004, S-1837-0129-0005, S-1838-0076-0003, S-1837-0136-0001, S-1837-0158-0001, S-1838-0161-0001, S-1838-0183-0005, S-1838-0192-0007, S-1837-0195-0004, S-1838-0177-0005, S-1838-0188-0003, S-1838-0192-0007, S-1838-0194-0005, S-1838-0205-0002, S-1838-0206-0004. New York, USA.

United Nations Documents: SCR 721, 27 November 1991, S/23280 ANNEX III, 11 December 1991, S/23513 ANNEX II, 4 February 1992, SCR 743, 21 February 1992, SCR 749, 7 April 1992, S/1994/291, S/24075, 6 June 1992, SCR 758, 8 June 1992, S/24188 26 June 1992, SCR 761, 29 June 1992, S/23777, 2 April 1992, S/23900, 12 May 1992, S/24000, 26 May 1992, S/24600, 28 September 1992, S/24767, 5 November 1992, S/24783, 9 November 1992, S/24810, 13 November 1992, S/24840, 24 November 1992, S/24870, 30 November 1992, S/24900, 7 December 1992, S/24923, 9 December 1992, SCR 795, 11 December 1992, SCR 816, 31 March 1993, SCR 821, 16 April 1993, SCR 824, 6 May 1993, 11 March 1994, S/1994/300, 16 March 1994, S/1994/333, 24 March 1994, SCR 908, 31 March 1994, SCR 914. 27 April 1994.

Wainhouse, David W. *International Peace Observation; A History and Forecast.* Baltimore: Johns Hopkins Press, 1966.

Wallenius, Claes, Gerry Larsson, and Curt R. Johansson. "Military Observers' Reactions and Performance when Facing Danger." *Military Psychology* 16, no. 4 (2004).

Zoutendijk, J. interviewed by Dion Landstra, January 29, 2018.

6 Turning "Enemies" into "Friends": The Role of the Military in Peacemaking in France after Napoleon (1815–18)

Archives Départementales de la Meuse, 8R/29. Bar-le-Duc, France.

Archives Départementales des Ardennes, 1J/486. Charleville-Mézières, France.

Archives Départementales du Haut-Rhin, 8R/1172, 1173, 1174. Colmar, France.

Archives Municipales de Sedan, H/70. Charleville-Mézières, France

Archives Nationales, F7/9904. Pierrefitte-sur-Seine, France.

Berdusis, John. "Crossing the Pond: How General Winfield Scott Adopted the British Model of Military Occupation for Use in the United States Army in the Early Nineteenth Century." MA thesis, University of North Carolina at Charlotte, North Carolina, 2021.

Bibliothèque Multimédia de Valenciennes, H7/38.

Blancpain, Marc. *La vie quotidienne dans la France du Nord sous les occupations, 1814–1944.* Paris: Hachette, 1983.

Breuillard, Jean. "L'occupation russe à Givet de 1816 à 1818, d'après les mémoires du Gén.-Baron V. I. Loewenstern." *Revue historique ardennaise* 12 (1977): 57–77.

Breuillard, Jean. "L'occupation russe en France (1816–1818)." Type script ms. for *Revue des Études slaves*, 1J/486, Archives Départmentales des Ardennes.

Bruchet, Max. "L'invasion et l'occupation du département du Nord par les allies, 1814–1818 (suite)." *Revue du Nord* 7, no. 25 (1921): 44–5.

Caruthers, Susan. *The Good Occupation: American Soldiers and the Hazards of Peace.* Cambridge, MA: Harvard University Press, 2016.

Cazin, François-Simon. *Les Russes en France: Souvenirs des années 1815, 1816 et 1817.* Avranches: J. Durand, 1880.

Dower, John. *Embracing Defeat: Japan in the Wake of World War II.* New York: W. W. Norton/The New Press, 1999.

Downs, Gregory P. *After Appomattox: Military Occupation and the Ends of War.* Cambridge, MA: Harvard University Press, 2015.

Duvivier, Jules. "La ville de Bouchain et l'Ostrevant de 1814 à 1818: L'occupation danoise." *Bulletin de la Commission historique du Nord* 34 (1933): 322–38.

Edelstein, David. *Occupational Hazards: Success and Failure in Military Occupation.* Ithaca: Cornell University Press, 2008.

Gazette nationale ou le Moniteur universel. February 25, 1818, 1–4. https://www .retronews.fr/journal/gazette-nationale-ou-le-moniteur-universel/25-fevrier-1818 /149/1332717/1.

de Graaf, Beatrice. *Fighting Terror after Napoleon: How Europe Became Secure after 1815*. Cambridge: Cambridge University Press, 2020.

de Graaf, Beatrice, Ido de Haan, and Brian Vick, eds. *Securing Europe after Napoleon: 1815 and the New European Security Culture*. Cambridge: Cambridge University Press, 2019.

Guérin, Yann. *La France après Napoléon: Invasions et occupations, 1814–1818*. Paris: L'Harmattan, 2014.

Hantraye, Jacques. *Les Cosaques aux Champs-Élysées: L'occupation de la France après la chute de Napoléon*. Paris: Belin, 2005.

Haynes, Christine. *Our Friends the Enemies: The Occupation of France after Napoleon*. Cambridge, MA: Harvard University Press, 2018.

Jarrett, Mark. *The Congress of Vienna and Its Legacy: War and Great Power Diplomacy after Napoleon*. London: I. B. Tauris, 2013.

Kissinger, Henry. *A World Restored: Metternich, Castlereagh and the Problem of Peace, 1812–1822*. Boston: Houghton Mifflin, 1957.

"Lecture par M. Duvivier d'un mémoire sur l'occupation étrangère de la région du Nord de 1816 à 1818: Journal du lt. danois Muller." October 24, 1938. *Bulletin de la Commission historique du Département du Nord* 36 (1948): 47–79.

Leuilliot, Paul. *L'Alsace au début du XIXe siècle: Essais d'histoire politique, économique et religieuse (1815–1830), vol. 1, La vie politique*. Paris: S.E.V.P.E.N., 1959.

"L'occupation russe de 1816 à 1818: les Mémoires du général-baron V. I. Löwenstern." Typescript ms., 1J/486, Archives Départementales des Ardennes.

Mikaberidze, Alexander. *The Russian Officer Corps in the Revolutionary and Napoleonic Wars, 1792–1815*. El Dorado Hills: Savas Beatie, 2005.

Nerland, Finn V. "Danish Troops in France following Napoleon's Fall." In *Danmark og Napoleon*, edited by Eric Lerdrup Bourgois and Niels Høffding, 233–47. Gjern: Forlaget Hovedland, 2007.

Nerland, Finn V. "Danske fresbevardende tropper I Frankrig, 1815–1818." *Krigshistorisk Tidsskrift* 39, no. 1 (2003): 3–27.

Ozaneaux, Georges. *La vie à Colmar sous la Restauration*. Bibliothèque de la Revue d'Alsace. Paris: Paul Hartmann Éditeur, 1929.

Rhinelander, Anthony L. H. *Prince Michael Vorontsov: Viceroy to the Tsar*. Montreal: McGill-Queen's University Press, 1990.

Sacrez, André. "Les Russes en 'Ardenne wallonne.'" *Ardenne wallonne* 97: 2–11, and 98: 10–17, 2004.

Service Historique de la Défense (Vincennes), 3D/19.

Stirk, Peter. *The Politics of Military Occupation*. Edinburgh: Edinburgh University Press, 2009.

Veve, Thomas D. *The Duke of Wellington and the British Army of Occupation in France, 1815–1818*. Westport: Greenwood Press, 1992.

Vick, Brian. *The Congress of Vienna: Power and Politics after Napoleon*. Cambridge, MA: Harvard University Press, 2014.

Wacker, Volker. *Die allierte Besetzung Frankreichs in den Jahren 1814 bis 1818.* Hamburg: Dr. Kovac, 2001.

Wauthier, Raphaël. "Les Russes à Givet, 1816–1818." *Revue historique ardennaise* 19 (1912): 155–61.

Wellington, Arthur W. and John Gurwood. *The Dispatches of Field Marshal the Duke of Wellington.* Edited by Lt. Col. Gurwood, 12 vols. London: John Murray, 1836–1839.

Zamoyski, Adam. *Rites of Peace: The Fall of Napoleon and the Congress of Vienna.* New York: Harper Perennial, 2007.

7 "War against War": The Anti-militarist Activities of Greek War Veterans (1922–5)

Akropolis. "Ta efedrika synedria" [Veterans' Conferences]. June 18, 1936, 5.

Alcalde, Ángel. "War Veterans as Transnational Actors: Politics, Alliances and Networks in the Interwar Period." *European Review of History* 25, no. 3–4 (2018).

Alivizatos, Nikos. *Oi politikoi thesmoi se krisi 1922–1974* [The political institutions in crisis 1922–1974]. Athens: Themelio, 1983.

Bacharas, Dimitris. "La Grèce Après la Guerre: Dictature et République dans un Monde en Mutation (1922–1925)." Ph.D. Thesis, Ecole des Hautes Etudes en Sciences Sociales, Paris, 2010.

Becker, Annette. "Faith, Ideologies, and the 'Cultures of War.'" In *A Companion to World War I*, edited by John Horne, 234–47. Chichester: Wiley-Blackwell, 2010.

Benaki Museum's Historical Archives. f. 145. Archive of Eleftherios Venizelos, Kriti, Greece.

Carabott, Philip. "The Greek 'Communists' and the Asia Minor Campaign." *Bulletin of the Centre for Asia Minor Studies* 9 (1992).

Ceadel, Martin. "Pacifism." In *The Cambridge History of the First World War*, edited by Jay Winter, .vol. II, 576–605. Cambridge: Cambridge University Press, 2014.

Central Service. f. 20.7. Diplomatic and Historical Archives of the Greek Ministry of Foreign Affairs, Thrace Army, Athens, Greece.

Clogg, Richard. *A Concise History of Greece.* Cambridge: Cambridge University Press, 1997.

Communist Party of Greece. *Episima keimena* [Official Texts], Vol. II. Athens: Sichroni Epochi, 1974.

Educational Centre Charilaos Florakis, Archive of the Communist Party of Greece. Athens, Greece.

Eghigian, Gregg. "Injury, Fate, Resentment and Sacrifice in German Political Culture, 1914–1939." In *Sacrifice and National Belonging in Twentieth-Century Germany*, edited by Gregg Eghigian and Matthew P. Berg, 90–117. Arlington: Texas University Press, 2002.

Gendarmerie Directorate of Patras to the Interior Ministry, Patras, February 16, 1925.

General Archives of Greece (GAK), Archive of the Prime Minister. f. 12, f. 738, f. 739, f. 877, f. 878, f. 879.

Hellenic Army General Staff. *Epitomos Istoria Ekstratias Mikras Asias 1919–1922* [History of Asia–Minor Campaign 1919–1922]. Athens: Army History Directorate, 1967.

Hellenic Literature and Historical Archive (ELIA), Archive of Andreas Michalakopoulos. Introductory reports f. 2. Athens, Greece.

Hering, Gunnar. *Ta politika kommata stin Ellada, 1821–1936* [Political Parties in Greece, 1821–1936], vol. II. Athens: MIET, 2004.

Isola, Gianni. "Socialismo e combattentismo: La Lega proletaria. 1918–1922." *Italia Contemporanea* 141 (1980).

Kamouzis, Dimitris. *Greeks in Turkey. Elite Nationalism and Minority Politics in Late Ottoman and Early Republican Istanbul.* London, New York: Routledge, 2021.

Koliopoulos, John S. and Thanos M. Veremis. *Modern Greece. A History since 1821.* Chichester: Wiley–Blackwell, 2010.

Kontogiorgi, Elisabeth. *Population Exchange in Greek Macedonia: The Rural Settlement of Refugees 1922–1930.* Oxford, New York: Oxford University Press, 2006.

Lefousis, Ilias. *To ergatiko kinima tou Volou 1881–1936* [The Labour Movement of Volos 1881–1936]. Volos, 1986.

Lenin, Vladimir I. *Collected Works*, vol. 21. Moscow: Progress Publishers, 1964.

Makris, Alexandros. "Oi kirikes tis ideas tou ethnous. Palaioi polemistes, anapiroi kai thimata polemou stin Ellada (1912–1940)" ['The preachers of the idea of the nation' Veterans and War Victims in Greece (1912–1940)]. Ph.D. Thesis, National and Kapodistrian University of Athens, Athens, 2021.

McMeekin, Sean. *The Russian Revolution. A New History.* London: Profile Books, 2017.

Millington, Chris. "Communist Veterans and Paramilitarism in 1920s France: The Association Républicaine des Anciens Combattants." *Journal of War & Culture Studies* 8, no. 4 (2015): 300–14.

Nation, Craig. *War on War. Lenin, Zimmerwald Left and the Origins of Communist International.* Durham, London: Duke University Press, 1989.

The National Archives/Foreign Office (TNA/FO). 371–9891, 371–10769, 371–10769, 371–8827, 371–8827, 371–9896. Richmond, United Kingdom.

Nikas, P. *To vivlio tou fantarou* [The Book of the Soldier]. Alexandria, 1925.

Orfanos, Philippos [Pantelis Pouliopoulos]. *Polemos kata tou polemou. Apofaseis tou Protou Panelliniou Synedriou Palaion Polemiston kai Thimaton Stratou* [War against War. Resolutions of the First Panhellenic Conference of Ex-Soldiers and Military Victims]. 3rd ed. 1924. Reprint, Athens: Diethni Vivliothiki, 2008.

Paloukis, Kostas. "I organosi Archeion Marxismou (1919–1934)" [The Organization 'Archeion Marxism' (1919–1934)]. Ph.D. Thesis, University of Crete, Rethymno, 2017.

Papadopoulos, Apostolos K. "The Drainage and Exploitation of Lake Copais (1908–1938)" "Polemos kata tou polemou" [War against war]. *Foni tou Efedrou* [Reservist's Voice], September 23, 1924, 1. PhD Thesis, University of Bradford, Bradford, 1993.

Pazis, Dimitris, "I drasis tou ypoyrgiou Pronoias" [The activities of Ministry of Relief]. *Dimokratia*, August 4, 1924, 2.

Pazis, Dimitris. "I drasis tou ypoyrgiou Pronoias" [The activities of Welfare Ministry]. *Dimokratia*, August 4, 1924.

Proia. "Oi efedroi polemistai" [The reservist warriors]. January 26, 1931, 2.

Rizospastis. "Barbusse's *Le Feu*." May 23 to July 25, 1921.

Rizospastis. "Diaggelma tis Diethnous" [Greeting of Veterans' International]. May 7, 1924, 1.

Rizospastis. "Diethnis traumation kai anapiron polemou" [Injured and disabled veterans' International]. January 23, 1922, 3.

Rizospastis. "Henri Barbusse." December 25, 1924, 1.

Rizospastis. "I Opospondia apanta" [The Federation answers], March 11, 1925, 2.

Rizospastis. "I organosis ton anapiron polemou" [The organization of disabled veterans], August 24, 1921, 1.

Rizospastis. "O agon tou gallikou laou enantion tou neou polemou" [The struggle of French people against a new war], April 29, 1921, 1.

Rizospastis. "Praxikopima kata ton anapiron" [A coup against the disabled], October 17, 1921, 4.

Rizospastis. "Yper ton anapiron" [For the injured and disabled], May 7, 1921, 3.

Tixier, Adrian. "The Evolution of International Relations between the Disabled and Ex-service Men's Organizations." *FIDAC. Bulletin of Allied Legions* 2, nos. 6–7 (1926).

Wolfe, Henry C. "War Veterans Who Work for Peace." *World Affairs* 98, no. 3 (1935).

8 Building Insecurity? Military and Paramilitary Forces in Postwar Czechoslovak Borderlands (1945–8)

Abrams, Bradley. "The Second World War and the East European Revolution." *East European Politics and Societies* 16, no. 3 (2002): 623–64.

Bechtel, Delphine and Xavier Galmiche. "Villes multiculturelles en Europe centrale." *Cultures d'Europe centrale* 8 (2009).

Čaplovič, Miloslav. *Armed Forces in Czechoslovakia 1918–1939 (with regard to Slovakia)*. Bratislava: Ministry of Defense of the Slovak Republic, 2001.

Czech National Archives. Prague, Czech Republic.

Dimitrijević, Bojan B. *Jugoslovenska armija 1945–1954: nova ideologija, vojnik i oružje*. Belgrade: Institut za savremenu istoriju, 2006.

Drtina, Prokop. *Československo, můj osud*, vol. 1. Prague: Melantrich, 1991.

Dullin, Sabine. "How the Soviet Empire Relied on Diversity: Territorial Expansion and National Borders at the End of World War II in Ruthenia." In *Seeking Peace in the Wake of War: Europe, 1943-1947*, edited by Stefan-Ludwig Hoffmann, Sandrine Kott, Peter Romijna, and Olivier Wieviorka, 217–46. Amsterdam: Amsterdam University Press, 2015.

Faure, Justine. *L'ami américain: La Tchécoslovaquie, enjeu de la diplomatie américaine, 1943-1968*. Paris: Tallandier, 2004.

Gerwarth, Robert and John Horne, eds. *War in Peace: Paramilitary Violence in Europe after the Great War*. Oxford: Oxford University Press, 2012.

Glassheim, Eagle. *Cleansing the Czechoslovak Borderlands: Migration, Environment, and Health in the Former Sudetenland*. Pittsburgh: University of Pittsburgh Press, 2016.

Goussef, Catherine. *Échanger les peuples: Le déplacement des minorités aux confins polono-soviétiques 1944-1947*. Paris: Fayard, 2015.

Horne, John. "Demobilizing the Mind: France and the Legacy of the Great War, 1919–1939." In *French History and Civilization: Papers from the George Rudé Seminar* 2 (2019): 101–19.

Jakl, Tomáš. "Povstalci, gardisté, vojáci a příslušníci SNB – vývoj ozbrojených složek ČSR v létě 1945." In *Od svobody k nesvobodě 1945-1956*, edited by Ivo Pejčoch, 50–69. Prague: MO České republiky, 2011.

Jíchová, Jana, Martin Ouředníček, and Lucie Pospíšilová. *Historický atlas obyvatelstva českých zemí*. Prague: Karolinum, 2017.

King, Jeremy. *Budweisers into Czechs and Germans: A Local History of Bohemian Politics, 1848-1948*. Princeton: Princeton University Press, 2002.

Lášek, Radan. *Velitelé praporů SOS*. Prague: Codyprint, 2009.

Lenormand, Paul. "Vers l'armée du peuple: Autorité, pouvoir et culture militaire en Tchécoslovaquie de Munich à la fin du stalinisme." Ph.D manuscript, Sciences Po Paris, Paris, 2019.

Mazower, Mark. *Dark Continent: Europe's Twentieth Century*. London: Penguin Books, 1999.

Miot, Claire. "Rentrer dans le rang? L'intégration des combattants issus de la Résistance intérieure dans la Première armée française (1944–1945)." In *Pratiques militaires et globalisation. XIXe-XXIe siècles*, edited by Walter Bruyère-Ostells and François Dumasy, 147–60. Aix-en-Provence: Bernard Giovanangeli, 2014.

Pucci, Molly. *Security Empire: The Secret Police in Communist Eastern Europe*. New Haven: Yale University Press, 2020.

Reklaitis, George. "Cold War Lithuania: National Armed Resistance and Soviet Counterinsurgency." *The Carl Beck Papers in Russian & East European Studies*, no. 1086 (2007): 1–43.

Slovak Military History Archives. Bratislava, Slovakia.

Snyder, Timothy. *Bloodlands: Europe Between Hitler and Stalin*. New York: Basic Books, 2010.

Svobodné Československo, June 16, 1945, 2.

Tenenbaum, Elie. *Partisans et centurions: Une histoire de la guerre irrégulière au XXe siècle*. Paris: Perrin, 2018.

Thiesse, Anne-Marie. *La création des identités nationales*. Paris: Seuil, 1999.

Vojenský ústřední archiv (VÚA - Military Central Archive). Prague, Czech Republic.

Ward, James M. *Priest, Politician, Collaborator: Jozef Tiso and the Making of Fascist Slovakia*. Ithaca: Cornell University Press, 2013.

Zückert, Martin. *Zwischen Nationsidee und staatlicher Realität: Die tschechoslowakische Armee und ihre Nationalitätenpolitik 1918-1938*. Munich: Oldenbourg, 2006.

9 General of the Russian Army Alexei Orlov: Military in the Service of Diplomacy

Airapetov, Oleg R. *Vneshnjaja politika Rossijskoj imperii (1801–1914)* [Foreign policy of the Russian Empire (1801-1914)]. Moscow: Publishing House Europe, 2006.

Archives des Affaires Etrangères, Russia. La Courneuve, France.

Arslanov, Rafael A. and Elena V. Linkova. *Strany Zapada i ih vneshnjaja politika v vosprijatii rossijskih konservatorov i liberalov XIX veka* [The Countries of the West and their Foreign Policy in the Perception of Russian Conservatives and Liberals of the Nineteenth Century]. Moscow: RUDN Publishing House, 2018.

Bagdasarjan, Vardan J. *Russkaja vojna: stoletnij istoriograficheskij opyt osmyslenija Krymskoj kampanii* [The Russian War: a Century-long historiographical experience of Understanding the Crimean Campaign]. Moscow: Izd-vo Moskovskogo otkrytogo universiteta, 2002.

Bor'ba imperij. "'Kruglyj stol' zhurnala *Rodina*, posvjashhennyj prichinam, itogam i posledstvijam Krymskoj vojny" [The struggle of empires. "Round table" of the magazine "Rodina," dedicated to the causes, results and consequences of the Crimean War]. *Rodina*, 1995.

Cherkasov, Petr P. *Nikolaj I i Lui Napoleon Bonapart (1848–1852)* [Nicholas I and Louis Napoleon Bonaparte (1848-1852)], vol. 3. Moscow, 2012.

Cherkasov, Petr P. *Rossija i Francija. XVIII-XX veka. Vypusk 9. Otvetstvennyj redaktor i sostavitel'*. Moscow: Ves' Mir, 2009.

Gosudarstvennyj arhiv Rossijskoj Federacii (GARF) [State Archive of the Russian Federation]. 672/1/198. Moscow, Russia.

Gradovskij, Alexander D. *Slavjanskij vopros i vojna 1877 goda. Pol'skij vopros* [The Slavic question and the War of 1877. The Polish question]. Moscow: M. M. Stasyulevich, 2017.

Linkova, Elena V. and Marc L. De Bollivier. "Francuzskaja istoriografija Krymskoj vojny (1853–1856 gg.): osnovnye napravlenija i tendencii" [French Historiography of the Crimean War (1853-1856): The Main Directions and Trends]. *RUDN Journal of Russian History* 19, no. 1 (2020): 240–53.

Muravyov-Amursky, Nikolay N. *Russkie na Bosfore v 1833 godu. Iz zapisok N.N.
Murav'eva (Karsskogo)* [Russians on the Bosphorus in 1833. From the notes of N.N.
Muravyov (Karssky)]. Moscow: Tipografija A.I. Mamontova, 1869.

"Parizhskij traktat, Parizh 18/30 marta 1856" [Treaty of Paris]; "Sbornik dogovorov
Rossii s drugimi gosudarstvami 1856–1917" [Collection of treaties of Russia with
other states]. *Histrf.ru*, December 15, 2015. https://histrf.ru/lenta-vremeni/event/
view/parizhskii-traktat.

Pogodin, Mikhail P. *Istoriko-politicheskie pis'ma i zapiski v prodolzhenii Krymskoj vojny.
1853–1856.* [Historical and political letters and notes in the continuation of the
Crimean War. 1853–1856]. Moscow: Tip. V.M. Frisch, 1874. http://elib.shpl.ru/ru/
nodes/8608#mode/inspect/page/142/zoom/4.

Pogodin, Mikhail P. *Rossija v otnoshenii k vostochnym plemenam* [Russia in relation to
the Eastern tribes], 1–4. Moscow: Moskvitjanin, 1856.

Rossija i Chernomorskie prolivy (XVIII–XX stoletija) [Russia and the Black Sea Straits
(XVIII-XX centuries).]. Moscow: Institute Ros. History of the Russian Academy of
Sciences, 1999.

Runivers. "Dogovory Rossii s Vostokom. Politicheskie i torgovye" [Treaties between
Russia and the East. Political and commercial]. Saint Petersburg, 1869. https://
runivers.ru/bookreader/book456128/#page/1/mode/1up.

Tatishchev, Sergei S. *Imperator Nikolaj i inostrannye dvory. Istoricheskie ocherki* [The
Emperor Nicholas and Foreign Courts. Historical Essays]. Saint-Peterbourg:
Tipografija I.N. Skorohodova, 1889.

Tatishchev, Sergei S. *Vneshnjaja politika Imperatora Nikolaja Pervogo. Vvedenie v
istoriju vneshnih snoshenij Rossii v jepohu Sevastopol'skoj vojny* [Foreign Policy of the
Emperor Nicholas I. Introduction to the History of Russia's Foreign Relations in the
Era of the Sevastopol War]. Saint Petersburg: I.N. Skorokhodov's Printing House,
1887.

Zajonchkovskij, Andrei M. *Vostochnaja vojna, 1853–1856* [Eastern War, 1853-1856].
Saint Petersburg: Poligon, 2002.

10 The Naval Officer, a Peacekeeper in Europe (1815–48)? Keeping European Peace Overseas and Consolidating French Naval Power

baron Tupinier, Jean-Marguerite, and Bernard Lutun. *Mémoires du baron Tupinier,
directeur des ports et arsenaux, 1779–1850.* Paris: Les Editions Desjonqueres, 1994.

Daget, Serge. "L'Abolition de la traite des Noirs en France de 1814 à 1831." *Cahier
d'études africaines* 41 (1971): 14–58.

Daget, Serge. *La Répression de la Traite des Noirs au XIXe siècle. L'Action des croisières
françaises sur les côtes occidentales de l'Afrique (1817–1830).* Paris: Karthala, 1997.

de Diesbach, Ghislain. *Ferdinand de Lesseps*. Paris: Perrin, 1998.

Laux, Claire. "La Construction d'une géographie de l'Océanie par les explorateurs, les missionnaires, les colonisateurs." In *L'Empire des géographes. Géographie, exploration et colonisation XIXe-XXe siècle*, edited by Pierre Singaravélou. Paris: Belin, coll. Mappemonde, 2008.

Laux, Claire. "Rivalités coloniales et rivalités missionnaires en Océanie (1688–1902)." *Histoire, monde et culture religieuse* 6, no. 2 (2008): 5–26.

Lentz, Thierry. *Le Congrès de Vienne : une refondation de l'Europe (1814–1815)*. Paris: Perrin, 2015.

Prou, Michel. *Malagasy," un pas de plus":--Vers l'histoire du" Royaume de Madagascar" au XIXe siècle*, vol. 1. Paris: L'Harmattan, 1987.

Renouvin, Pierre. *Histoire des relations internationales Tome 2 de 1789 à 1871*. France: Hachette, 1994.

Schmidt, Nelly. *L'Abolition de l'esclavage. Cinq siècles de combats (XVIe–XXe siècle)*. Paris, Fayard, 2005.

"SHD Vincennes, CC7 alpha 347, Bruat (Armand-Joseph)." Paris, February 9, 1843.

"SHD Vincennes, CC7 alpha 863, Despointes (Auguste-Febvrier dit Febvrier-Despointes), Fort Royal" [letter from the Governor of Martinique to the Minister of Marine and Colonies]. Paris, May 19, 1823.

"SHD Vincennes, CC7 alpha 863, Despointes (Auguste, Febvrier dit Febvrier-Despointes), Fort-Royal" [report by M. Febvrier, einseigne de vaisseau]. Paris, February 24, 1823.

Thésée, Françoise. "La Révolte des esclaves du Carbet à la Martinique (octobre–novembre 1822)." *Revue française d'histoire d'outre-mer* 80, no. 301 (1993): 551–84.

Vencent, Hélène. "Les Ecoles flottantes sous l'Empire et la formation des officiers de marine, 1810–1816." *Revue de l'Institut Napoléon*, no. 197 (2008): 21–57.

Vencent, Hélène. "Les Elèves officiers de marine sous l'Empire et leur destin." In *Thèse de doctorat en Histoire, Ecole doctorale d'Histoire modern et contemporaine*. Paris: Université de Paris-Sorbonne, 2016.

Wanquet, Claude and Jullien Benoît eds. *Révolution française et océan Indien. Prémices, paroxysme, héritage et deviances*. Proceedings of the colloquium of Saint-Pierre de la Réunion from October 22 to 27, 1990, organized by the International Historical Association of the Indian Ocean, Saint-Denis, l'Harmattan, 1996.

11 Soldiers versus Veterans: Peacemaking in Britain after Napoleon

Beckett, Ian F. W. *The Amateur Military Tradition, 1558–1945*. Manchester: Manchester University Press, 1991.

Brodsky, Stephen G. W. *Gentlemen of the Blade: A Social and Literary History of the British Army since 1660*. New York: Greenwood Press, 1988.

Daly, Gavin. "British Soldiers and the Legend of Napoleon." *The Historical Journal* 61, no. 1 (2017): 131–53.

Hay, George. *The Yeomanry Cavalry and Military Identities in Rural Britain, 1815–1914*. Basingstoke: Palgrave Macmillan, 2017.

Haynes, Christine. *Our Friends, The Enemies: The Occupation of France after Napoleon*. Cambridge, MA: Harvard University Press, 2018.

Hayter, Tony. *The Army and the Crowd in Mid-Georgian England*. Totowa: Rowman and Littlefield, 1979.

Hobson, James. *Dark Days of Georgian Britain: Rethinking the Regency*. Barnsley: Pen and Sword, 2017.

Jolliffe, S. William. *The Charge of the 15th Hussars at Peterloo (1845)*. Edited by F. A. Bruton. Reprinted in *Three Accounts of Peterloo*. Manchester: Manchester University Press, 1921.

Kennedy, Catriona. *Narratives of the Revolutionary and Napoleonic Wars: Military and Civilian Experience in Britain and Ireland*. Basingstoke: Palgrave Macmillan, 2013.

Manchester Observer, April 29, 1820.

Mansfield, Nick. "Military Radicals and the Making of Class, 1790–1860." In *Soldiering in Britain and Ireland, 1750–1850: Men of Arms*, edited by Catriona Kennedy and Matthew McCormack, 57–75. Basingstoke: Palgrave Macmillan, 2013.

Morris, Thomas. *The Napoleonic Wars*. Edited by John Selby. London: Longman, 1967.

Myatt, Frederick. *The British Infantry, 1660–1945: The Evolution of a Fighting Force*. Poole: Blandford Press, 1983.

The National Archives, Kew. WO 33/18. Richmond, United Kingdom.

Old Bailey Proceedings Online, April 1815, trial of James Ripley, Robert Herbert, Richard Burton, Richard Mathews (t18150405–13). www.oldbaileyonline.org.

Palmer, Stanley H. *Police and Protest in England and Ireland, 1780–1850*. Cambridge: Cambridge University Press, 1988.

Shelley, Percy B. *The Masque of Anarchy*. London: Edward Moxon, 1832.

Smith, Harry and George C. M. Smith. *The Autobiography of Lieutenant-General Sir Harry Smith, Baronet of Aliwal on the Sutlej*. London: John Murray, 1903.

Thompson, Edward P. *The Making of the English Working Class*. London: V. Gollancz, 1963.

The Times, March 13, 1815.

Uglow, Jenny. *In These Times: Living in Britain Through Napoleon's Wars, 1793–1815*. London: Faber & Faber, 2014.

White, Reginald J. *Waterloo to Peterloo*. New York: Russell and Russell, 1957.

Wilson, Evan. *The Horrible Peace: Britain at the End of the Napoleonic Wars*. Amherst: University of Massachusetts Press, 2022.

12 The Price of Disobedience: The Eastern French Army in Albania (1918–25)

Archivio storico diplomatico del Ministero degli Affari Esteri. Serie affari politici 1919–1930. Rome, Italy.

Descoins, Henri V. *Six Mois D'histoire De L'albanie - Novembre 1916- Mai 1917*. Paris: A. Costes, 2021.

Dorlhiac, Renaud, and Fabrice Jesné. "Une alliance de circonstance: l'Italie et les musulmans d'Albanie (1912–1920)." *Revue des mondes musulmans et de la Méditerranée* 141, no. 61 (2017): 51–67.

Ministère des Armées, Service Historique de la Défense. Vincennes, France.

Ordioni, Jean-André. *Un officier français dans les Balkans, 1917–1925*. Dominique Danguy des Deserts, 2014.

Puto, Arben. *Çështja shqiptare në aktet ndërkombëtare pas Luftës së Parë botërore*. Tirana, 2001.

Puto, Arben. *La question albanaise dans les actes internationaux de l'époque impérialiste*, Tirana, 1988.

Salle, Henri. "L'occupation française en Albanie." *Revue politique et parlementaire*, Septembre 10, 1920.

Sarrail, Maurice. *Mon commandement en Orient (1916–1918)*. Paris: E. Flammarion, 1920.

Contributors

Editors

Beatrice de Graaf is Distinguished Professor at the Faculty of Humanities at Utrecht University. She is a historian and a security and terrorism researcher. Her research focuses on how states and societies try to maintain high levels of security and how these attempts relate to core values and institutions (democracy, freedom, rule of law, and constitutional and responsible government). As a strong science communicator, Beatrice appears on (international) television and radio stations, and in newspapers. Her recent work includes *Radicale verlossing. Wat terroristen geloven* (2021) and *Fighting Terror after Napoleon. How Europe Became Secure after 1815* (2020).

Frédéric Dessberg is Associate Professor at Paris 1 Panthéon-Sorbonne University, detached at Saint-Cyr Military Academy. He is heading the Research Department "European Defence and Security" at Saint-Cyr Research Center, is a member of UMR SIRICE (Sorbonne), and holds a Jean Monnet European Chair. He is interested in the French policy in Central and Eastern Europe between the two world wars. He recently published *Diplomates et militaires français en Europe centrale* (2017), *L'Européanité en Europe médiane* (2018), and *Frontières en Europe depuis le Congrès de Vienne (1815)* (2020).

Thomas Vaisset is Assistant Professor at Le Havre University (France) and a member of UMR IDEES-CNRS 6266. He is interested in the history of the French navy between 1870 and 1945, investigating the role played by the navy in a global dimension including politics, international relations, and social and cultural matters. He teaches and researches on contemporary naval issues and on the history of French external resistance during the Second World War. He is the author of *L'amiral d'Argenlieu. Le moine-soldat du gaullisme* (2017) and the co-editor of *Militaires en résistances en France et en Europe* (2020) and *Cessez-le-feu, cesser les combats ? De l'époque moderne à nos jours* (2022).

Contributing Authors

Sir Hew Strachan, FBA, FRSE, has been Wardlaw Professor of International Relations at the University of St Andrews since 2015. He is a Life Fellow of Corpus Christi College, Cambridge, where he was successively a Research Fellow and Fellow from 1975 to 1992, and an Emeritus Fellow of All Souls College, Oxford. He was Professor of Modern History at Glasgow University 1992 to 2001, and Chichele Professor of the History of War at the University of Oxford 2002 to 2015. He was a Commonwealth War Graves Commissioner 2006-18, a Trustee of the Imperial War Museum 2010-18, and member of the national committees for the centenary of the First World War of the United Kingdom, Scotland, and France. His recent publications include *The First World War: To Arms* (2001); *The First World War: a New Illustrated History* (2003; based on his 10-part series for Channel 4); and *The Direction of War* (2013).

David Fitzgerald is Lecturer in the School of History, University College Cork, Ireland. He is the author of *Learning to Forget: US Army Counterinsurgency Doctrine from Vietnam to Iraq* (2013), which was a finalist for the Society of Military History's Edward M. Coffman Prize. He is the co-author of *Obama, US Foreign Policy and the Dilemmas of Intervention* (2014) and co-editor of *How the United States Ends Wars* (2019). His most recent publication, *Militarization and the American Century: War, the United States and the World since 1941*, was published in 2022. He is currently working on a cultural history of the US Army between the Cold War and the War on Terror.

Wietse Stam studied History at Leiden University and Sciences Po Paris. He is currently a Researcher at the Netherlands Institute for Military History and a PhD candidate at the History Department of Leiden University, where he writes his dissertation about UNTAC, the United Nations peacekeeping operation in Cambodia (1991–3). He was a visiting scholar at Columbia University while doing his research in New York.

Major Dion Landstra, MA, of the Royal Dutch Army, is Lecturer of Military History and Strategy at the Netherlands Institute for Military History (NIMH). He currently holds a position as a PhD candidate facilitated and supported by the NIMH and the University of Leiden. The chapter is based on his thesis, defended in 2022: Dion Landstra, Informatiemakelaar en schietschijf. De inzet en effectiviteit van waarnemers in vredesoperaties op de Balkan, 1991-1995 (Amsterdam: Boom, 2022), PhD Diss, Leiden University.

Thomas Wijnaendts van Resandt, MA, is a graduate of Military History at the University of Amsterdam. He contributed to the writing of this chapter as part of a traineeship at the NIMH.

Christine Haynes is Professor of History at the University of North Carolina, Charlotte (United States). She has written on a variety of topics in nineteenth-century French history, including the literary marketplace, roller coasters, war indemnities, and military occupation. Her most recent book is *Our Friends the Enemies: The Occupation of France after Napoleon* (2018). Past co-president of the Society for French Historical Studies, she is now a co-editor of *French Historical Studies*.

Alexandros Makris is Postdoctoral Researcher at the University of Patras. He completed his PhD at the National and Kapodistrian University of Athens (2021). His research interests focus on veterans' studies, welfare politics, and social history of interwar Greece. He is author of the book *"The preachers of the idea of the nation." Veterans and War Victims in Greece (1912–1940)* and co-editor of the collective volume *Greek Soldiers and Asia Minor Campaign: Consequences of a Painful Experience* (in Greek, 2022).

Paul Lenormand is Assistant Professor at Paris-Nanterre University and a member of UMR-ISP CNRS 7220. He was a research fellow at the French Service Historique de la Défense (military archives) and is Associate Researcher at Sciences Po Paris. His research interests focus on the history of warfare, international history, and Central and Eastern Europe. He has published on the military, resistance, collaboration, and the early Cold War in Czechoslovakia. His recent publications include *The Palestinian Triangle: Czechoslovaks, Jews and the British Crown in the Middle East, 1940–1943* (2020) and *Les aviateurs tchécoslovaques dans la bataille de France (1939-1940)* (2021).

Elena V. Linkova, PhD in History, is Associate Professor at the Peoples' Friendship University of Russia (RUDN University), Moscow, Russia. Her research currently focuses on the history of conservatism and the intellectual history of Russia in the eighteenth and nineteenth centuries, and the history of diplomatic and cultural relations between Russia and France. She is also the co-ordinator of the double master's degree program jointly with the University of Grenoble-Alpes (France).

Hélène Vencent, PhD in History is teaching at Sainte-Ursule-Louise-de-Bettignies Highschool, Paris. Her research interests focus on history of navy and naval officer training, colonial history, and history of science. Her recent publications include the chapter "Du Premier au Second Empire, l'évolution du métier d'officier de marine" in the book *La Marine sous le Premier et le Second Empire* (2017) and "La selection des élèves des écoles spéciales de marine face aux enjeux de la Restauration (1814–1817)," *Revue d'Histoire militaire* (2017).

Evan Wilson is Associate Professor in the John B. Hattendorf Center for Maritime Historical Research at the US Naval War College. In 2018, he won the Sir Julian Corbett Prize in Modern Naval History. His most recent book is *The Horrible Peace: British Veterans and the End of the Napoleonic Wars* (2023). He is the editor of four books and has published articles in a number of journals, including the *English Historical Review* and the *Journal of Military History*. Before coming to Newport, he was Caird Senior Research Fellow at the National Maritime Museum (UK) and Associate Director of International Security Studies at Yale University. He holds degrees from Yale, Cambridge, and Oxford.

Renaud Dorlhiac is Research Associate at the Center of Turkish, Ottoman, Balkan and Central Asian Studies (CETOBAC, EHESS-Paris) and a teaching assistant at the Institute of Political Studies (IEP Toulouse). His main fields of research include military occupations, national engineering, paramilitary phenomenon, and mass violence. His publications include "Muslims of Epirus, Muslims of Empire? The Cham issue in relation to the Albanian, Greek and Turkish national projects (1912–1925)," in Severin-Barboutie and Horel (eds.), *From Empire(s) to Nation-States: Population Displacements and Multiple Mobilities in the Late Ottoman Empire*, to be published in 2023 and "Frontière nationale, régionale, fédérale, impériale? L'établissement de la frontière albano-yougoslave," dans Laloux, Dessberg et Palaude (dir.), *Frontières en Europe depuis le Congrès de Vienne (1815)*, 2020.

Index

www.ingramcontent.com/pod-product-compliance
Lightning Source LLC
Chambersburg PA
CBHW071856270326
41929CB00013B/2251